TransformNational

Journey of a Bastard

Lamont Robinson

Hilton Publishing Company
Chicago, Illinois

Praise for Lamont Robinson and TransformNational

"'Don't block my path' is Lamont Robinson's battle cry in this moving account of his determination, perseverance and resilience—against all odds—in his journey to personal and professional success."

Sandra E. Timmons
President, A Better Chance

"What an inspiring, humbling and incredible journey! We have always known that this story is powerful enough to change the lives of those who come to know it. Lamont, you are a model citizen and an amazing human being. There is no doubt that you have been placed here for a real and solid purpose. May the man upstairs continue to shine his goodness on you, so that you can continue to transform many more lives!"

Shara Pathak, President of Price Chopper
Deven Pathak, Managing Director of Medical ID Solutions

"Work hard, never give up, never settle, stay focused and always be true to yourself—these are simple lessons that Lamont's profound story is built upon, and ones we should all aspire to live by. He is a model of success—in every sense of the word—and his book shares how anyone can live their life with the same positivity and faith to achieve greatness and, above all else, a life full of love and happiness."

Hilton M. Hudson MD
CEO of Hilton Publishing, Cardio Thoracic Surgeon

Hilton Publishing Company
Chicago, IL

Direct all correspondence to:
Hilton Publishing Company
1630 45th St. Suite B101
Munster, IN 46321
(219) 922–4868
www.hiltonpub.com

Copyright © 2014 by Lamont Robinson
TransformNational: Journey of a Bastard
ISBN 978-0-9904283-0-5

Designed and edited by Angela Vennemann
Cover illustration by Tifani Carter
Photographs courtesy of Lamont Robinson

Notice: The information in this book is true and complete to the best knowledge of the author and publisher. The author and publisher disclaim all liability in connection with the specific personal use of any and all information provided in this book.

All rights reserved. No part of this book may be reproduced or transmitted in any form or by any means, electronic or mechanical, including photocopy, recording, or any information storage or retrieval systems, including digital systems, without written permission from the publisher, except by a reviewer who may quote brief passages from the book in a review.

Printed in the United States of America.

Library of Congress Cataloging-in-Publication Data

Robinson, Lamont, 1972–

TransformNational : journey of a bastard / Lamont Robinson. Munster, IN : Hilton Publishing Company, 2014.

p. cm.

ISBN 978-0-9904283-0-5

1. Robinson, Lamont, 1972-. 2. Robinson, Lamont, 1972--Childhood and youth. 3. African-Americans--Biography. 4. Illegitimate children--United States--Biography. 5. Successful people--United States--Biography. 6. Poor children--Illinois--Chicago--biography. 7. Self-actualization (Psychology).

E185.97.R6625 A3 2014   LCCN: 2014017135

Contents

Foreword · vii
Acknowledgments · ix
Introduction · xiii

Part I: Foundation
Lula · 3
Fatherless · 10
Music · 17
Siblings · 26
Movies and Television · 48
Social Holocaust · 55
Education: My Way Out · 62

Part II: TransformNation
Summer of 1986 · 73
A Better Chance · 79
3 Strikes? · 96
Lake Forest College · 102
The Real World · 117
The Church · 129

Part III: Maturation
The Turnaround · 141
2001 · 150
Supplier Diversity · 163
Transition · 178
Rejuvenation · 196
The 12 Disciplines · 208

Foreword

LAMONT ROBINSON IS IN A unique position to stimulate growth and level the playing field for historically disadvantaged communities. As a young man, he grew up in one of the most poverty stricken and violent areas of inner city Chicago. Within that environment, he was able to use the seeds of strength gleaned from role models who may not have been classically seen as heroic. Without a traditional father figure, he cultivated gems of wisdom from the men and women who worked hard to ensure his survival, enabling him to transcend the environmental pitfalls associated with such a volatile set of circumstances. These unsung heroes—single mothers, stepfathers, neighborhood hustlers and other neighborhood soldiers—enabled him to receive a tremendous opportunity for a top education through the A Better Chance college preparatory program. They also enabled him to attend college which led to him obtaining his Master of Business Administration (MBA) degree. His mother created an escape plan for him that established a blueprint for his success, which is chronicled on the following pages to help others. She branded this blueprint on his heart and mind and it endeavors to serve as the living legacy that will help advance the overall condition of mankind.

Lamont is now ready to embark upon one of the most exciting projects of his life, offering his living legacy, his inspiring motivational story, the skill sets he has mastered, and the fire in his soul, which has given birth to a transformational movement. However, in a global environment, where all of humanity is intricately linked together, it must give rise to a transcendent movement. No longer can we afford to focus on our own specific corner of the world. All nations must unify and bond to ensure progressive evolution.

TransformNational

In a global economy, we need to devise ways we can all prosper. We must look beyond the standard of success, or what we do for ourselves, and instead pursue the goal of greatness, or what we do for others. Lamont's remarkable journey, although not fully completed, will inspire others on similar paths to strive for the greatness that resides in all of us.

Dr. Randal Pinkett
Chairman and CEO, BCT Partners
Entrepreneur, speaker and author of *Black Faces in White Places*

Acknowledgments

BEING ABLE TO THANK EVERYONE who has impacted your life is impossible. However, I will try my best by acknowledging those who have contributed to positive moments in my life.

Family

I would like to first thank my children: Jacqui, Malik, Antonio, and Payton. You've been my driver for success. I pray that I can continue to be the best father I can be while preparing you to be successful men and women and great contributors to society. Michelle, thanks for your help in raising our kids the right way and, in your own way, pushing me to finish this project.

To Mom and Dad, thanks for bringing me into this world. My life has always had a purpose because of your involvement. I look forward to continuing my efforts to make your lives happier.

To Bob, thanks for being my father figure when I was alone, and for being the reason I wanted to be successful. Even though we aren't biologically connected, you've always made me feel loved as if I was your son.

To my sisters, Ronetta, Renee, Sheila, and Shanee, thanks for your love. To my one and only brother, June, may your soul rest in peace. I know you're smiling down on your little brother.

To my niece, JaQueah, and nephews, Jerome, LaMonte, Germaine, and Timothy, as well as nephews and nieces from the Miche and LaRue families, thanks for always making me feel like a special uncle.

To the remaining derivations of family members consisting of my living aunts and uncle including Aunt Vernice, Dorothy, Jeannette, Annette, Gwen, Lottie, Pauline and Cheryl; my Uncle Butch; and, my remaining family members from the Adams, LaRue, Armstrong, Miche, Wells, Evans, Walker, Washington, Brown, Gates and Robinson families, I appreciate your never ending support and love.

Friends

To my Awesome Force brothers Rashied, Walter, Jermaine, Donnell, Antron, Quamie, Dashan, Rob, Maurice, and my cousin James. I was blessed to have a brotherhood that also served as my guardian angels. Our legs always kept us clean and safe.

To my Rockwell Gardens family, I've always felt your support and will continue to push boundaries some of us may not have had the chance to achieve. Your spirits are always with me.

To my friends at my employers Lake County Forest Preserves, Abbott Laboratories, Hospira Inc., Cardinal Health, VHA/Novation/UHC, and Nielsen, thanks for making the workplace an extension of home.

To my church friends at the Church of Jesus Christ of Latter Day Saints and Mars Hill Baptist Church, I appreciate your true following of Christ to provide the spirituality I needed to escape my mental Hell.

To my fellow alumni, staff and board members of the A Better Chance program, thanks for keeping me on the path to receiving a better chance at life. Specifically, I'd like to thank my ABC brothers Joe, Teo, Mark, Brian, Danillo, Carlos, Alfredo, Nashid, and our unofficial neighborhood ABC Caucasian student, John.

To my friends at Lower Merion High School, thanks for introducing me to different cultures and religions. Hopefully I'll add to Kobe's legacy to further place you on the global map. Thanks for your friendship, Jim "J.G." Pollard.

To my friends at Lake Forest College, thanks for all the memories as well as the platform to mature. Thanks also for supporting 2 'Uva Kynd with Enuff. Renee Burgess, thanks for your unwavering and unconditional support since Day 1. I love you, big sis!

I would also like to specifically thank the following individuals who have been instrumental in my life and vital to this story being told: Shara and Deven Pathak, Joe and Danielle Reubel, Lorena Valencia, Karen Greene, Eddie and Kentone Wells, Dr. Hilton Hudson, and Mrs. Janice Bryant Howroyd.

Acknowledgments

In addition to those I've mentioned I have met other outstanding people throughout my life. For those not listed, please know it was an oversight and not on purpose. Thanks to Preston and Patricia Scott, James Danforth, Lisa Washington, Ernest Roarke, LeRoy Mobley, Reverend Clarence E. Stowers, Jr. and family, Frederick Jones, Donald Moran, Angela Jackson, Dina Cox, Jeff Lockett, Eric Cunningham, Dana Christmas, Joe and Jennifer Rosello, Nicole Fleming, Nicole Reeves, Shaneen Travis, Kelli Stanley, Shelia Northington, Hanelle Culpepper Meier, Melissa Clark and family, Kijuan Ward, Lornell Grayson, Ron Labrum and family, Brik Eyre and family, Nate/Lori Emery and family, Jeremy/Lili Stephenson and family, Maria Guerrero, JV, Denise Greenwald, KB, Charles Brazil, Indria Hollingsworth, Jolene Anderson-Rau, LaSheia Strong, James Williams, Kevin Price, James Duke, Angela Wilkes, Shirelle Magee, Cheryl Pearson-McNeil, Joyce Reubel, Andrea Reubel, Kathy Benn, Martha Holmes, Heidi Hannes, Angela Talton, Paul Ochsner, Greg Serafin, Sarah Catterson, Mike Sterbenz, Yvette Mejia, Dwight Thaggard, Bill Cooper, Stacia Gowens, Kathryn Kimbrell, Melzie Robinson, Sonya Cunningham, Mark Cartwright, Susan Wan, Knitasha Washington, Kenneth "Jabo" Dean, Reggie/Joelle Hannah and family, Andreas/Jill Lex and family, Joe Koziol, Kathy Kalmon, Rebecca Blaesing, Don Lowery, Monica Gil, Kathryn Roberts Goldstein, Andrea McCarther, Laz Reese, Tavares Duckett, Yvonne Odimgbe, David Gillan, Barb Raines, Russell Hall, Louis Williams, Candy Wolff, Tru Thornton, Carrera family, Tim Smith, May Boyer, Vesheta Rennie, Ryan Walcott, Randy Byrd, Kenny Brown, Nicholette, Anthony Ray, Sandi Blue Savarese, Richard Manson, Steve Pemberton, Martin C. Jones, Mark Harris, Margaret Byrne, JT Mueller, Crystal Ann Robinson, Doris Dean, Jonah Cooper, Sumalya Sundaram, Jesse Crawford, Kelly Abcarian, and Robbie Lopez.

And finally, my life has been filled with many losses. For that reason I honor and respect the following that have left this world to be with our Father in Heaven: June, Jerome "Spot" Wells, Mudea, Grandma LaRue, Earl Reubel, Corris Boyd, Will Stewart, Bibian Cornell Soldevilla, Ronald Robinson, Sr., Granddaddy Henry Adams, Aunt Sam, Aunt Sis, Aunt Cat, Miss Robinson, Floyd Robinson, Sr., Doris, Calvin, Cathy, Oscar, Aunt Deebie, Thomas "Chubby" O'Leary, Willie, Odiaraye LaRue Phlegm, Deborah LaRue, and Eddie Charles LaRue.

—Lamont Robinson

"If it is to be, it is up to me."

—William H. Johnsen

Introduction

I ENTERED THIS WORLD IN the early morning of April 4, 1972, as a child that was, in society's eyes, lower than a bastard: undesired by a separated mother of three who was enjoying her newfound freedom after an abusive marriage; unknown to a biological father of two who was married and focused on raising his own family; undefined by society's definition of what constitutes a legal relationship; but, most importantly, unfazed by dogmas typically used to deter desires to destroy complacency and acceptance of the status quo.

When attempting to classify myself, I believed being defined as a bastard would have been an improvement. However, I couldn't be called a bastard because of society's definition, which defines a bastard as a child born to a couple not legally married. In my situation, my mom and dad *were* married, but not to each other. The blank space after "Father" on my birth certificate is a constant and painful reminder of an unwanted ejaculate conception that took place on an uneventful night in the summer of 1971. In addition to not being considered even a bastard, I couldn't be called a love child either, because there was no love between the two adults that conceived me. The sacred act of sex was used as their succor to temporarily escape painful relationships and not as a physical manifestation of a holy matrimony with celestial and eternal blessings.

I left the hospital the next day to go "home" to a place where violence was an everyday occurrence. While living in that home, I would be prematurely exposed to drug use, gang life, racism, infidelity, and pornography. Easily, I could have been victimized by the vicious cycles plaguing children in similar situations, which included accepting the hand I was being dealt.

However, I knew that my life had a purpose, regardless of how it started or its lack of a societal classification. Even though I could not define success, I knew that through hard work I could achieve it by overcoming all of the unfair obstacles I faced.

Instead of giving in to the accepted temptation of dwelling on shortcomings, I was grateful for my assets. The name of my father may have been undefined on my birth certificate, but the one that followed "Mother" was *all* I needed. I was blessed with a mother who sacrificed her own freedom and dignity to provide me with an opportunity to at least pursue *her* vision of success, which was simply escaping the physical, mental, and financial tortures of the ghetto. She knew that in order to rescue her baby from that world, she would need to do something radical. There would need to be a level of sacrifice not performed before by anyone in her circle. In order for her plan to succeed, however, she needed me to accept it as well. This wasn't easy, considering I was actually comfortable in my uncomfortable surroundings. Even though the daily violence was stressful, the ghetto was the only environment I had known.

Although our escape plan promised great rewards, it was filled with risks neither of us were fully prepared to tackle. The plan involved sending me thousands of miles away from our roach- and rat-infested comfort zone to an economically and culturally different environment to receive a level of education that would challenge my ability to adjust. Our plan hit a few road bumps along the way, but we knew we needed to stay the course at all costs. To continue with our plan, the same blood-traced drug dollars that would later claim the physical and/or emotional lives of close family members were also partially used to fund the necessary education.

My mom adjusted to her difficult life as a single parent and, by any means necessary, provided me with all resources she had in her power to allow me to pursue my dreams after realizing I was special. She had to be willing to make deals with the devil in order for me to escape our earthly hell. We both needed to be willing to lay our close relationship on the altar as a necessary sacrifice and cost for success.

A vital element of our plan was for me to be completely committed to not allowing anything or anyone to block my path. I had to come to grips

Introduction

with the reality that my decisions could impact relationships with family and friends. I had to maintain internal desires that would not allow me to take anything for granted. I had to have a stalwart approach in refusing to accept the status quo of most children raised in the ghetto. I could not allow an elementary school deprived of necessary resources to determine my level of success. I also needed to reject the mentality of others later in life that purposely attempted to deter me from reaching my aspirations. Instead of responding with anger, I had to develop an amount of sympathy for those people, realizing they did not have the same dreams or any dreams at all.

My mental fortitude provided the motivation to fight for success and to overcome challenges that would have destroyed weaker individuals. My mom influenced me to believe my life had a purpose, which is why I constantly worked hard to avoid complacency. To see people struggle through life without hope sickens me. To see people constantly take advantage of life's loopholes without hard work angers me. Although we are all presented with challenges on various scales of life's continuum, we are also provided with the knowledge to escape. Hope should be the light that constantly flickers inside of us. For some, escape comes in the form of athletic talent. For others, intellectual capacity provides the platform. For me, an unrelenting tenacity as well as fear of returning back to a life of poverty, drugs, and violence kept my fire burning. With zero excuses, I had to work harder than students who were raised with social, financial, and educational privileges I did not enjoy.

While most would find my upbringing a detriment, I look at it as a blessing. I truly believe I received a PhD in the real world, regardless of my need to be defined by society. I was blessed with a mom who was unafraid to take chances as well as put her life on hold to see me succeed. Through my eyes, I was able to see the dangers of drugs and gang violence, which allowed me to avoid both later in life. I was blessed with an eternal motivation that could only be obtained by surviving the increasingly violent Chicago streets.

My level of motivation and background became an asset for me later in life while battling other professionals in corporate America. Growing up without a father provided me with an unwavering and unquestioned support in the lives of my children. My life allowed me to refuse any of the ready-made excuses for why I should avoid pursuing success as well as accepting the cyclical lives of generations before me. Being able to change my perception of unfortunate shortcomings into fortunate pieces of an overall plan would potentially be the difference between success and failure.

This is a story of how to use pain, survival, and negative experiences to develop a path to personal success. It is also a story of ways to be driven in the midst of external and uncontrollable forces. Although at times I felt less than human because of my unclassified existence, my belief and faith in God pushed me to overcome most challenges placed on the roads ahead of me. Many times during my life all I had was God and my mom, and they both manifested their presence by assuring me I wasn't alone during key moments on my journey.

While some may see my survival as heroic, the main heroine in my life is my mom. Without her sacrifice, encouragement, and support, it would have been impossible for me to witness any amount of success. My mom's story is in itself one of survival. She has successfully rebounded from years of mental and physical abuse, financial hardship, and the pain from various deaths in her life. As much as her struggles were my struggles, her story is also *my* story, which is why I am dedicating this book to her. This book is also dedicated to the single parents and children in poor and violent areas that continually seek ways to obtain better lives in the middle of their own Armageddon.

Through examples, I will emphasize the vital role of a parent in the life of a child in negative or positive ways. My mom made sacrifices many would not emulate because she saw something special in me. She knew I *wanted* to be different. She knew I had the desire and dedication to change my future. She also knew it was too late to steer my siblings in different directions because of the free agency in the choices they made. And even though my mom assisted with guiding my life towards a different and more positive path, her methods of sacrifice would also have negative influences on my life even though the original intent was positive.

Life is obviously difficult, but we are all given the ability to fight for survival. We are all equipped with an inner desire and outward ability to change our

Introduction

future paths regardless of the challenges faced. Instead of stepping off a path entirely, we often shy away from paving a completely different one to follow, almost as if we are resigned to an internal reality that there is only one path open for us to venture. I will describe how I created new paths regardless of how far behind I started versus others. I share examples of ways I used negative surroundings as motivation to succeed instead of license to fail.

Through my eyes, I've seen the eternal consequences of decisions as I approached various forks in the road. I've seen ways to chart entirely different courses than ones initially destined for me. In order to pursue different courses, I had to believe that failure was not going to be an option. I knew my journey was not going to be easy if I was going to eliminate stereotypes and societal patterns that destroyed the mentality of most in similar circumstances. I also understood that my decisions and sacrifices were going to be impactful not only to my life but to a future generation.

Take a journey with me through a set of eyes that have seen events that could have altered my life in completely different directions. Walk in my shoes while marching on unknown paths that changed courses, leading into what initially appeared to be an abyss but turned out to be paradise. Hear through my ears the doubts purposely placed to poison me into thinking my less-than-bastard identification was a reason to accept the status quo. And feel the pain inside a mother's heart as she struggled with balancing her love and concern for her children with the need to enjoy the life she rightfully earned. While walking you through my journey, I will describe how I was able to transition from a mentality of *learning to live* while adapting in a violent neighborhood to a life in which I was *living to learn* as I was able to expand my world academically, financially, and emotionally.

Part I

Foundation

Left: Me, Renee, Ronetta, and June

Below: Me pretending to be a Chicago Cub (my favorite baseball team)

Above: Me and Mom

Right: At my tenth birthday party with Lamont White, Steven Cobbs and Tim Anderson

Lula

My story begins with my mother Lula, who was born on April 24, 1942, in Brinkley, Arkansas, to parents Henry and Malissie "Mudea" Adams. She was the third of five girls born to Henry and Mudea. To seek a better life, Henry and Mudea migrated to Chicago in the mid-1940s. Mom followed her parents to Chicago along with her sisters when she was three years old. Mom stayed in Chicago until 1949, when she returned to Arkansas with her three sisters Vernice, Ora Lee, and Dorothy. She and her sisters stayed with their maternal grandparents while both parents remained in Chicago because of its improved employment opportunities in comparison to Arkansas. Mudea and Henry produced their fifth daughter, Jeanette, in November of 1949.

Henry's alcoholism and philandering contributed to his physical and emotional abuse of Mudea. However, Mudea shared the same philosophy of marriage as many women in the South during that time, which was to ignore the shortcomings of her husband, even while in an abusive relationship. Finally, after several additional attacks, Mudea and Henry divorced shortly after Jeanette was born.

Because of the promising job market, Mudea and Jeanette stayed in Chicago while my mom and the rest of her sisters remained in Arkansas. As a struggling single parent, Mudea made the decision to send Jeanette to Arkansas to live with her sisters while she was only nine months old. Mom's maternal grandparents, uncle L.W., and older cousin Pauline raised the five girls while Mudea continued to work and live in Chicago. During this time, Mudea found new love with a man named Floyd Robinson. She decided to give marriage a second try and married Floyd. The relationship produced three additional children: Floyd, Jr. ("Uncle Butch"), Annette, and Gwen. Mom, Ora Lee and Dorothy visited Mudea in Chicago every summer. They had to pick cotton during the year to pay for their Chicago bus ticket, but they happily obliged because they were happy to see their mom and her new husband.

Mom, Vernice, and Dorothy traveled back and forth between Arkansas and Chicago until they officially moved to Chicago in 1959. The girls lived with Mudea, Floyd, and their three younger siblings while Mom was a junior in high school. Ora Lee and Jeanette remained in Arkansas. In Chicago, the family moved into the Cabrini-Green housing project. Cabrini-Green, built in 1942 and located on Chicago's Near North Side, was one of the most well-known housing projects in the country after being featured in the 1975 movie *Cooley High* as well as the 1970s television show *Good Times*. While a resident of Cabrini-Green, they lived near famous soul singers Major Lance (who sang "The Monkey Time"), Curtis Mayfield (composer of the classic song "Super Fly") and Jerry Butler (who wrote the song "For Your Precious Love"), who all attended Wells High School together with my mom. Mayfield and Butler performed in a neighborhood church choir together before forming the legendary group The Impressions.

Mom enrolled in Wells High School as a senior, during which time she met Ronald Robinson (no relation to Floyd) at a dance held at an Episcopal church near Union Park (Ashland and Madison Avenue). One of the main attractions about him was that he was a good dancer. My mom and Ronald developed a relationship shortly after the dance. After courting for a year, she and Ronald were married on June 26, 1960. My mother and Ronald moved in with her older sister Vernice before moving to the home of Ronald's grandmother and mother on the West Side near the Chicago Stadium. They lived there until the birth of their first child, Ronetta, on October 22, 1960. Shortly after Ronetta's birth, they finally moved into their first apartment on the West Side.

As with my mom, Ronald's upbringing wasn't ideal. He was mostly raised by his grandmother while his mother patrolled the Chicago streets. His dysfunctional family life severely influenced his perception of women. During their marriage, he was physically, verbally, mentally and emotionally abusive towards my mom, mostly because of his inability to maintain employment and his jealousy of the attention she received from her good looks. While my mom worked, instead of searching for jobs, Ronald typically stayed home to watch television and sneak women in and out of their home to have multiple affairs. His mother's hatred and jealousy of my mom influenced her to assist Ronald with keeping his affairs a secret.

Mom and Ronald received meager support from state aid as well as weekly drop-offs by the milkman, who delivered milk, butter, and eggs every Saturday. Ronald's extreme jealousy was displayed when he forced my mom to stay indoors while he partied during the weekends. He often put flour on the floor of the apartment before leaving to attempt to capture Mom's footsteps in case she left for her own enjoyment. Ronald's mistrust of my mom stemmed not only from his own infidelity but also from her appearance. My mom was a very beautiful woman with physical attractions that garnered attention from interested men and spiteful women. Ronald despised the looks my mom received for her appearance and tried hard to control her. He refused to allow Mom's family to visit, fearful that they were delivering secret messages between my mom and other men.

To boost her self-esteem and temporarily escape from Ronald's torment, my mom sought comfort from relationships outside of their marriage with guys who appreciated her internal and external beauty. Ronald caught my mom engaging in one of her affairs, which enraged him to the point of brandishing a knife and threatening her life. Although he enjoyed a multitude of affairs himself, one of which led to additional children, he couldn't stand the thought of my mom repeating his immoral behavior. He couldn't stand the thought of another man touching his prized possession.

Mom became pregnant again and gave birth to her second child and first son, Ronald, Jr. (June), on February 22, 1963. They then moved to another apartment on the West Side where they stayed until separating in 1964 while my mother was carrying her third child. After the separation, she then moved back with her mother before moving in with her aunt Mildred. She then gave birth to their third child and second daughter, Renee, on October 17, 1964. During this time she applied to live in the Chicago Housing Authority housing projects. In December 1964, she received a letter stating her approval to move into the recently constructed Rockwell Gardens housing project on the West Side of Chicago. She and Ronald reunited and moved into the Rockwell, apartment 603, in the building located at 340 South Western Avenue on December 26, 1964.

Unfortunately, the relationship between my mom and Ronald didn't last long after the reunion. During one of Ronald's physical attacks, my mom finally defended herself by stabbing him. Knowing my mom was the actual victim in the relationship, the investigating police decided to look the other way. One of the policemen even encouraged my mom to kill Ronald the next time he struck her. My mom knew she had to leave Ronald for good or else someone was going to die. One of Ronald's abusive tactics was to tell Mom that no one would want a single mother of three kids. Ronald's hurtful words were effective—he got my mom to believe she wasn't attractive, even though she was always a very beautiful woman who won local beauty pageants. He also convinced her that life without him would be lonely.

Mom knew she needed to leave Ronald to find happiness. Her decision to stay with him was probably a result of witnessing her own mother's refusal to leave abusive relationships. Fortunately, she found great inner strength in deciding to separate from Ronald for good. Ronald then found employment with the Cook County Sheriff's Department after briefly moving in with his mother.

Freedom was a new concept for Mom. As a youth, her mother and grandmother did not allow her to have as much freedom as her other sisters. As a young wife, Ronald controlled Mom's life on a daily basis. This was the first time in her life when she felt she could make independent decisions on what she wanted in life. Consequently, Mom's newfound freedom and discovery of her beauty led her to date multiple men at the same time. In addition to her looks, Mom was a great dancer and often hung out at a local club called The Pole, where she gained additional attention from men regardless of whether they were accompanied by a date that evening. Mom dated Pimpin' Sam, a popular West Side pimp, as well as Sonny, a Chicago policeman, at the same time. Unsuccessfully, Sam attempted several times to convert my mom into one of his workers. Mom's staunch refusal to become a lady of the evening intrigued Sam, who instead treated Mom like a queen.

Sonny, who never knew about Mom's relationship with Sam, also appreciated Mom. There were times he provided Mom with money seized from various drug busts. He was the first man to take Mom to expensive clothing stores to buy quality clothes. Unfortunately, Mom discovered Sonny was having a secret relationship with a friend she had allowed to move into her apartment. After the discovery, Mom evicted her friend and decided to leave Sonny.

Because of his passion towards my mom, Sonny was not going to allow the relationship to end quietly. He drove mom to a vacant lot and brandished a gun, threatening to kill her if she left him. He couldn't live without my mom and was willing to take her life if she didn't change her mind. Screaming and begging, my mom was able to convince Sonny to spare her life. Mom and Sonny dated a little longer before mutually deciding to end the relationship with no further threats to her life.

After Mom and Ronald's final separation, she and several members of her family established a vacation club, where they traveled to Nassau, Bahamas, every July. The annual vacation allowed my mom to mentally escape from the abusive life she had with Ronald as well as spend time with her mom and sisters, who accompanied her on many of these trips. My mom's love of reggae music also allowed her to hear the authentic sounds from the island.

After returning home from their annual trips, my mom struggled with supporting her kids as a single parent. Her independence forced her to start working for a manufacturer of pay phones in the suburbs of Chicago while dating a man named Leroy, who had recently returned from Vietnam. Leroy was nice and, similarly to Sonny, tried to assist my mom financially. He was a hard worker and liked by my siblings, but he didn't have the charisma to maintain my mom's interest in a long-term relationship.

During my mom's relationship with Leroy she became pregnant. She contemplated abortion but couldn't go through with it because she was already in the late stages of her pregnancy. My mom didn't know she was pregnant for months because she was still having her monthly menstrual cycle and didn't gain an extraordinary amount of weight in her first few months. She became concerned about raising a child for many reasons. First, she was approaching 30, which was beyond what was perceived at that time to be her child-bearing years. And, even though she was involved with Leroy, my mom was still a single mother of three because of their volatile relationship. Ronald wasn't fulfilling his responsibility as a parent, which placed a great burden on her financially. Her pregnancy was a tremendous surprise and one that could have destroyed the world she was starting to build as a single parent.

After moving forward with her pregnancy, my mom delivered me on April 4, 1972, at the Presbyterian Hospital in Chicago, Illinois. She named me after the son of the main character in the television show *Sanford and Son* (which spawned countless Fred impersonations of "Hey Lamont, you big dummy!" throughout my life). After I arrived home, Renee welcomed me by accidentally dropping me while trying to hold me for the first time. Up to that point, Renee had been the youngest and hadn't been around a baby in our home.

My siblings were excited to have a baby in the home. June was happy to have a little brother, while Ronetta and Renee were looking forward to testing out their early maternal instincts by assisting with my care. Since we lived in Rockwell with other family and friends, my mom received help caring for me. She also got help from my Aunt Dorothy, who lived nearby and always enjoyed having me at her house. I spent a lot of time with Aunt Dorothy and her husband, Oscar, who treated me like I was one of their biological children.

I had always been told that Leroy was my father, but Leroy knew I couldn't have been his child as the result of his impotence developed from an injury sustained during his Vietnam tour. He initially thought I was Ronald's son because of my light complexion and eyes, which were similar to Ronald's. My mom and Ronald officially divorced in 1974, so technically there could have been a chance I was Ronald's. Regardless, the uncertainty of who my father was added to the complexities surrounding my mom's life during this period of time.

I vaguely remember Leroy and, from the pictures of him, never noticed a resemblance. Leroy was about 5'8", while I now stand 6'3". He also didn't have any of my prominent facial features, including my sleepy eyes and large earlobes. Most importantly, I didn't believe he had any love for his supposed son, walking out on me when I was four years old. I could have looked beyond our lack of similarities if he showed any desire to be in my life. I grew up angry at Leroy and fathers in general because he wasn't in my life. I also grew jealous of my siblings, since they knew their father and had the luxury of living with him at some point in their lives.

Since my mom had already invested into her annual Bahamas vacation, she decided to continue the tradition in 1972, even though I was only three months old. During that 1972 trip, my mom met Bob, who was an insurance salesman and prominent politician in the city of Waukegan, a neighboring suburb north of Chicago. Back home, I was left with Leroy, who used this moment as an opportunity to escape by leaving me with my mom's stepfather, Floyd. Leroy knew that he wasn't going to be in our lives knowing that I wasn't his biological child. It was also discovered during this time that he had resurrected his relationship with his ex-wife while still in one with my mom.

My feelings for Leroy changed from hatred to sympathy. Even though it was obvious to him that I wasn't his biological son, he and my mom maintained a relationship for three years. Eventually, he left for good in the late '70s after deciding to move to Florida. Initially, he attempted to take me with him, claiming to have an intention of only visiting his father. After he was denied in bringing me along, he disappeared from our lives forever. I can't blame Leroy for leaving us after having physical proof of my mom's lack of commitment to their relationship. Also, his intuition probably revealed that my mom's heart was elsewhere and not focused on growing a stronger relationship with him.

Fatherless

EVEN MORE THAN SONNY, BOB was the first man to show my mom the finer things in life. He taught her how to be financially independent as well as the value of managing money by showing her how to manage a savings account while also being able to wine and dine. He used a tough love approach, forcing my mom to give him her paychecks as he helped to sort the "needs" versus "wants." My mom enjoyed buying a lot of "wants" through the usage of credit cards. Bob forced her to give him all of her credit cards then subsequently cut them all up so that she couldn't use them anymore. My mom still found creative ways to make purchases by obtaining new cards after convincing stores she left her card at home.

Bob also encouraged me to save, and he taught me how to hide my money inside the socks occupying my drawers, knowing my snooping family wouldn't think to look there as they searched my room for money. He also influenced me to keep a ledger that included all amounts borrowed by my mom. In addition to the amount borrowed, I kept track of the due date I assigned to the loan and constantly reminded my mom about her obligations if payments were late.

Although previous boyfriends also took care of us financially, Bob was the first to bring a structure to our home. My mom's kind heart allowed others to take advantage of her because of her inability to tell them "no." Bob stopped the family and friend freeloaders who freely borrowed items from my mom's kitchen or lived in our home along with their kids. This didn't make Bob popular among the family, but it was necessary in order for my mom to maintain her path towards financial freedom.

Bob always seemed to carry an extraordinary amount of cash for an insurance salesman, usually sporting a wad consisting of $20, $10 and $5 bills. His large bills, $50s and $100s, were kept in his wallet. Renee later admitted she used to sneak inside my mom's bedroom, as she and Bob rested, to steal some of his cash. Renee believed Bob wouldn't miss the cash since he had such an abundance of it. Bob was proud to display his wad, confident that no one would attempt to take it from him. Because of his financial security, family members frequently borrowed from him, which turned him into the de facto family "Godfather." However, unlike Don Vito Corleone, family members received no comeuppance after frequently failing to pay him back. I am sure Bob knew exactly how much others owed him but allowed them to deal with their own conscience as they often found ways to change the subject when money was mentioned in conversations.

Unfortunately, Bob couldn't be our full-time dad because he was married with three kids. Even though he had a family of his own, Bob became the father figure desperately needed by my family. Even with his morally unorthodox leadership of the family, he was the father every child ever wanted. He gave us gifts for Christmas and birthdays, attended the majority of our graduations and other special occasions, entertained the family by taking us to downtown restaurants, and provided physical and financial protection. I desperately wanted Bob to be in our home every day but I was too young to understand the significant logistical and ethical conflict we were presenting to his primary life as a married father of three.

When Bob took us to the downtown restaurants for dinner, we felt as if we were going out of town because of the new and different experience. We were fascinated while watching the way people dressed, talked, and looked—genuinely happy about life. We had that same feeling of escaping our reality when we visited our relatives in Waukegan, which now included Mudea and husband Floyd, my aunts Dorothy, Annette, and Gwen, as well as Uncle Butch. Our view from our insular ghetto world was so myopic that any expansion outside of our vicinity seemed like a world away. Although my relatives stayed in Waukegan's version of the projects, we felt as if their tiny townhomes were mansions compared to our ghetto living quarters just because they had two levels with stairs.

Bob was also the first person to allow my Mom to see that Chicago was not the only city in the world. He took my mom on Wednesday "movie nights," invited her to travel out of town during his business trips, and eliminated her financial debt even though he was still supporting his family in Waukegan. Bob allowed us to feel like we were ghetto royalty because we were exposed to more than the average families in Rockwell. Because I focused so much on the positive things Bob provided us, I never thought much about his situation at home.

I never thought how strange it was that each time I visited Bob's home in Waukegan, it seemed as if no one was living there with him. I discovered later that my visits corresponded with the times his wife and kids were traveling. However, I ignored the strange feelings because I was excited I was able to spend time with my "dad." Since Leroy had walked out of my life, having a male role model was exciting. Because of this void in my life, I often got attached to many of the males visiting our home, constantly looking for positive father figures to replace what I didn't have.

Although the relationship between my mom and Bob was immoral, Bob was a very spiritual man. He influenced my mom to go to church after noticing she wasn't grounded in the gospel. He promised that if she went to church every Sunday, he would buy her anything she wanted for Christmas. She started attending a local neighborhood church, but didn't like having a woman preacher. She then started to attend her mother's church, Mars Hill, which was on the West Side of Chicago. She was eventually baptized on December 6, 1974, and has remained a strong and active member of the church since that day. True to his word, Bob purchased a new car for my mom, which wasn't standard in Rockwell.

Growing up in the church was difficult in my early years. Church services seemed to last forever, and every Sunday my mom caught the "Holy Ghost", which is a phrase used for obtaining the spirit. Almost like clockwork, I knew when the Holy Ghost was approaching. Typically when the choir was singing a powerful hymn and the minister was rhythmically screaming, Mom started to shake. She then rocked back and forth in her seat before belting "Thank you Jesus!!!" Immediately after her vocal announcement of the spirit, she leapt from the bench, walked around in a circle, and then chanted indescribable words while her eyes rolled to the back of her head. As a child, this was daunting and embarrassing, knowing that my mom's performance was being viewed by everyone in the church. To reduce the horror, I purposely found a spot in back of the church and stretched across the bench with the intent of sleeping throughout the ceremony and avoid the spiritual spectacle.

I developed a disdain for ministers that begged for their mostly financially inept members to contribute to the church, or to the ministers directly. While I always believed in tithing, I did not believe in furnishing the minister with his latest and greatest Mercedes-Benz while the majority of his congregation struggled to keep food on their tables. I also struggled with being involved in a church that did not look for ways to assist their struggling members. Although I had a physically impressive Bible, I rarely found the need to study the gospel written inside of it. Later in life, I stopped going to church for a period of eight years. I knew there was a better alternative than going to a church that made tithing a public spectacle and whose congregation suffered financially while the minister profited. However, our home benefited as a result of my mom having a spiritual foundation. Bob's influence on her as well as his dedication to forcing us to believe we were different than our surroundings was beneficial too.

Bob always had a special focus on me. He became my surrogate father and supported me with any necessities. He was also the major influence with my interest in corporate America. Visions of him preparing for work by shaving, slapping on the good-smelling aftershave and cologne, then donning nice suits before going to important meetings were all great memories and key drivers for me to want the same level of success, even though I didn't truly understand his profession. Even though Bob was an insurance agent, I always thought he and all men in suits were accountants, since I had no one explaining to me the differences between careers within corporate America. This could have occurred after seeing a program on television that featured an accountant who happened to be wearing a suit.

I spent the majority of my early scholastic life training to be an accountant. This fascination was also the reason I enjoyed watching movies and television shows pertaining to business as it looked like an enjoyable profession. One of my favorite television shows growing up was *The Jeffersons*. Seeing the diminutive George Jefferson in a suit and owning his own company (a line of dry cleaners) as a minority would later provide inspiration for my career path.

To get me into the mind frame of a businessman, I often created and played a pretend game by myself for which I called "The Executive." To play this game, I set up a makeshift executive office in my small bedroom, with my backpack serving as my attaché and my mom's unused check register as my pretend work ledger. I imagined various negotiation sessions and involvement with key board meetings. I had a pretend phone on my pretend desk, calling pretend clients to ask for pretend opportunities. Since I didn't think other friends would be interested in playing my pretend game, I opted to maintain my solo performance and continued to negotiate deals against myself.

Along with watching *The Jeffersons*, playing "The Executive" provided the initial spark which led to the desire to become a business executive. I often wondered how it would feel to have the power to make decisions in a business setting since I was, at that time, on the other side of that success as a poor kid on the West Side of Chicago. I also wanted to see how it felt to be one of the most important people in the company, if not the leader of that pretend company.

I always wondered what each day was like for Bob. I wondered what he did on his lunch breaks, what he discussed during work meetings and even what his secretary looked like. Even though I had all of these questions in my head, I never asked him. I believe I didn't want to be disappointed that his real work life was nothing similar to the pretend world I created.

Bob visited our family every Wednesday night. Since the majority of my friends did not have a father in their household, Bob gave me a sense of pride and envy among some of the neighborhood kids. He often arrived at our building and immediately started distributing money to the local kids as if he was the Rockwell Santa Claus, mostly because of his soft spot for kids. No one bothered Bob mostly because of his intimidating personality as well as the muscular physique he developed as a former wrestler in high school. If all else failed, many knew he also carried a handgun and a stun gun, and was not afraid to use either. Bob had a loud, powerful voice that demanded attention, which augmented his aura. Unfortunately, his loud voice was also directed frequently towards my mom, sometimes in abusive ways, which intimidated me when I was young. Although I loved Bob, I also feared him during my early years because of his strong and controlling personality.

Although Bob aggressively attempted to provide the needed father figure, growing up without a father inside the home provided additional challenges. Without a father to give me the proverbial *birds and bees* father/son discussion, I had to learn on my own. Since most of the Rockwell boys were also without fathers, we sometimes allowed our curiosities about our changing bodies to teach ourselves about sex, or at least what we thought encompassed sex. Because there were always scintillating record album covers or pornographic videotapes inside our homes that were easily accessible, we often allowed our curiosity to educate ourselves about sex.

On a few occasions, a small group of us explored our bodies not knowing the reasons for our curiosity. While none of these experimentation sessions actually led to sex, we knew our exploration was reaching a level of taboo none of us could explain or even discuss among each other today. To my knowledge, none of us received counseling for these formative experimentations. I always firmly knew I was heterosexual during this period in my life mostly because I was able to suppress any curiosity for further "experiments" for my strong desire for female companionship (even at an early age)—unfortunately, a result of the vivid pornographic images of women from the videos embedded in my mind. However, I strongly believe some of the participants in these sessions pursued same-sex relationships later in life even though on the surface they maintained relationships with females. The problem with this isn't the fact they are interested in same-sex relationships as much as it is they were confused about their situations in life and had no one to talk to during this physically volatile period.

Another early exposure to sex came at the hands of a babysitter who was the daughter of a very close friend of my mom. While watching the Charlie Brown Christmas special around the age of five, my teenaged female babysitter convinced me to lie on top of her. As the program continued, she kissed me on my lips which, initially, I thought of as being innocent. When she continued to kiss me I knew something was wrong and different. Although our kisses did not progress to anything beyond our initial interaction, I never realized until later that I had been molested, or understood the impact this event would have on my sexual growth.

Child molestation wasn't new to our family as there were known molesters in our family. Even though everyone knew which relatives to avoid because of their sexually abusive tendencies, there was never any counseling for them or the victims, which led to even more destructive behaviors and divisiveness within the family. Often the abusers had been earlier victims themselves. As usual, the nature of secrecy in our family incorrectly suppressed behaviors and horrible memories that could have been healed through proper counseling.

Without a solid way to verbally externalize the various challenges we faced on a daily basis, we often turned to our own security blankets, similar to the Linus character in Charlie Brown movies. Some of us used drugs as our security blanket, while others were drawn towards gang families and criminal activities. My comfort was, and always has been, music. While music did not serve as a ghetto panacea, it always provided a therapeutic way for me to escape or cope with my struggles. Music gave me a connection to a blissful world that I had always yearned for and believed to have existed.

Music

MUSIC HAS ALWAYS PLAYED A vital role in my life. Mom often listened to music based on her mood. Reggae was often played while she was cleaning around the house, even though it hadn't yet gained popularity in America. The blues played while she was in a sad mood, usually the result of a relationship problem. Doo-wop was also often heard when she was reminiscing about her youth in Arkansas and Chicago. Motown was reserved for the happy times, especially when we had visitors, which was always a favorite time of mine. My mom and her sisters frequently sang selections from The Supremes, with my mom often taking the lead as Diana Ross overshadowing her background singers.

One of my favorite songs to hear Mom playing was the blue-eyed soul group Hall & Oates' 1976 hit "Sara Smile." To this day, "Sara Smile" brings a smile to my face each time I hear the opening guitar riff. My mom played that song over and over, while sometimes closing her eyes and singing out loud. While she was enjoying the song, she didn't realize I was in my room enjoying it as much as she did. I was also shocked to find out that Hall & Oates were white. I thought for sure that song with such a powerful soul was only reserved for black singers. Other songs from that period bring happy feelings today when I think of the positive memories surrounding my family and those songs.

My siblings were also great music lovers. Ronetta used to sing Deniece Williams' "Free," while hitting all of the insanely high notes. June imitated the falsetto voices popular during songs of the late 1970s male soul groups. Renee often pretended to sing in a group, usually the Mary Jane Girls, with several of her girlfriends. I watched their performances sometimes and pretended I was at their concert, allowing them to allow me to escape for that one brief moment. Similar to my mom, Renee often took the lead for most of the performances, which later influenced my musical group leadership as well.

Other family members, such as my Uncle Butch, often imitated The Temptations with my older cousins, which greatly influenced me to dream about being in a singing group. I enjoyed performing Gladys Knight & The Pips' "Midnight Train to Georgia" in front of my Aunt Dorothy, even though her album was scratched during the part when Gladys sang "I'd rather live in his world…I'd rather live in his world…I'd rather live in his world." She had me repeat the words over and over until it eventually advanced to the next line. Even though it was annoying that she didn't advance the scratched part of the song, I enjoyed the positive attention I received from her and Oscar as well as the joy she displayed in seeing how her young nephew was appreciating good music.

Growing up in the all-black development of Rockwell didn't prevent me from having a diverse taste in music. I believe I was the only kid in the projects that liked Elvis Presley, which developed the moment I heard my mom play her Elvis 45-speed record, and Mudea gave me an 8-track of *Elvis' Christmas Album*. I performed "Hound Dog" and "Don't Be Cruel" in front of our apartment while enjoying the neighborhood cheers. At the end of "Hound Dog," I jumped in the air and landed on my knees, timing my leap with the drum roll at the end of the song. This repeated performance is probably the reason I have bad knees today. Again, I enjoyed the small piece of joy my performances provided to family and friends during our tumultuous stay in Rockwell.

Even though most of us were too poor to attend major concerts, we enjoyed our own impressive Rockwell talent. On different occasions, the neighborhood June Mallory Band performed on the large concrete field in front of our building. We were entertained hearing flawless imitations of soulful '70s and '80s bands such as Earth Wind & Fire, Kool & the Gang, The Commodores, and others. The free JM Band concerts were enjoyable to listen to and displayed the amount of talent from kids that essentially were given no hope. Even though the performances were partly for our enjoyment, they were also conducted for a hopeful discovery as if music executives were walking the broken Rockwell grounds to search for the next big act. In the late '80s and early '90s, we were often entertained by scratch sessions from Maurice "DJ Waxmaster," one of my childhood friends who established himself as a force to be reckoned with on the Chicago DJ scene, especially in the '90s.

My largest musical influence during that period was from a neighborhood quartet called the Chi-Boys, which consisted of some of the greatest singers and performers I had ever seen perform. The Chi-Boys often sang in the urine-stained hallways, snapping their fingers and belting out melodic and reverberating sounds that I would have easily paid to hear. In addition to their incredible sound were their smooth moves. The Chi-Boys were Rockwell's version of The Temptations. Even though as a group they never realized stardom, one of their lead singers, Dave Hollister (who is also the cousin of K-Ci and JoJo, the lead singers of the R&B group Jodeci), became the lead for Teddy Riley's 1990s group Blackstreet.

I was inspired to pursue a career in entertainment as a result of attending my first concert. On August 28, 1981, Renee took me to The Jacksons concert during their *Triumph* tour at the old Chicago Stadium. I had always been a huge fan of The Jacksons and did not know what to expect. We arrived late but were still able to catch Stacy Lattisaw, the opening act, who was joined on stage by a young Johnnie Gill. I enjoyed Stacy's performance, but anxiously waited to see the kings.

When it was time for The Jacksons to perform, four large screens covered the entire stage. The Jacksons' video for "Can You Feel It" played on the large screens as the crowd screamed louder and louder. After the video, the crowd's level of anticipation reached unbelievable depths. While the crowd screamed and waited for the show to begin, one of The Jacksons screamed into his microphone "Caaaan you feeeeel it?????! Caaaaaaaaaan yooooooooou feeeeeeeeeel iiiiiiiiiiit?????!" The large video screens then rose slowly, revealing The Jacksons, who were all standing on stage in still poses. I had never heard a building get as loud as The Stadium that evening while I cheered for my heroes. After a few decibel increases, The Jacksons kicked off their concert, singing the live version of "Can You Feel It." Watching Michael glide across the stage and capture the hearts of fans greatly influenced me to want to pursue a career performing in front of others. My mom took me and Renee to see The Jacksons again in 1985 at the old Comiskey Park during their *Victory* tour. Jermaine reunited with his brothers during that tour, which gave me the chance to see the entire musical clan and hear the sounds that used to blast from my room as I played my various 45-speed Jackson 5 records on the blue Motown label.

Shortly after returning home from the 1981 concert, I went into my room and began to practice the dance steps seen at the concert. I became fascinated with Michael as he possessed the ability to mesmerize audiences in ways I had never seen an artist do then or even now. For months, I came home from school, closed my bedroom door, and practiced routines I had seen at the 1981 concert or on their music videos. The Jacksons were gods to me after seeing how they influenced hysteria in others through music on that August evening.

Like most kids from that era, I was caught up in the Michael Jackson craze once the *Thriller* album was released. When I visited Mudea, she had me dance in front of everyone at her house. One of her favorite routines was "Billie Jean." As everyone was gathered downstairs in her living room, I stood at the top of her stairs. Once the famous drum beat and subsequent baseline of the song began, I started walking down the stairs, emulating Michael's careful and rhythmic walk on the lit-up tiled floor from the music video. I always enjoyed the thrill I got while watching everyone witness my performance as I pretended, for that moment, to be the biggest pop star in the history of music. The attention was definitely exciting and worth all of the repetition and numerous practices to perfect the performance.

My solo performances continued until May 16, 1983, while watching the television special *Motown 25: Yesterday, Today and Forever*. It was then that the world saw Michael perform the moonwalk for the first time after reuniting with all of his brothers on stage. After the program, I decided to form a group imitating The Jacksons. I knew that my neighborhood friend Rashied was a good dancer, as well as his cousin Quamie and my friend Dashun. I also asked my cousin and best friend, James, to join the group. James wasn't a good dancer but he worked hard. The decision also allowed me to avoid any family political drama if he was left out of the group.

Music

I took my fascination of Michael to another level. My Members Only jacket was covered with Michael Jackson buttons while my bedroom wall was blanketed with his posters. I participated in various dance contests while wearing my pleather *Thriller* black and white imitation jacket, flooded pants, white socks, black penny loafers with a quarter lodged inside, cheaply imitated solo white glove and a mini-afro Jheri curl. Also like most youths, my eyes were glued to the television every Friday night to watch *Friday Night Videos*, hoping to catch a Michael video. We couldn't afford cable, so MTV wasn't an option. However, even without seeing Michael's videos consistently, my memory allowed me to perform his moves. I perfected the moonwalk and even taught it to some of the neighborhood break dancers.

We performed in front of crowds at Rockwell Gardens as well as in talent shows, pageants, and other events. Dashun moved from Rockwell, after which we replaced him with two brothers, Antron ("Cook") and Walter. In our group, Cook was Tito, Walter was Jermaine, Rashied was Marlon, James was Jackie and Quamie was Randy. It was a thrill to see people cheer for us, which made all of us work even harder. We wanted our "fans" to believe we were actually The Jacksons, which meant our performance had to be memorable.

As music continued to define my life during that time, the summer of 1983 gave me my first experience away from home for a significant amount of time. My mom decided to send me and James to stay with her Aunt Sis in Hot Springs, Arkansas for a month. I was not excited at all about this "vacation" mostly because I am, and have always been, a true city boy. I had, up until that time in my life, never embraced the back-in-time feel for rural living, feeling more comfortable in the constant hustle and bustle of the big city, even with its daily dangers. Chicago had become my world and Arkansas seemed closer to being its own country to me than just a couple of states away.

My angst in going to Arkansas was made easier in knowing that James was joining me. Because we were almost identical in age and lived in apartments directly above one another, we had a brotherly bond. In addition to being in the same dance group and sharing the same friends, we used to find various ways to entertain each other, including prank calls. One particular call involved James randomly calling someone from the Yellow Pages phone directory. When the recipient of the call answered, James would ask to speak to Roach. After the person stated there was no one in their household by the name of Roach, James facetiously replied, "With all of those damn roaches in your home, you can't let me speak to ONE?!" I knew our Arkansas summer would be filled with additional memories.

After arriving in Arkansas, it was everything I knew it would be…hot, boring and slow. I felt as if I was transported to a world 100 years ago when horses pulled carriages that occupied easygoing southerners. While carriages were replaced by cars, I was still not comfortable with being in the South. I often saw movies or television shows portraying black southerners as laid back and even lazy, while portraying white southerners as being evil and racist. The ghetto nature inside my soul kept me on edge for any activities I felt displayed racism.

Aunt Sis enjoyed her frequent games of bingo. She used to force me and James to pick out the "good" bingo cards and actually gave us a small portion of her winnings if our boards were victorious. When she realized she was a winner, which was rare, she stomped loudly on the floor, shouting out "Baaaannnnngoooo!!" James and I were more excited because our earnings would allow us to purchase our favorite treats. When we realized the price differences of candy and other delicious Arkansas treats versus Chicago, we worked hard to earn enough to support our savory habits.

Living in Arkansas allowed me to temporarily conquer one of my biggest fears…swimming. Living in the city did not allow many opportunities to swim as most of us in Rockwell were too poor to afford memberships at the local YMCA, and many of the city pools were often dirty with vicious combinations of feces and urine, or used as bathtubs for lazy kids washing off dirt from their playful activities. I also believed death by drowning would be the worst way to die. However, James was a good swimmer and we had access to a clean pool nearby, so I decided I would conquer this fear.

Each day, James and I went to the YMCA pool to escape the torturous sun and boring lifestyle. I was jealous and amazed of the way James maneuvered the waters while I was concerned more with learning how to hold my breath at the bottom of the pool. A near-drowning of another swimmer didn't add to my level of confidence, but I knew if I didn't learn how to swim I would never have the desire as an adult. While I was able to learn the basics of swimming that summer, I lost confidence once I went back home to Chicago. I have never regained that confidence even as an adult.

After each afternoon filled with swimming, James and I went inside the nearby recreation center to enjoy a nice bowl of soup and a stick of cheese. The soup was always hot and the cheese provided a great flavor once melted inside the bowl. The delicious soup and cheese allowed us to ignore the other diners that seemed to ignore good hygiene, and one evening we found out why this was the case. After Aunt Sis returned from work, it was obvious that she was visibly upset. After slamming her purse on the kitchen table, she screamed out at us, "Why would you embarrass me in front of my neighbors?!?!?"

Even though James and I were never angels, we both believed we had been acting appropriately every day at the pool and around town. Our days only consisted of swimming and eating the hot meals provided at the recreation center. We then found out from Aunt Sis that we had been enjoying soup provided in a soup line that was intended for the homeless. Since we were both known around town as Aunt Sis nephews, word quickly spread back to her that we were taking advantage of the system. Although neither one of us wanted to embarrass our aunt, I was extremely disappointed that we would no longer enjoy the delicious offerings of the warm soup and cheese.

As I later reflected on the summer of 1983 in Arkansas, I realized that the experience of being away from home and daily violence would benefit me in ways I could have never imagined at that childish period in my life. My eyes were opened to a new world. Until that Arkansas "vacation", I believed everyone lived in neighborhoods that were controlled by drugs and gang violence. I also realized that not all whites were racist and there were some southerners that actually moved hastily. With my generalizations conquered, it was time for us to return to reality by returning to Chicago.

Violence not only impacted my neighborhood and family, it also found its way into my music. On April 1, 1984, I found out that Marvin Gaye, who is currently my all-time favorite singer, had been killed. What made the news worse was to find out that he was killed by his own father. Since this was on April Fool's Day, I thought it was a horrible joke until all of the radio stations and television broadcasts confirmed the killing. Not only was the news of Marvin's death difficult to swallow, to hear it came at the hands of his own father tormented me. Marvin had triumphantly returned to America after a self-exile in Belgium, rediscovered success with his hit song "Sexual Healing", won his first Grammy award for the song, performed his emotionally-stirring rendition of the National Anthem during the 1983 NBA All-Star Game, and elicited positive reviews after his *Motown 25* performance. My hope in the value of fathers diminished significantly on April 1, 1984. *How could a parent commit such a heinous crime to a child they've been blessed with?*

I didn't fully appreciate Marvin's greatness until I matured, but I would find several similarities between me and him. Marvin wrote and sang songs based on events that impacted his life. In addition to being Aries, both of us constantly battled our desires to follow Godly examples only to find ourselves influenced by sin surrounding us. Sex and drugs were Marvin's escape from various pains in life, which he made evident in the lyrics of his songs. Although my appreciation of Marvin was not developed at that time, I vividly remember the bereaved feeling after receiving the shocking news of his death. This was unlike my typical reaction upon hearing about the death of other singers and celebrities.

I knew the world had lost a musical prophet. The pain in Marvin's voice spoke to generations. One of my favorite Marvin songs is called "I Want You," which deals with the pain of loving someone who didn't love him the same way. I related to these lyrics later in life, but my immature mind only knew of a man that sang of wars and sex. As the song begins, seductive sounds of the violin set the mood while the steady bass and perfectly placed horns are a prelude to Marvin belting the lyrics which include the line "but half a love, is all I need". He was clearly in need of someone making *at least* a half-hearted effort to show their love for him as he was giving 110% of himself to that person. His cry of "I want youuuuu baby…but I want youuuuu to want me too baby" at the end validated the outpouring of his soul to fans through his music.

While still trying to make sense of Marvin's death, I noticed a shift in my music tastes in the middle of 1984 after seeing one of the most influential musical movies of my time. *Purple Rain*, the semi-autobiographical movie about the singer Prince, debuted in July that year. After seeing the movie (which was extremely inappropriate for 12-year-olds) at least ten times at the theater, my group decided that we needed to change our inspiration. I stepped to the background as Rashied took the lead as Prince. Even though he was the darkest of us all, Rashied was the ideal imitator of Prince because he was the best dancer and raunchiest among us. I was actually happier to take a back seat for this group, as I don't know if I would have been brave enough to sensually gyrate in front of the others the way Rashied was able to do.

Since the group provided an opportunity for all of us to lead, we decided to break off a group to imitate Prince's offshoot group The Time, which was led by Quamie. Just like in *Purple Rain*, we often had The Time versus The Revolution (Prince's group) battles. Just like with everything else, I put my heart completely into imitating Brown Mark from The Revolution. I researched Prince's previous work, borrowing long trench coats from friends, influencing my mom to buy a plastic guitar, and using broken synthesizers some of us received originally as Christmas presents to fantasize we were playing actual instruments. We couldn't afford real wardrobes or instruments, so we used our imagination to improvise. Although we never performed in formal contests, we practiced every day, which kept all of us out of trouble from the mean and unforgiving Rockwell streets. Unfortunately, my siblings didn't have the same diversions as I did with my friends, which had a direct impact on their lives.

Siblings

Like most housing projects, Rockwell Gardens started as a great concept for poor families. The discounted rent allowed parents to support their children while enjoying the benefits of having a neighborhood "family". Some decent residents, including my mom, took great pride and care in keeping their "home" presentable by cleaning their apartments and mopping the small porch area in front of their doors. Unfortunately, some residents didn't maintain the same level of pride in their homes. Some apartments were so filthy that its stench could be smelled from the outside.

To get to our sixth floor apartment you could ride the elevator (when it was working), or walk up the stairwell that typically included broken lights, glass, and urine puddles. Occasionally, violent entrepreneurs used the darkened and urine-scented hallways to sell drugs or rob tenants and visitors. By the time you reached your destination, you had survived most of these elements without even knowing they existed.

My mom never accepted the stigma of a single, welfare mother who lived in the projects. Although we lived in the projects, she always maintained an immaculate apartment. She allowed no one to sit on the vinyl-covered couches in her tiny living room, and was constantly seen mopping the floors inside and outside our apartment while listening to reggae or other inspirational music. Even though my mom was a single mother, she always prepared a hot breakfast and dinner for us every day and night. I still remember how we used to hear her resounding shouts travel above all of Rockwell's nightly mayhem, summoning me and siblings to come home for dinner. It seemed like she could make an impressive dinner spread with just a few ingredients as if she was Jesus feeding the poor. Some of her meals were Rockwell legends such as her baked macaroni and cheese casserole or sweet banana pudding dessert. She even made meatloaf an enjoyable treat. My mom was also known for her sense of style and class even though her income was in the poverty range.

My mom was the best I knew at making the most with the hand she was dealt. She was very influential among some of the other women in the neighborhood as they saw how hard she worked to bring joy to her kids and the neighborhood as well. To keep my siblings out of trouble as well as expand their world, she sent them to an annual summer camp in Algonquin, Illinois. She hoped their exposure to nature would influence them to explore life outside of the city, or at a minimum take their minds off the Rockwell violence. To bring entertainment into Rockwell, she led an annual parade which featured my siblings and other neighborhood kids dressed in their Sunday best outfits while dancing and singing for the audience.

I never knew we were poor since not only was everyone else around us poor, we always received what we needed. We never had an empty refrigerator and never had to worry about having clean clothes. Periodically my mom had to get assistance from Public Aid, but she worked hard to avoid the additional support. She was able to attend Westinghouse Vocational School to obtain her G.E.D. She then went to Daniel Hale University to receive a certificate in typing, which was the extent of her education.

My mom worked hard and did the best she could in maintaining a solid family life as a single parent. Before I started elementary school, my mom's early morning routine consisted of her wrapping my long-legged body into a warm blanket, carrying me down six flights of stairs, and then whisking us away towards the Les Finch Learning Tree preschool I attended while she worked. Most of the time I was already awake, but I enjoyed the comforting feeling in my warm blanket with my mom's loving and embracing arms protecting me.

Violence always found ways to rear its ugly head in my family. One of its victims wasn't actually physically hurt, but was forever impacted nonetheless. My oldest sister Ronetta is one of the sweetest people you could ever meet. Ronetta, at that time, was a beautiful, quiet person, but also one of the fiercest fighters if she was provoked. She enjoyed sports and was sometimes viewed as a tomboy because of her desire to hang with the boys while playing softball and jumping on the dirty mattresses left outside. As a pre-teen, Ronetta was molested by a much older family member. The incident was, like most negative situations in our family, never addressed, and Ronetta was never provided proper counseling. Since Ronald wasn't as active in Ronetta's or my other siblings' lives after the separation, they often sought replacements. In the late 1970s, Ronetta developed a relationship with Jerome ("Spot") Wells, a tall, slender boy from one of the nearby apartment buildings, 2515 West Jackson.

Spot was the sixth child of nine kids, of which there were three girls and six boys. Because of their parents' upbringing, they were all raised in the church. The Wells boys were known as the neighborhood Jackson 5, as they started singing at early ages in a family group which originally focused on gospel music before shifting to more secular R&B. The Wells brothers used to compete against other neighborhood groups, such as the early formation of the Chi-Boys.

Violent gangs existed in Rockwell but weren't as dangerous during that era and weren't as popular as the singing groups. The groups used their competitive drive to battle on the various stages at high school talent shows and the local Beacon House community center. Ronetta and Spot met during one of those talent shows, where she was charmed by this handsome, well-built, intelligent and talented young man. Spot and his brothers sang The O'Jays ballad "Cry Together," while he charmed Ronetta, directing his attention towards her. Ronetta was mesmerized and almost instantly fell for him that night.

Spot had a very kind heart, but he had a violent streak in him as well. He loved to collect guns and even knew how to take them apart only to rebuild them. He would give the shirt off his back and didn't start fights, but would respond in a severe manner if something was directed towards him or his biological or gang families. Drew, Spot's right-hand man, joined him on missions to visit other projects like Cabrini-Green, assisting the local undermanned Vice Lords gang with battles against their rival, the Disciples.

As a teen, he was arrested and sent to the Saint Charles Juvenile Correctional Facility after Ronetta became pregnant with their first child. While he was still incarcerated, Ronetta delivered Jaqueah "Queah" in December of 1981. Spot had to celebrate the birth of his first child and daughter at Saint Charles, but that didn't take away his excitement of being a father.

Even though they had a volatile relationship, Spot and Ronetta enjoyed being parents. Spot was especially excited to be around Queah, who was also my mom's first granddaughter (June had a son, Timothy, who lived in a nearby building with his mother) and the first grandchild to live in our home. When Queah was born, I was excited to have someone younger than me inside our apartment. I used to watch her sleep peacefully while amazed at God's work to produce such a beautiful child. She had a warm and welcoming smile, similar to Ronetta's, even at an early age. I was enamored with my niece and was always eager to showcase her in front of my friends. Since Queah was the only grandchild inside our home, she was treated like the family trophy, which was fine with me. I didn't have a younger sibling, so she became my de facto little sister. I protected her to the extent any nine-year-old could do in the face of danger. I always enjoyed going places with Queah in tow because of the positive attention she always received.

When Spot was released from Saint Charles, various factions of the Black Souls and Folk Nation gang enterprise, which included the Gangster Disciples, had integrated closer to his building, which had been historically dominated by the rival Vice Lords. There were also Imperial Insane, Mafia Insane, Conservatives and Unknown Vice Lord factions. Spot was the original chief of the Renegade Vice Lords (RVLs), and was unfazed by the threat of the increased population of the Disciples.

As Disciples and Black Souls started occupying more territories in Rockwell, Vice Lords were pushed further back into the less-populated gang areas in the northwest part of the neighborhood. Impact from the violent clashes weren't relegated to gang members. While Queah was playing on Spot's front apartment porch, one of the rival gang members fired a shot from the other end of the floor towards her direction. Fortunately, she wasn't hit by the stray bullet, but the incident caused Spot to seek unspecified but severe retaliation as he couldn't believe someone would attempt to kill his helpless and innocent child.

Because of Spot's gang leadership, police often raided the Wellses' apartment. The Wellses also constantly lived in fear of the rival gangs. In addition to his violent tendencies, Spot experimented with drugs, with his favorite selection being a "syrup" drink, which is a drug made from cough syrup typically mixed with ingredients such as Sprite or Mountain Dew and pieces of Jolly Rancher candy. Its impact is similar to heroin, causing a drowsy sensation and the user nodding half-asleep. Ronetta often supplied him with the syrup while working for a doctor's office. Spot and his friends used to smoke marijuana in their house, which was often overlooked by his mom because of her preference in wanting him to stay indoors and away from the Rockwell violence.

As the violence and threats increased around him, Spot and Ronetta brought another life into this world. In September 1983, my nephew Jerome "Casper," was born. Casper developed his nickname because of his very light complexion like the eponymous character from the old cartoon show *Casper the Friendly Ghost*. Now blessed with a girl and boy, Spot realized that it was time to mature into a father. Unfortunately, he would find out that leaving that life behind isn't easy to do.

One day, an older gang chief for the Black Souls was hanging around Vice Lords territory, openly flaunting his gang affiliation by keeping his baseball cap tilted to the right (which was one of the gang symbols for Chicago gangs). After refusing to turn his hat straight after being respectfully ordered to do so by a group of Vice Lords, he was shot and killed. When the news traveled about the chief's murder, it became known that the Black Souls targeted the chief of the RVLs, who, at that time, was Spot. Again unfazed by the threat, Spot continued to freely roam Rockwell.

On December 8 of that year, a member of the Black Souls nicknamed Tags was in front of Spot's apartment building, screaming up towards Spot's apartment with threats that he was going to kill him. After hearing enough of the threats directed towards his family, Spot began to leave the apartment to approach Tags before being stopped by his mom. Spot knew that his life was in danger but he didn't allow it to change any of his daily routine.

The next night, Spot was in a neighboring building visiting his aunt. As he headed home that evening, some of his friends offered to walk him home, knowing the Black Souls were seeking revenge for the murder of their chief. However, Spot refused his friends' suggestion as he never liked to be accompanied. When Spot arrived at his apartment building, someone told him that a group of guys, including Tags, were waiting for him. Still defiant, he proceeded to enter the elevator.

Spot's apartment building had an elevator that stopped on all the even-numbered floors while the other was for the odd-numbered ones. Spot lived on the seventh floor but decided to take the even-floor elevator. One of the Black Souls got on the elevator with him and started a confrontation. Spot then exited on the eighth floor, where other members of the Black Souls were waiting for him. He then proceeded to walk down the stairs towards his seventh floor apartment. As he approached his apartment with his key in hand to open his door, he knew what was about to happen and started adamantly knocking on his door to enter. Unfortunately, he was ignored by his dad, who thought it was a relative being facetious. Not able to enter his home, he stood at his door while the gang started shooting at him several times.

When they were done, Spot had eighteen bullet holes covering his body, including the fatal blow that traveled from the back to front of his head. When his dad finally opened the door, Spot's bloody body fell inside. His father held him in his arms and covered him with his trench coat, then watched his son's transition. His father blamed himself for not allowing Spot to enter the apartment. His guilt was so severe that it destroyed his soul and may have led to his own broken-hearted death a few years later.

While events from that night were unfolding, Ronetta and Renee were getting dressed in our apartment to attend the local high school talent show while blasting the music extremely loud. I was in my bedroom, which had a clear view of the front door, with my friends Dashun and Buffy. As Dashun and Buffy were plotting a sleepover that night, I enjoyed the sight of my sisters dancing happily before going to the talent show.

As Renee continued in the living room, one of her friends stormed inside and proceeded to share something with her. The loud music prevented me from knowing what was developing inside our apartment. Immediately after Renee received the message, she released a piercing scream of "Nooooooo!!!!" that penetrated the loud music. She then told Ronetta, who was in their bedroom getting ready for the talent show. Immediately, Ronetta put on a coat to cover her half-naked body before rushing out of the apartment with Renee towards Spot's building. When Ronetta arrived at Spot's apartment, she witnessed the horrific destruction of his body along with the remnants of his blood and bullet holes all over the porch. He was only eighteen years old and due to turn nineteen on January 8, as well as a father of two with Ronetta.

After Spot's murder that evening, an eerie calmness pervaded the Rockwell streets. Mysteriously, the street lights were turned off that evening, almost as if everyone knew what was about to happen. The pending retribution was so obvious that the police, while at the crime scene, asked the Vice Lords to wait to seek revenge until after they were done investigating. Revenge didn't take long to manifest itself. Retaliation towards the Disciples and Black Souls was so severe that it was unlike any previous Rockwell gang war. Although another routine killing took place that night with Spot's murder, this time was different because of how well liked Spot was in the neighborhood, even among the police.

That night, Spot's leaders were all ordered to eliminate as many Disciples hanging out in Rockwell as they could. Gunfire was heard all night while the RVLs paid immediate retribution for their leader being killed. Everyone stayed indoors as Rockwell was transformed into a war zone that dreadful evening. There would be many funerals over the next few weeks because of the violence that ensued from the murder of Spot.

Allegedly, the day after Spot was killed, one of the RVLs loaded one of Spot's guns, donned the same blood-soaked trench coat that was placed on his lifeless body the night before, and proceeded to travel to a neighboring building where the Black Souls and Disciples often hung. After seeing one of the rival gang members, he approached the youth and calmly stated, "You're one of *them*, aren't you?" before pulling out his gun and boldly killing him in broad daylight. He was never convicted of the crime because of the unwritten rule of allowed retribution, which was even accepted by the local police. After Spot's death, Vice Lords took over most of Rockwell and the rival gangs never fully recovered. Unfortunately, many

RVLs left their faction to join the Traveling Vice Lords (TVLs), who were more into selling drugs than engaging in violence, introducing a new set of problems that would plague the neighborhood.

The morning after Spot's death, Renee woke up around 5 a.m. to Ronetta staring out of their shared bedroom window, calling out "I'll be there soon… I'm coming…" She was telling Renee that Spot was calling for her to join him because he needed her. This went on for months and concerned Renee as it was obvious Ronetta had lost her mind. She was speaking as she looked up towards the skies as if she was still talking to Spot. Ronetta was never the same.

Shortly after Spot's murder, female Disciples started teasing Renee and Ronetta about the successful hit on the RVLs' chief. After the incessant pestering from a girl named Tina, Renee decided she had heard enough and borrowed a gun from a friend. She then went to the girl's building and started to shoot, hoping to hit one of the girls but not caring if she struck anyone else. After her unsuccessful assassination attempt, she returned home. As she was cleaning the gun the next day, a bullet accidentally discharged and almost shot Queah in the head, missing her by two inches. Realizing how close she was to killing her niece, Renee became overwhelmed by her emotions and she decided to stop her pursuit.

When Spot was alive, Ronetta didn't use heavy drugs. She dabbled in marijuana but never developed a craving, mostly because of Spot. He adored Ronetta and enjoyed her purity in regards to drugs. After his death, her drug usage increased. She sought drugs as a comfort to deal with her loss while most people would have gone insane. She was never the same from that dreadful night. Her stress level increased after she realized she would be a single mother raising her kids while the love of her life was no longer alive. Her sweet spirit gave way to a mind that seemed as if it was getting younger and more immature with each passing year, almost as if that was her automatic mechanism for coping with her extraordinary loss. Ronetta was a lost soul after this traumatic event without any professional help to guide her through her challenges. In black culture during that era, it was taboo to admit mental sicknesses or the need for psychological assistance. Because of this, there were many lost souls trying to cope with their mental challenges alone or, similar to Ronetta, through the assistance and comfort of drugs.

Society often finds it easy to quickly judge someone for their addiction to drugs. Ronetta's usage culminated from enduring unbelievable pain after the molestation and murder. Drugs provided a way for Ronetta to escape the pain. Drugs also influenced her to make decisions that placed her children's lives in jeopardy. As a teenager, I often visited Ronetta's apartment only to find her kids home alone at the tender ages of 8 and under. Occasionally at those tender ages, the kids decided to walk the dangerous West Side streets late at night, hungry and searching for their mother. During my unplanned visits, I spent hours waiting for Ronetta to return, only to find her in a drugged state and with no idea of the severity of leaving her kids alone. Some of Ronetta's male drug buddies, who constantly frequented her apartment, sexually abused Queah, which, similarly to her mother, would have a significant negative impact on her life.

In 1988, one of Renee's boyfriends, Ray-Ray, introduced Ronetta to a man nicknamed Boo, saying he was a good man. Boo instantly fell in love with Ronetta. However, this "good" man was married and a successful drug dealer. Ronetta became pregnant, and was happy that she and Boo were going to build the life that she couldn't with Spot. Ronetta knew the dangers involved with being around Boo while his drug business became more successful. She would often hide (and use) some of his supply. She was finally in love and was starting to become herself again.

One night Boo hadn't come home, which wasn't typical of his behavior. Ronetta called around searching for him, but couldn't call his house because of his wife. A friend of Boo told Ronetta he had been missing for days. When police eventually went to his house on the north side of Chicago, they found him dead from a shot to his head with a pillow covering his face. Apparently, a rival drug dealer planned the hit because of his jealousy that Boo and Ray-Ray had the prettiest women in Rockwell. Again, Ronetta was left with tremendous pain, realizing that she was going to deliver a baby without the love of her life and, again, become a single parent.

Ronetta's drug usage continued to spiral out of control, and she began experimenting with heroin and other drugs. During some of my visits to Ronetta, I discovered many cut straws and bent spoons, which were obvious signs of cocaine and heroin usage. Her children would wait hours for Ronetta's return while she was searching the streets for drugs. While it hurt me tremendously to see my sister degenerate before my eyes, I understood her pain and the fact that she needed comfort, even though I disagreed with her method. In a strange way, I believe many in the family excused Ronetta's addiction not only because of her traumatic experiences but also because of their unwillingness to help.

I always admired my only brother, June, who was muscular, handsome, and had a light complexion, but he constantly found himself on the wrong side of the law. For most of my years at Rockwell, my brother June spent a lot of time in juvenile homes or prison. He called himself the "bad boy" and "black sheep" of the family. Unfortunately, I have more memories visiting him in penal institutions than being with him at home. His violent rage surfaced as a result of unfortunate circumstances involving abuse. When he was around eight years old, while my mom hung out with friends and family, an adult friend of my mom forced him to have sex with her while she babysat my siblings. June also witnessed his father's constant abuse of my mom, which drove him to get stronger so that he could protect the family from his father.

June often committed violent acts just for the sake of it, such as when he poured a pot of hot chili on a neighborhood friend, Johnny Boy from the Chi-Boys. But even though he had violent tendencies, he always showed love for his family. Renee and June had a tight bond and often snuck out to have late night talent shows while Mom was out of the house. When they got caught sneaking out of the house to attend local high school dances, June often volunteered to take Renee's punishments, which never fazed him. His protective love for his siblings went to the extreme when he burned a stray dog to death after it bit Renee.

Because of June's violent behavior and disdain towards any house rules established by my mom, he was often kicked out of our home. His street instincts helped him find comfort at night, when he often slept in parked cars. I used to think he was having fun being independent as I saw him resting in parked cars on my way to school, not understanding the reasons why he wasn't home. In 1976, June was put into a program called Big Brothers after my mom gave up her parental rights as a result of not being able to raise him alone. While in the program, which was located on a farm in a Chicago suburb, he was molested by the same older big brothers that were supposed to protect and help him. Again, he was hurt by someone he was supposed to trust. The unpunished and ignored molestation led to June's rebellion while in the program, which culminated with him setting one of the ranch horses on fire.

After June was sent home from the program after the horse incident, he returned to his troubled ways. When he was 16, he was charged with raping a Caucasian woman on a Chicago El platform. June vehemently denied raping the woman, claiming to have only robbed her while his accomplice performed the dreaded violation. As a 17-year-old in 1980, he was sent to a program for juvenile delinquents before being sent to a jail at 26th and California in Chicago. June was then formally tried as an adult for the 1979 rape. Because of an agreed plea bargain, he received a twelve-year prison sentence.

After serving a few years, he was released in the summer of 1983. I was excited that I would finally get the chance to establish a relationship with my only brother, and I was hoping that his years of incarceration would have a positive influence on him so that he could remain free to be with his family. Unfortunately, returning to the same violent neighborhood and friends was not a good influence for him.

Before June went to prison, he often searched to find a "family" that accepted his violent ways. One of our cousins, Donald, introduced him to the Disciples, who he was also associated with. However, when June returned home, Ray-Ray convinced him to join the Vice Lords. Ray-Ray was one of the biggest drug dealers in Chicago, and a 5 Star Universal Supreme Chief Elite for the TVLs. I always thought he resembled former middleweight boxer Thomas "The Hit Man" Hearns with his eager eyes and Jheri curls. King Neal, the founder of the TVLs, and Ray-Ray made June prove that he was one of theirs. In order to prove his loyalty to the TVLs, he had to commit a violent act, which June obliged willingly. He was then officially "blessed" by King Neal into the TVLs. June was always strongly committed to any decision, which wasn't any different with his membership in the Vice Lords.

Siblings

Shortly after reestablishing his neighborhood presence, June quickly ascended among the local TVLs as they fought to control their territory, which consisted of our apartment building . Although June often displayed his violent behavior, he had a tremendous heart in a way that made him similar to Spot. His goal was to protect our entire building from being taken over by the Disciples. I also felt safe visiting other Vice Lord territories, knowing June was well respected among the gang. I knew, however, I had to stay away from the Disciples, not wanting them to know my family's strong Vice Lord alliance with June, Ray-Ray, Spot and King Neal.

I often came home from school to find June polishing off his sawed-off shotgun before warning me to stay indoors. As a curious kid, I ignored his warnings and followed him outside where I witnessed him shooting at his rival gang recklessly in broad daylight, not caring if an innocent bystander was present. I feared that June's violent streak would result in an unfortunate ending with him going to prison or, even worse, to his grave. I worried that we would lose our protector since June was the man of the house. Unfortunately, one of my fears would come true on a cold evening during the fall of 1984.

While my mom and I were enjoying a peaceful evening, we heard a firm knock on our door. Upon opening the door we noticed two detectives waiting to enter. My heart raced, and I prepared to hear the worst news I could hear about my brother. Even though my sisters were not home during this time, I knew this visit was about my brother. The detectives proceeded to inform us that June had been arrested for armed robbery and would have to go back to prison. June received a thirty-year sentence for his armed robbery, mostly because of his violent past. Again, my mom would experience pain in her heart because of this disappointment. Again, June would be separated from the group that loved him. And again, my siblings and I would experience the loss of a prominent male figure inside our home. While I have never condoned any violent behavior of June, I understood how his past led to his decisions.

When he went to jail, Disciples and Vice Lords mistrusted him because of his decision to change gang affiliation. Vice Lords couldn't trust him, not knowing if he was still loyal to the Disciples, and the Disciples were angered that he changed affiliations. To order protection for June in prison,

King Neal, Ray-Ray and other TVL leaders Dickie, Jewel, and Jettie "Bo Dilley" Williams (King Neal's chief enforcer), came to our apartment to start the process of officially declaring June as a member of the TVLs. While this would anger the Disciples, June needed to be protected by his new Vice Lord family. They waited on a phone call from the penitentiary to begin the process. When it came, King Neal sanctioned June over the phone so that he would have 24-hour security from the Vice Lord guards.

Knowing that June would be gone from the family for a long time and that my sisters were struggling with their own challenges, I turned my attention back to music. Unfortunately, on one memorable night in the winter of 1984 during one of our Prince practices, another violent act would have a direct impact on my family. As we were working on The Time's "The Bird" routine, we heard a loud shotgun. We looked downstairs and noticed three young boys sitting in the playground as if nothing happened. While we were inside Rashied's apartment, Quamie entered in tears telling us that a close family friend (and the brother of Johnny Boy), Thomas "Chubby," was just murdered.

Chubby, who was 17 at the time of his murder, was always close to my family and was what we often called a "pretend cousin" (a close friend who was considered family even though there were no biological ties), which made this news extremely emotionally disturbing to me. We found out later that the three boys in the playground (ages 20, 17 and 14) were Chubby's killers. Chubby was associated with the Vice Lord gang, while the two killers were from the rival Disciples gang, although his mother denied he was directly involved in any gangs. After coming to grips with the news that Chubby was dead, I sat in a nearby neighbor's apartment, stunned, while listening to DeBarge's "All This Love" on the radio.

While listening to the song, I thought a lot about my brother because of the love he had for Chubby, whom he treated like a little brother. I had always prepared myself for receiving similar news about June, which added to the pain I was feeling from Chubby's death. June was extremely saddened after finding out about Chubby's murder while watching the news on television in prison. In just two years, two close family friends were murdered while my brother received thirty years in prison. Three men in my life, all of whom had great potential to legitimately succeed, were taken away from me.

Violence in Rockwell occurred so often that not only was it was expected, there was uneasiness in the air if everything was calm. The numerous senseless killings desensitized me to violence, which was somewhat necessary in order to mentally deal with the constant fear that I could be main feature at the next funeral. While the television news occasionally talked about victims from Rockwell, for every story told there were at least five other known murders in the neighborhood that never made it to the media.

Often, while people sat in the park enjoying a beautiful summer night, rival gangs randomly shot into the innocent crowd. As children, we developed a sense of invincibility, often laughing while we were running away from flying bullets. Chubby's death was the first time I lost my virtual shield since he was so close to me in age and considered family. In the past, the neighborhood gangs met in a large field near our house and had fist fights to determine the winner. Rarely would someone draw a weapon, which usually was a knife. Guns became more prevalent in the early and mid-80s when money from drug sales allowed the drug-dealing members to purchase them. Once guns became more accessible, and the new breed of gang members entered the landscape, violence became a standard way of life.

Because of June's temper, he was involved in many fights in prison that would lead him to serving his thirty years in the majority of Illinois' prisons, including Statesville, Pontiac, Joliet, Danville, Canton, Pinckneyville, and Menard. He was placed in protective custody for threats to his life from rival gang members. His history with prison guards wasn't positive either, as he physically attacked them, further supporting his internal rage. While still in protective custody in 1993, the prison guards allowed a rival gang to enter June's cell, where he was stabbed, suffering a punctured lung and almost losing his life. After the stabbing, Disciples were afraid of the retaliation because of June's association with Ray-Ray, King Neal and Bo Dilley. His lengthy prison life was filled with violence, loneliness and even unconventional reunions, such as when he was briefly a cellmate to his only son, Timothy, as well as being in the same prison where his father served as a guard. Purposely, Ronald ignored June for fear that other prisoners would use this relationship as motivation to harm June. From June's perspective, Ronald ignoring his son led to more unnecessary violence as June acted out his pain on others.

Of all of my siblings, I had the closest relationship with Renee, who was the family princess. She was beautiful and had a welcoming personality. Renee was a great dresser and was always outgoing and engaging around others, which earned her many friends. The Robinson girls turned many heads and were great catches in the neighborhood. My mom did a great job of instilling confidence in all of her children, which gave us an air of arrogance at times. However, our down-to-earth personalities helped us avoid many enemies.

The negative impact of living in the projects didn't escape Renee. When she was 16 years old, she became pregnant and was forced to get an abortion, even though she was seven months pregnant. Bob requested that my mom take Renee to a clinic in New York where late-term abortions were performed. Neither Mom nor Bob told Renee what was going to happen. Mom took her to the hospital where she was given fluids to initiate the abortion. She felt excruciating pain that night. They had given her a portable toilet, telling her to sit on the toilet if she felt the worst pain. While on the toilet in unbelievable pain, she noticed a stillborn fetus inside the toilet. After the doctors were summoned, the umbilical cord was cut and Renee went back onto the bed. There were other girls inside going through the same procedure. There was never any communication between the patients or doctors regarding the purpose of the procedures, which increased the level of strangeness inside that facility.

The next morning, they went back to Chicago, where Renee struggled with not having had a choice whether or not to keep her baby. A couple of years later, Renee became pregnant again, then had a miscarriage while in her high school history class. She went home and almost hemorrhaged to death from the amount of blood lost. Instead of worrying about the threat to her life, she felt bad that she had let Bob down by getting pregnant for the second time. Again, she struggled to find comfort after realizing she had lost another child.

For the most part, Renee dated boys in the neighborhood that were kind and respectful towards her as well as my mom, but things changed dramatically when she met Ray-Ray. One day as she was entering 340, she was introduced to Ray-Ray by one of his friends. Everyone knew about his reputation and warned her to not get involved with him, which actually intrigued Renee even more since she had only dated clean-cut boys. She and Ray-Ray became a Rockwell power couple and were frequently seen together. She was beautiful and always dressed in the latest fashion, and he was becoming a very successful drug dealer. Ray-Ray saw his empire grow from $200 a day to roughly $40,000.

Three years into their relationship, Renee found out that Ray-Ray was married—a similar scenario to Mom and Ronetta's relationships. Like Bob and Boo, Ray-Ray constantly told Renee he would leave his wife for Renee, which he said just to maintain the relationship. Also like Bob and Boo, Ray-Ray's fast lifestyle appealed to Renee. He exposed her to the finer things in life (also similar to Bob and Boo) such as enjoying expensive restaurants, flying to exciting places like Miami, going to the race tracks, and attending high profile sporting events. Even though Renee enjoyed the materialistic elements of the relationship, she fell in love with the man as well.

However, Renee tired of Ray-Ray's empty and false promises to leave his wife. The pain she endured from these broken promises led her to search for a different type of comfort than the high-level materialistic binges she'd typically make after an argument. Ray-Ray stored kilos of cocaine and cash under Renee's bed in a safe. After one of their fights, she purposely went into her room, pulled the safe from under the bed, removed an ounce of cocaine from the safe, and then decided to snort it for the first time. She enjoyed the high, mostly because it took away the pain of knowing Ray-Ray wasn't going to leave his wife for her.

Similar to the men in my mom's relationships, Ray-Ray was emotionally, physically and verbally abusive towards Renee. He lied to her often and, because of his jealousy, forced her to be a prisoner in her own home (similar to Ronald and my mom). If she left the home, Ray-Ray's sycophant workers in the building called him, which caused him to react by coming to our apartment to attack her. Even though Renee's black eyes were proof of the abuse, Mom ignored the signs because of the "hush money" and other material items Ray-Ray would provide, which increased the level of hurt Renee was going through during this dark and depressing period of her life. When she had no one else to turn to, she suffered from knowing Mom was willing to accept materialistic bribes over helping her daughter.

One night, Renee was convinced to go to Mister Gee's, a local nightclub, with Ronetta and a next door neighbor to get her out of a depressed state. Unbeknownst to Renee, inside the club were some of Ray-Ray's friends, who promptly called to tell him of her arrival. Ray-Ray immediately drove to the club, where inside he attacked her so severely that Ronetta pleaded for him to stop. After this unfortunate event, Renee went home and used drugs again as a way to not only comfort herself but to punish Ray-Ray. Again, Mom overlooked the beating because of the money Ray-Ray provided. Renee was living in constant fear—afraid to leave the house, not knowing if it would lead to another violent outburst. It was difficult for her to have male friends because of their fear that Ray-Ray would accuse them of sleeping with Renee.

As Ray-Ray's drug empire grew, he and Renee made frequent trips to Miami for various transactions. Renee accompanied him not only as his girlfriend but as a carrier of his drugs as well. During one Miami trip, they were joined by two other women. While on the plane, a senseless argument escalated into Ray-Ray attacking Renee verbally in front of the passengers. She went to the bathroom in order to escape the humiliation and seek a temporary reprieve. Inside the bathroom, she removed Ray-Ray's $30,000 worth of jewelry from her neck so that she could more easily snort coke. In her drug-induced state, she accidentally left the jewelry in the bathroom. Renee was deathly afraid in thinking about the potential severity of Ray-Ray's punishment. Fortunately, one of Ray-Ray's family members convinced him to not hurt Renee.

In the mid-1980s, my mom developed a strong relationship with Earnest, a former Arkansas elementary school classmate and auto mechanic. She spent a lot of time with Earnest, which often left me and Renee at home. When Renee was out with Ray-Ray, I usually waited for her to return home, regardless of how late it was, to make sure she was safe at home. Once she returned, my relief allowed me to go to bed. I often sat on the porch waiting for her to return, even if it meant staying up until 3 a.m., when no one else was outside. I wasn't thinking about the danger of sometimes falling asleep alone on our porch outside, because I had a greater fear of something happening to my sister. Since Renee knew I was waiting up for her, she constantly reminded Ray-Ray that she couldn't stay out late because her brother wouldn't sleep until she was safe at home.

My time with Renee allowed me to observe her physical and emotional changes in life. Even though she was living a "glamorous life", I could tell she wasn't happy. She rarely smiled when she was with Ray-Ray, making it obvious that something was wrong. I never saw the physical abuse, but I still remembered the verbal assaults he directed towards Renee. Ray-Ray was like Jekyll and Hyde: his calm and polite demeanor often took a back seat to his violent and tumultuous temper. Her increased drug usage started impacting her beauty, which concerned me. I could always tell when she was high and would give her looks to show my obvious displeasure.

While dealing with all of her pain, Renee developed a relationship with King Neal. When King Neal's wife discovered pictures of Renee that confirmed the affair, she informed Ray-Ray. In a jealous rage, Ray-Ray brought Renee to King Neal's home to question him about the relationship. King Neal, surrounded by his henchmen, laughed off Ray-Ray's accusation, denying anything between both of them. King Neal then strongly encouraged Ray-Ray to leave his home—he was obviously outmatched as King Neal's henchmen were loaded and ready to strike if the argument escalated. Ray-Ray left without receiving any confirmation from Renee or King Neal about the affair.

During this time, the Federal Bureau of Investigations started investigating Ray-Ray, which would last for five years. As the FBI focused on four of his accomplices, two were mysteriously killed. Also during this time, Renee met Gerald, who, unlike Ray-Ray, was a basketball player and college graduate. Unfortunately, Gerald was also married, like the other men in the Robinson women's lives. However, Gerald brought out the best in Renee because she was able to be herself. For the first time in years, I saw the smile and positive countenance she used to have before she got involved with Ray-Ray. Even though Gerald and Renee understood the potentially fatal consequences of their relationship, they continued to see each other.

As their relationship intensified, they became more paranoid in trying to hide it from Ray-Ray. Things changed in 1991 when Gerald was told that Renee was pregnant with his baby. When Ray-Ray found out, he angrily ordered for Gerald to be killed. As both went into hiding, Renee moved in with Ronetta in her apartment on Homan and Douglas, which is on Chicago's West Side. Desperately trying to find Renee, Ray-Ray convinced one of her friends to reveal her location in exchange for drugs.

While in hiding, Renee walked to a nearby Popeye's Chicken. As Renee walked, a car abruptly drove onto the sidewalk and stopped next to her. Ray-Ray stepped out of the car and quickly approached Renee. He then pulled a gun on her and forced her to go to Ronetta's apartment. Inside the bathroom, he made Renee strip naked to confirm the pregnancy, and then threatened her to get an abortion or else he would kill Gerald. Not wanting Gerald to die, she agreed to get an abortion in the morning.

The next day, Ray-Ray ordered his workers to take Renee to get the abortion. When she spoke to the doctor, she found out she was already seven months pregnant. Because of Renee's irregular menstrual cycles, she didn't know she had been pregnant for that long. The late-term abortion would cost $1,500, which was paid by Ray-Ray's workers. During the initial assessment, Renee was instructed to not eat anything the night before.

That night, Renee struggled with her hunger as well as the pain of losing her third potential child. Unfortunately (or fortunately for her), she capitulated to her needs and decided to eat an egg roll, thinking it wasn't big enough of a meal to make an impact on the abortion. As they returned to the clinic the next day, Renee anxiously awaited for the right moment to tell the doctor she had the egg roll the previous night. Luckily, Ray-Ray's workers waited in the lobby while Renee entered the room alone where the procedure was to take place.

Before performing the abortion, the doctor asked Renee if she ate anything, which she eventually admitted. Angrily, the doctor chastised Renee for not obeying his instructions to avoid eating, as now the abortion could not be performed. Since Ray-Ray's workers waited in the lobby, when they saw Renee re-enter the waiting room, they thought the abortion was successfully done. They then made a call to Ray-Ray to inform him of such, which satisfied him. He instructed them to take Renee to one of his homes on the West Side to wait for him. As she waited inside the home, she knew that she didn't want to feel Ray-Ray's wrath, even though he thought the abortion had been accomplished. She waited for the right opportunity then escaped from the home, returning to Ronetta's.

Renee risked her life to have the baby. She also knew she was taking a chance with Gerald's life, but didn't want to endure the pain of losing her third child. She also wanted to build a life with Gerald, even though she knew it would be difficult to get him to leave his wife. When Renee went into labor, she was staying with a friend of the family. After being rushed to the hospital and delivering her baby, she was devastated to hear the doctors tell her the baby was stillborn. Miraculously, the baby was revived, and she was able to enjoy her new baby boy, Germaine, who was born on November 18. Renee felt horrible for almost aborting him. She also felt guilty that Germaine was born with drugs in his body from all of the years of her usage. Once reality kicked in, she felt even worse that she didn't know how to care for a baby. She couldn't believe she was able to have a baby after the drugs and physical abuse she received throughout her life. Fortunately, after Mom visited Renee and Germaine in the hospital, she asked Renee to move back in with her.

Ray-Ray's physical and emotional abuse had a severe impact on Renee. Drugs were her comfort. Struggling with her mom looking the other way as she was going through her abuse, Renee sought comfort from drugs. Struggling with the fact that she was in love with a married man who wasn't going to leave his wife, Renee sought comfort from drugs. Struggling after the thought of potentially losing three babies, two by forced involuntary abortion, Renee sought comfort from drugs while trying to take care of a new child. Gerald's wife fought Renee often, claiming that Germaine wasn't Gerald's, but anyone seeing both would not be able to deny the resemblance. Gerald eventually left his wife for Renee so he could to help her raise Germaine, but their relationship struggled. Unfortunately, Gerald also developed a habit with drugs, which obviously wasn't going to help Renee or their relationship.

Drugs played a significant role in my family over the past thirty years. Because of the influence of drugs on my family, I witnessed my sisters transform from beauty queens to walking zombies. I used to come home from elementary school to see my sisters and their boyfriends smoking marijuana. I then saw them escalate from marijuana to cocaine and even heavier drugs. While they thought they were hiding their addictions from me, I often discovered their drug paraphernalia. I could easily have also been influenced to use the drugs because of the accessibility and my own need for comfort. However, after seeing the negative impact of drugs on my sisters, I was never tempted.

Drugs impacted both Renee's appearance and her mind. Renee was always smart and inspired me to learn how to type because of her keen ability. During her heavy drug usage, Renee became a shell of her former self. This was often ignored because Ray-Ray always kept money in our pockets and always showed great respect for my mother. Ray-Ray always had the nicest clothes and cars and was envied by all of the kids in the neighborhood, including myself. I could easily see how a child seeing this image of "success" would be drawn to sell drugs. It was actually an honor to know Ray-Ray and for the neighborhood to know that he was dating my sister, even though they also knew he was married.

Ray-Ray often showed up to our apartment with large brown bags of money collected from drug transactions, dropping the stacks onto our kitchen table for me and some of my friends to count. As impressionable and poor kids, we were fascinated to see all of the money, not caring about the means of how he obtained the stash. After a successful count, Ray-Ray paid us for our services. Not until later in life did I realize the dangers involved with this activity. A rival gang or drug dealer could have followed Ray-Ray into our apartment and murdered everyone inside for the drugs and the money. I held an unforgiving grudge towards Ray-Ray for introducing Renee (and indirectly, Ronetta) to the various means of accessing drugs. While he did not condone Renee's drug usage, I felt his influence allowed others to provide her with the product. Also, I thought the drug-induced glamorized lifestyle he introduced to Renee forced her to keep searching for that next high.

Ray-Ray started selling marijuana, delivered in tiny Ziploc bags, in the late 1970s, when he earned the nickname "Short Bag". In the early 1980s, he progressed to powder cocaine and later learned how to skillfully cook up "rock" (which is known by others as crack), using baking soda, powder cocaine and water. After boiling and hardening the mixture, he chipped rock pieces off the 12-inch sized ball, then distributed the rock among his workers to sell for $10 a bag. The crack epidemic of the 1980s turned him into one of Chicago's all-time most successful drug dealers. His headquarters was located in a building on the 2700 block of Flournoy, which was on the West Side of the city.

In 1995, Ray-Ray was arrested, along with nineteen of his workers, under "Operation Flournoy." He, along with a younger brother, was given a life sentence. His empire included Chicago police officers and amassed annual gross sales over $14 million. The operation was taken down by an undercover cop who frequently traded "law protection" for guns, cocaine, and heroin. During the trial, Ray-Ray was condemned by the judge for not using his ability to influence to do something positive in the neighborhood. He was a leader, but unfortunately he led others down a destructive path. I always thought Ray-Ray wanted to do something constructive with his life but found it difficult to walk away from the lifestyle, which became his own drug. He was the neighborhood Donald Trump, who controlled a multi-million dollar enterprise.

Some of the smartest business people I have ever met were drug dealers. Drug dealers often run complex supply chains involving multiple levels of corruption within the streets and municipalities. Some of them use brutal methods of intimidation, which was needed in order for them to maintain their effectiveness, as the game was all about geographic dominance. Most of them employed neighborhood kids and others desperate for money to provide de facto security systems to avoid police interference. If drug dealers were given a different route in life and focused on legitimate and legal ventures, their contribution to society would have had a great impact, especially within the African American community. We have lost myriad potential diverse CEOs and other positive contributors to society because of the drug trade and gang violence. Fortunately, I continued to shield myself mentally from the chaotic and dangerous surroundings through movies and television.

Movies and Television

IN ADDITION TO MUSIC, MY fascination for movies developed while I lived in Rockwell. Movies allowed me to temporarily escape my world and walk in the shoes of people in different worlds. I was taught various life lessons while watching movies. My friends and I used to travel on the Chicago El when we were as young as ten to see a movie downtown. We would travel to McVickers Theater and watch kung fu movies while large rats nibbled on the popcorn in chairs next to us. The McVickers floors were always sticky with butter and Lord knows what else, which attracted rats and allowed the popcorn to stay in place after falling from frantic fingers. We got excited to view kung fu films, mistakenly believing that we were actually learning martial arts for future protection in Rockwell.

Movies led to my love for rap music the moment I saw *Krush Groove*, starring Run-DMC, LL Cool J, The Fat Boys, Kurtis Blow and my favorite group, New Edition. I was blown away by the energy I felt while listening to the songs or seeing the performances. Rap provided music that spoke about the life I was familiar with. I could relate more to DMC rapping "People in the world try to make ends meet, you travel by car, train, bus or feet…" versus love songs that promised a blissful life with family and kids.

Krush Groove was also inspirational in its portrayal of Russell Simmons becoming an entrepreneur and helping to build a record company that would produce timeless rap songs such as LL's "Rock the Bells," which was performed in the movie, as well as later hits such as "I'm Bad," "I Need Love," and others. Russell allowed his adversity to influence him to create something that was unheard of in the black community. His persistence to succeed gave a blueprint to future entrepreneurial success for hip hop moguls Jay-Z and P. Diddy.

I have been truly blessed to witness rap grow, especially when it impacted Rockwell. The Village Crew, a Rockwell rap crew, inspired many of us to dream after they were able to get songs produced which talked about our way of life. We never thought it would be possible to hear rappers from our very own neighborhood featured on the radio. We also felt proud that our story was being told.

Living in Chicago, we were drawn to movies that were filmed there as well. One Saturday afternoon on September 28, 1985, a group of us were almost in one of these Chicago classic movies. As we were walking downtown heading to see *Rambo: First Blood Part II*, we noticed a crew filming a movie on the corner of Dearborn and Randolph during the Von Steuben Day parade. We did not wait to see which movie was being filmed but later found out it was the float scene in *Ferris Bueller's Day Off*. Not one of us knew how successful that cult film would become, and we would have all been ecstatic to participate in the "Twist and Shout" and the "Danke Schoen" routines during that famous parade scene.

While movies offered me great entertainment, they also opened the door to various emotions, including unsavory thoughts and behavior. At a very early age, I was inappropriately exposed to adult language, horror films and pornography through film. Movie theaters were not very strict with preventing underage viewers from entering without adults, and what would be considered rated R today was sometimes rated PG then. Parents were not strict either, so the advent of VCRs allowed children to enjoy these types of movies in the privacy of their own homes. Porn movies were easily found in our apartment, so as a child I naturally gravitated towards watching these types of movies without any feelings of guilt. Without a male figure explaining the purpose of sex to me, pornography incorrectly taught me behavior which I thought was appropriate. I grew up without a true appreciation for making love because of my insensitivities to the act of sex developed through pornography.

Movies that elicited sadness were typically ones that closely resembled my life at that time. Seeing the violent way Lawrence Hilton-Jacobs' character Cochise died in the 1975 black cult classic *Cooley High* reminded me of the senseless murders of Chubby, Spot, and other neighborhood victims. The movies *Sparkle* and *Lady Sings the Blues* are frank and sad reminders of the drug addictions that continued to plague my family. My life was a movie and it continued to evolve beyond the real world that existed in front of my eyes on a daily basis.

My love for movies pertaining to business was developed during these early years of visiting Chicago movie theaters. Movies such as *Wall Street* and *The Secret of My Success* gave me a great desire to become a businessman and to learn business terminology. Since I grew up poor, I was always attracted to rags-to-riches movies such as Will Smith movie *The Pursuit of Happyness* because of the hope it provided. *The Pursuit of Happyness* remains the only movie during which I cried while watching inside a movie theater. I became emotional during the ending as I placed myself inside the shoes of the main character played by Will. To see him overcome all of the struggles endured to raise his son in unpleasant situations and finding that first opportunity…that first hope…was too powerful to hold back tears.

While I did not know the specific area of business in which I was interested, movies gave me confidence that my life as an adult would involve wearing suits and making powerful decisions on a daily basis. I wanted that life portrayed on the screen. I wanted to have the financial security to not have to worry about whether or not we would have enough money for rent or to decide whether or not to borrow money from the neighborhood drug dealers. I also wanted to establish my own boundaries beyond what anyone else from Rockwell had established in corporate America, which was to become an executive. I wanted to have my own office, be able to travel to other cities, stay in executive hotels, conduct meetings while enjoying a meal at a quality restaurant, and meet goals and objectives that are important to the company. I also wanted to expose my children to a world I wasn't exposed to while young myself.

Eddie Murphy's 1983 movie *Trading Places* first exposed me to the stock market. I saw how daily commodities such as orange juice, coffee and wheat were used not only for consumption but also as ways to allow financially savvy individuals to become wealthy through the buying and selling of those commodities. *Trading Places* remains a favorite to watch, but now because of the financial lessons taught versus its comedic element in the early '80s.

The 80s was the ideal decade for anyone hoping for stardom. Music videos introduced musicians into the homes of millions that would not have purchased their material. Michael Jackson showed all entertainers how hard they needed to work to be successful. The style from '80s bands glamorized loud colors and wild hair. Television was also influential during this decade of decadence. One of my favorite television shows during this period was *Miami Vice*, which did a great job of emphasizing fashion and music while at times glamorizing the drug dealing. Any fan of the show will admit to dreaming about driving a white Ferrari Testarossa down a darkened highway with Phil Collins' "In the Air Tonight" blaring through the speakers. One Easter Sunday my attire consisted of a white suit jacket, white pants, no socks, white dress shoes and a turquoise netted see-through top, to pay homage to the show.

Other television shows impacted me in various ways. Since television provided a new world for me and other ghetto kids, we were heavily influenced by its messages. *Sanford and Son* provided my name, as the popular show featured a junk collector and his son, Lamont, whom I was named after once the show debuted in 1972. *The Jeffersons* was another favorite because of its lead black character, George Jefferson. George was the first example I had seen of a powerful black business owner. George never succumbed to the stereotypical financial plight of blacks, opting instead to "move on up" to the East Side, where whites were appalled that a black family would be able to reside. I looked at George as my hero. I wanted to own my company one day and have the ability to tell anyone, regardless of their race, how I truly felt.

The '70s hit show *Good Times* was always enjoyed by other Chicago ghetto kids because it told our story. The Evans family lived in a Chicago housing project and often found ways to enjoy the good times of life instead of dwelling on their daily depressing challenges. Although the show revolved around the Evans family, the Robinsons could have easily provided substitutes. We struggled in similar manners, but the Evanses had something we didn't—a father that lived in the same home. When the father, James, was killed on the show, it provided a weird sense of comfort for me because the Evanses would more closely resemble the Robinsons: fatherless and filled with struggles.

Later in the '80s, *The Cosby Show* would be groundbreaking for black families. For the first time, we were able to see a black family portrayed in a positive and professional manner with both parents maintaining successful careers. The common complaint about the show was that it wasn't possible to have a black male doctor and female lawyer under the same roof, which was ridiculous. *The Cosby Show* also allowed me to see a black family eating at a dinner table together without it being a holiday. Rarely did I recall our family sitting down on an ordinary evening to eat together. Bill Cosby inspired me to have my own family one day. I wanted to share life experiences with my sons and daughters while at the dinner table, free from the stress of neighborhood violence or drugs. I wanted to be a fun parent, and one that my kids' friends would enjoy being around. I wanted to have kids that focused on education. I wanted to be able to take my wife on dates without worrying about the financial impact on the family's budget. More importantly, I wanted to be a father that was active in the lives of my children. *The Cosby Show* allowed me to dream and plan for a future that had not yet been realized in my family.

The media's positive and negative influence on my early childhood was instrumental in shaping the person I am today. Without those small, temporary suspensions in life, I would not have been able to dream of escaping the horror I was facing as a child. Although mostly fictional, the movies and programs I watched allowed me to peek inside the homes of others while serving as various goals for my future. Fortunately, many of my friends enjoyed the same love for movies, probably for similar reasons.

On Easter Sundays our tradition was to go to the downtown movie theaters. We would get dressed in our Sunday best, go to church (sometimes), and then go downtown to see a movie. One Easter Sunday, April 7, 1985, would be a monumental moment for me and a few of my friends. After watching the thriller *Friday the 13th: A New Beginning*, Rashied and I decided to stop inside a local record store. While randomly searching for music, I came across the New Edition cassette tape *New Edition*. New Edition was my favorite group of all time. They sang hit songs like "Candy Girl," "Mr. Telephone Man," "Cool It Now," "My Secret," "Count Me Out," and others. It was at this moment during which Rashied and I had the same thought about our next project: develop a group to imitate New Edition. Before that day, we had been practicing and performing songs from Prince and The Time, but the excitement from *Purple Rain* had faded. We were also bored with the lack of opportunities for choreography which New Edition was always known to have as their strength. While performing New Edition songs would bring greater excitement to others, we knew it would be a great challenge because we had to make sure we had to have the right members.

Shortly after arriving back at Rockwell, Rashied and I started to recruit for our new group, which we now called Awesome Force. We transitioned Cook and Walter into the group as well as Quamie. However, I decided to not include my cousin James in our new group. Because of New Edition's well-known tight choreography, we needed five strong dancers, and dance was not an area of strength for James. This was a tough decision because of the potential family impact, but during our first practice I received confirmation of the chosen five.

Imitating New Edition increased our popularity, especially with the girls, at school and in our neighborhood. Awesome Force performed in front of large crowds in and around Rockwell. We were successful in neighborhood talent shows and auditioned for the 1980s television contest *Puttin' on the Hits*. Unfortunately, our lack of funds cost us an opportunity to advance. While other New Edition imitators were able to don suits that resembled the actual group's wardrobe, we could only piece together a few dollars to purchase mix-matched mariachi band tuxedos. Although I believed we performed the best of all New Edition groups, we were not presentable or professional enough in comparison to the others in our white and off-white mariachi tuxedos.

The concept of Awesome Force was not restricted to our singing group. Awesome Force became our escape. It allowed all members to seek ways to provide enjoyment for a neighborhood that needed a break from its daily struggles. Awesome Force also provided a hopeful future of escaping the ghetto for members that did not focus as much on education or were not good enough for sports. Most importantly of all, Awesome Force created a brotherhood bond that still exists today. I am proud to say none of the original members of Awesome Force experienced drug addiction. We looked out for each other because we kept our eyes on the bigger picture of overcoming the dark experiences of the ghetto.

I enjoyed participating in groups because of the camaraderie formed with friends that were more like brothers. I am the youngest in my family by at least eight years, making me more of an only child. Having *group* brothers allowed me to experience life with others that were going through the same challenges during the same period of time in their lives. The same reasons that influenced June and Spot to seek brotherhood with gang families were why I was always drawn towards group families. Our almost-daily disciplined practices kept most of us out of trouble.

I found the great strength needed to survive the mental challenges Rockwell provided because of my Awesome Force brothers. They became even more successful after my eventual departure, incorporating more complex dance routines and performing on Chicago television programs. Awesome Force spawned talented individuals such as Donnell Jones (who is known by many in the spoken word community as the artist Sphinxx), Jermaine Phillips (a rapper known as Jay Rockwell), Rashied (Chicago's DJ Rated X) and Maurice Garrett (well known Chicago DJ Waxmaster). We had other non-performing, but still positive, friends that were part of the Awesome Force family such as Rob, Gene, Red, Paris, Big Dave, K-Smooth (now a chef called "Cookin Daflava") from the Village Crew, Walter "Truly", Lovell, and Jeff. My experience in Awesome Force provided me with the necessary skills and confidence to be successful.

While the concept of ghettos in American cities could have had positive intentions, the end result continues to negatively impact lives across the country. Seeing Rockwell transform from a community to a psychological concentration camp was disheartening. Ghettos used to consist of families all working together to support each other's struggles. Residents often helped to raise each other's children and proactively sought ways to aide fellow tenants. Once violence in ghettos increased, the theory of using a neighborhood to raise a child went by the wayside, replaced by an insular focus solely on an individual family's survival.

Social Holocaust

ACCORDING TO WIKIPEDIA, THE TERM "ghetto" originates (amongst many debated derivations) from a Venetian word for waste, which was "gheto" or "ghet." It was typically used to describe the foundry where waste was stored on the same island as the area of Jewish confinement. The term grew in usage in the late 1930s and early 1940s to describe the areas to which Germans confined Jews before they were sent to concentration and death camps during the Holocaust. Although the word is usually used today to describe poverty-stricken urban areas, the German usage still applies.

Ghetto tenants are socially, economically, and sometimes mentally confined, struggling with constant doubt of being able to survive the social holocaust that awaits them outside of their ghetto walls. In America, northern ghettos emerged as a result of two major movements in the mid-twentieth century: the Great Migration and white flight. A plethora of southern African Americans moved to midwestern and northern urban areas between 1914 and 1950 in search of the American Dream. Automotive manufacturing and steel mill jobs in the north lured blacks that struggled with unemployment and racist segregation in the south. Because of clever and discriminatory practices by the banking and insurance industries, blacks were confined to specific areas within the cities they migrated to, unable to move to better areas even though many could afford to do so.

As the black population increased in urban areas, many whites fled to nearby suburbs, rural areas and the South. Suburbs increased as a result of highway and rail construction as well as the availability of federally subsidized homes, improving the process mostly for whites looking to buy new homes versus renting in the cities. The white movement from cities to predominately white suburban communities led to an even greater percentage of blacks in urban areas as well as an increase in the amount of affordable, urban public housing.

Decrease in consumer demand as well as discriminatory labor practices contributed to a significant decrease in the once-promising manufacturing jobs at steel mills, auto plants, and other factories. Since many of the employed tenants in public housing worked in manufacturing, they were negatively impacted by the economic downturn. The process of urban decay began to take shape once unemployment increased amongst the residents in public housing, which eventually led to an increase of alternative (but illegal and violent) revenue-generating methods to survive. An increase in urban drug usage resulted from black Vietnam veterans who returned to urban homes only to find significant unemployment as well as untreated mental issues resulting from fighting in the war. In the '70s, the black unemployment rate typically doubled that of the national rate. While many civil rights leaders such as Dr. Martin Luther King, Jr. fought against the discriminatory policies in housing and labor, the social holocaust had already begun.

I was part of the second generation of those that migrated from the South. Hope had already dissipated into an accepted reality that the ghetto was our home and poverty was our economic status. My generation didn't witness firsthand the black activists of the '60s such as King, Malcolm X, Stokely Carmichael, or Huey P. Newton. Outside of the occasional "Keep Hope Alive" saying from the Reverend Jesse Jackson, Sr., we didn't attach to any political figure, which is why our heroes were typically professional athletes, entertainers, or our neighborhood drug dealers. Our sports heroes were even watered down, which may have led to a greater desire to follow the career paths of the drug dealers. Global icons such as Muhammad Ali and Jim Brown were replaced by neighborhood legends such as Ray-Ray and King Neal in the eyes of a young boy, since the lifestyle and wealth of the latter were more tangible to us.

My generation was also removed from the mentality of our parents and grandparents who had sharecropping parents or were actual ones themselves before heading to the Promised Land of the North. Our level of poor was now on par with society's definition instead of the inhumane economic conditions faced in the South. Even though we were considered poor, we still enjoyed luxuries such as running water, electricity, bathrooms, televisions, microwaves, and deep freezers, which were not imagined by the migrating class. Living in the ghetto was all we knew since most of us were born there.

The late 1970s and early 1980s saw the structure of traditional families suffer as a result of most family units having two working parents. The lack of parents in the household left many of us alone, which led to increased mischievous behavior. We were able to explore without much parental guidance, which was unprecedented and unimaginable for the previous generation that migrated from the South with strong family bonds still intact. Gangs were able to take advantage of the weak family structures by preying on kids that didn't enjoy the love and affection normally received at home. Rockwell served as a breeding ground for many of these wayward young boys and girls.

Rockwell Gardens was the first public housing development in the United States that was constructed using both federal and state funds. Constructed in 1961, it was located three miles west of Chicago's downtown, occupied seventeen acres of Chicago's West Side, and housed 1,126 apartments. The irony of Rockwell Gardens was that I don't remember seeing any actual gardens. However, I'm sure it would have been impossible to grow anything of value since it would have been surrounded by hard dirt and glass. Living in Rockwell was similar to storylines seen on movies such as *Boyz n the Hood, Menace II Society* and *New Jack City*. Gunshots were a daily and nightly occurrence.

I attended Ulysses S. Grant Elementary School, which was nestled in the middle of Rockwell at 145 S. Campbell Street. If you were not home soon after school ended, you were almost assured of being in the middle of a gang war between the Disciples and Vice Lords, who constantly battled to control the buildings in Rockwell. As children, we knew most of the apartments that served as the "dope houses," which facilitated the neighborhood drug transactions and served as the location to test out the newly purchased supply.

Because of the lack of cleanliness displayed by many Rockwell tenants, we had to endure living amongst rats and roaches. The rats were about the size of kittens and were not afraid of people. Unlike mice, rats did not scurry when lights were turned on or at the thunderous sound of a large adult stomp. Matter of fact, rats scared the cats. As a child, I often slept with pillows or blankets completely covering my body to prevent the rats from nibbling on my head or toes, a habit I continue today.

Roaches were also severe in Rockwell. One of the tenants who had a lack of desire to clean her apartment would have so many roaches and maggots blanketing the walls of her cupboard that it was impossible to place any food items inside without a "visitor" becoming permanently placed inside. Because of her situation, I refused to eat anything created by that household. There was another neighbor who used to periodically smash roaches with her hand while stirring food contents and then resumed cooking without washing her hands. Needless to say, I NEVER ate anything made by her hands either.

Large cockroaches, which we called water bugs, were also present and would sometimes find themselves on shoulders of unexpected tenants after wearing coats that were previously hung in roach-infested closets. Our "ghetto pets" forced us to keep most lights on in our apartment. You were guaranteed to see a group of roaches or occasional rats if lights were kept off for a lengthy period of time. My discomfort in complete darkness probably originated because of the rats and roaches. It was difficult to avoid embarrassment around guests, not knowing when a roach or rat would make its nightly appearance. If the guests were also from the housing projects, they completely understood. When outsiders visited our apartment, we found ourselves constantly eyeing every corner for those miniature creatures.

Mostly because of my mom, I never knew we were poor. I thought all kids in America stood in long lines to enjoy the free summer lunches that consisted of cold sandwiches, a milk carton and fruit (which was typically discarded because of its unpopular pro-nutritional value). My mom never dated anyone that could not assist her financially with her kids. She also conducted herself in ways that were not typical for some of the women in the ghetto. When around whites or business professionals, she dropped any usage of Ebonics and spoke articulately as if she were Harvard educated. This often embarrassed me as I initially saw this as an attempt to speak like Caucasians. Fortunately, later in life I saw this act as a way for her to educate me on the essentials of utilizing proper grammar to be successful.

For all of Rockwell's dark, dangerous, and disgustingly violent history, I actually had more fun memories. While most children in America didn't have to dodge bullets, I'm sure that my fun memories were similar to theirs. Most likely to keep our humor in place, we helped to project myths such as the cat with the human head that, supposedly, went around asking for cigarettes.

Nicknames in environments like Rockwell are used more than actual birth names. Colorful names such as "Fat Cat," "Woolight," "DoDo," "Chalk," "Bookie," and "Papa Daddy" were used so often that I couldn't tell you the real names of most of those individuals. Some, like Woolight, even had *double* nicknames. In addition to his primary moniker, he was often called "Happy Stick" because of the happy stick drug (marijuana joints laced with PCP) to which he was addicted. Colorful nicknames weren't limited to the neighborhood as I had relatives such as "Cat," "Rabbit," "Pookey Slim," "Dirty Red," "Buddha," and "Boone."

One of my fondest childhood memories was seeing the peeking sun's rays shining brightly against the orange bricks on the south side of our building—it provided hope that it would be a great day. Since violence was a daily occurrence, the sun also confirmed to me that I was able to survive another dangerous evening. Each day of survival provided another opportunity to dream and escape to worlds beyond the violence we faced.

As a child, I loved playing childhood games such as "Mother May I," "Simon Says," "Cops and Robbers," "Cowboys and Indians," or "Red Light/Green Light." I believe my constant failure in "Simon Says" contributed partly to my inability to allow others to tell me what to do. Being the youngest in the family, I often rebelled when forced to do something contrary to my desires. Our intrigue with "Cops and Robbers" and "Cowboys and Indians" was influenced by our excitement about the cap guns we used during those games. Interestingly, the cap guns posed a slight danger of being mistaken for real guns in the dark, which actually thrilled us as we were mimicking the Disciples and Vice Lords fighting against each other. We all sought to find the biggest, most realistic looking cap gun.

Another favorite game involved one of my favorite cartoons, *The Super Friends*. I always enjoyed playing the Apache Chief character because I was one of the tallest. I would yell out Apache's famous phrase "Inyuk-chuk," and then pretend to grow to astronomical heights before battling the pretend Legion of Doom and my pretend arch-nemesis Giganta. I never wanted to be Superman because he was the popular and commercial choice. I wanted to turn a lesser-known choice such as Apache Chief into the key hero, which may have contributed to my desire to always seek ways to help the little men and women.

Since sports were one of the ways to escape from the ghetto, they were embraced by most of the Rockwell boys. Every summer day was filled with numerous games including softball, baseball, basketball, and football. Since all of us were poor, we often shared baseball gloves, leaving them on the concrete ground in the field for the opposing player playing the same position to use. Pickup softball games would continue for hours until darkness prevented anyone from seeing the ball. Basketball games were exciting to watch because most of the best neighborhood athletes were also great basketball players. Rockwell athletes from families such as the Willifords, Cobbs, Andersons, and Johns entertained us as if we were watching a classic, grinding NBA Finals in the 1980s between the 76ers and the Lakers. Football was also played on the same concrete field, which didn't necessarily mean tackling was avoided.

Unlike children today, we saw it as a blessing to be able to get outside and play sports versus staying indoors. Our parents constantly yelled for us to come inside at night to eat dinner, since we would have stayed outside all night if it were possible. We would opt to get hit with belts or small tree branches instead of being forced to stay inside. There were no "time out corners" to go to as the only options were pain for punishment or staying inside. Since organized sports were not as developed as they are today (and because we didn't have money to join those leagues), we battled each other on our neighborhood field. We played until darkness came, ignoring any feelings of exhaustion. The euphoria and adrenaline from the nature of competitive sports allowed us to compete for that day's bragging rights.

Life in the ghetto has many positive and negative memories for residents. Because of the consistent violence and small-minded mentalities, it is difficult to dream beyond those streets. Striving to escape the ghetto is often more daunting than dealing with the dangers inherent in the neighborhood. Because of the violence and common diseases associated with blacks such as hypertension or diabetes, you never assumed to live a full life and die of natural causes. This myopic mentality made it bearable as a child to have children of your own. Establishing a family (typically as single parents) before graduating from high school wasn't necessarily frowned upon. In fact, to graduate from high school then proceed to college without bearing children was a significant achievement.

Unfortunately, environments such as Rockwell force you to focus on short-term goals because of your uncertainty of seeing the next day. Because of this mentality, I strongly believe dreams were ruined for individuals who could have contributed greatly to society through new inventions, tremendous business deals, or other positive facets of life. Ghettos also have a way of stripping away the responsibilities individuals should have in controlling their own lives, making it easier for them to blame the environment as a way of coping with their own failures. Once excuses are eliminated, more time could be devoted to developing exit strategies. I knew that education would need to be my driver for future success.

Education: My Way Out

SINCE I WAS THE YOUNGEST in my family by at least eight years, I was able to see the negative impact of drugs and crime through the actions of my siblings. This early exposure helped my decision to avoid both, instead focusing on a legitimate road to success. My mom and Bob also constantly reiterated the importance of education, as they knew this could be my ticket out of poverty. I did not realize how vital education was until I entered the seventh grade. It was there that I met one of the most influential individuals in my early life.

Because of my educational success, I was placed in an experimental class for academically gifted seventh- and eighth-grade students. Our teacher, Mr. Aloysius Bottom, always instilled pride in his students and demanded nothing short of greatness from all of us. As a seventh grader, I was able to measure myself against Grant's cream of the crop. His class taught us that the world was larger than just Rockwell Gardens. He made us believe that we were able to reach that previously unreachable destination if we believed in our own abilities to succeed.

My life aspirations came from an inspirational quote Mr. Bottom constantly repeated to us. Each day in class, he repeated his favorite phrase—"If it is to be, it is up to me"—which meant that any of my successes in life would have to be created, implemented, and maintained by *me*. This phrase gave me a purpose in life beyond the red, orange and yellow bricks of Rockwell. Mr. Bottom was a man of great faith and had a sense of dignity I never saw from any man in the ghetto. I looked at Mr. Bottom as a knight in shining armor who came in to rescue those of us looking for success. I always wondered what inspired Mr. Bottom to have that level of pride. I also wondered

Education: My Way Out

if Mr. Bottom truly understood the impact he made on many lives. He gave all of his students hope in the middle of chaos and despair. I am forever grateful for Mr. Bottom's impact on my life and consequently the lives of my descendants.

I developed my competitive spirit while in Mr. Bottom's class. I fought hard academically to compete against other students in his class, specifically an eighth grader named Stephen and fellow seventh graders Sabrina and Carolyn. I especially envied Stephen because of his athletic ability in addition to his natural intelligence. Sabrina was not only very smart but well-grounded in her faith and always helpful to others. Carolyn had a quiet confidence about her that was respected by other students in the class. Many of the students knew I was serious about education, but not until I entered Mr. Bottom's class did they see me in action.

Transitioning to the eighth grade was exciting for me because it meant I could be the top student at Grant. I worked hard all year to maintain an "E" average (which stood for the top grade "Excellence"), sacrificing many of the daily enjoyments of other kids in the neighborhood. After arriving home from school each day, immediately I completed my homework assignments while listening to the happy screams of my friends playing outside in the beautiful weather. Even though I was a latchkey kid, which meant I often returned home from school with no supervision since Mom worked each day, I knew I had to discipline myself to complete my homework and other assignments. Relatives often questioned my mom why I spent a lot of time after school doing homework instead of having fun outside with the other boys. My mom always knew I had bigger goals in life and was willing to make the sacrifices to change the status quo.

As my academic career started to blossom in the winter of 1985, the city of Chicago was taken over by the Chicago Bears. Long-suffering Chicago sports fans had not celebrated a sports championship since the 1963 Bears. The 1985 Bears provided great sports entertainment through their dominance of the NFL. They also supplied an endless amount of characters to cheer for: Walter "Sweetness" Payton, William "The Refrigerator" Perry, Jim "Mad Mac" McMahon, and Coach "Iron" Mike Ditka. While the "Winning Ugly" White Sox disappointed fans in 1983, and the 1984 Cubs continued to break fans' hearts after Leon Durham allowed the ball to roll under his legs in the National League Championship Series against the San Diego Padres, the Bears were poised to bring a championship back to the city.

The most endearing element of the Bears to fans was their cocky attitude. Even though they were far from winning in previous years, the championship in 1985 became an afterthought. The climax of the regular season came in the form of a music video and song entitled "The Super Bowl Shuffle," which featured performances by some of the Bear players. The irony of the video was that it was filmed the day after the Bears only loss that season. I am confident in believing all Chicago kids knew the words to the Shuffle. The Awesome Force even performed a "Stay in School" version of the Shuffle at a neighborhood recreation center.

When the Bears finally won the championship in January of 1986, a few of us celebrated the achievement by attending a downtown parade for the champs. The frigid, 20-below February temperatures did not dampen our moods as we enjoyed watching the players sitting on top of the team buses while carrying the Lombardi trophy and circling the massive crowds. The 1985 Bears gave great pride to Chicagoans, which is why we continue to talk about that season as if it occurred last year. Even more important to me, the 1985 Bears allowed me to temporarily forget about the challenges faced on a daily basis in Rockwell. I always find it amazing the way sports galvanize communities and races, especially if a favorite team wins the championship. The Bears weren't just cheered by white Chicago fans. They weren't the favorites of only the Rockwell residents. The 1985 Chicago Bears brought great pride to *everyone* that considered Chicago home.

My commitment towards excelling in education started to pay off in 1986. During the last few weeks of school, Mr. Bottom informed me that I was going to be Grant School's Class of 1986 valedictorian. I could not wait to tell my mom as I knew she needed some positive news in her life after her many trials and tribulations. My mom was very proud of my accomplishment and made sure to inform everyone that criticized my academic commitment. As a result of being the valedictorian, I was going to provide my first speech in front of a large crowd during our graduation. Although I had never spoken in front of a large group, my previous dance performances prepared me well. My speech would also set the foundation for future aspirations in regards to my career.

I worked hard in trying to get accepted into Lane Tech, one of the best high schools in Chicago. Lane was on the North Side of Chicago and was used as the school in the 1986 Goldie Hawn and Wesley Snipes movie *Wildcats*. If I attended Lane, I would have had to take the Western bus several miles each day between hope and despair. However, I was informed that although my grades and achievement tests results were the best among all the students, I was not accepted into Lane Tech along with Grant's salutatorian, even though all of my grades and accomplishments were more impressive. This was devastating news to me and my family as it would result into me attending the neighborhood's Crane High School.

Crane was similar to East Side High in the '80s movie *Lean on Me*. Metal detectors were positioned in the front of the school to prevent guns and other weapons from entering. Drug dealing and gang violence were rampant inside and outside the school. After telling my siblings and assuming they would be happy that I was following their academic footsteps, they were extremely disappointed, knowing that Crane was not the appropriate school for me to achieve success. Crane produced athletic talent such as former and current NBA players Ken "the Snake" Norman, Will Bynum, and Tony Allen, as well as legendary coach and owner of the Chicago Bears, George "Papa Bear" Halas. Crane was a charter member of the Chicago Public League in 1913 and was second in the city for most league titles for basketball. However, Crane wasn't known for manufacturing academic stars. Knowing that my future path would not involve sports, I worried about the impact of attending Crane.

While feeling depressed about the recent change to my academic future, I received great news. Grant's vice principal, Mr. Jones, gave me hope by giving me an option for school. Mr. Jones urged me to apply for a program called A Better Chance (ABC). ABC is a college preparatory program that takes academically gifted students and places them into better high schools across the country. Since most of the participating ABC schools were located on the East Coast, it was obvious that I would have to move in order to attend the program. To get accepted into the program, I had to take the Secondary School Admission Test (SSAT) then select my top three schools.

Preparing for the SSAT was difficult, because I have never been a great aptitude test-taker. However, I knew that my future was in the hands of this program. My top three school choices were a high school in the Boston area, one in New York, and Lower Merion High School, which was near Philadelphia. Lower Merion was my first choice mostly because of its proximity to Philly and my childhood hero, Julius "Dr. J" Erving of the 76ers.

Dr. J maintained endless eloquence whether gliding on the court or conducting an interview off of it. He is in a class by himself in my eyes because of his smooth mannerisms and extreme confidence without coming across as arrogant. I enjoyed watching his commercials and became so fascinated with him that I wanted to emulate his style in walk and speech, since I knew I couldn't match his athletic abilities. Because of his influence on me and other young black males in the late '70s and early '80s, he remains my favorite basketball player, even though my favorite team, the Chicago Bulls, enjoyed championship years while being led by the great Michael Jordan.

Lower Merion consistently ranked as one of the top public or private high schools in the United States, and it continues to graduate students each year to prestigious colleges and universities around the world. Its motto, "Enter To Learn, Go Forth To Serve," was a perfect complement to Mr. Bottom's quote and philosophy. Lower Merion is located in Ardmore, which is one of the suburbs on Philadelphia's Main Line, a historical region of towns built along the Main Line of the Pennsylvania Railroad. Its communities include some of the wealthiest families in the country. The school's most famous alumnus, Kobe Bryant, would later star on a Lower Merion basketball team that enjoyed multiple state championships. Other sports such as football and lacrosse also found great success.

To my surprise, I was accepted into the ABC program at Lower Merion around the same time Bob informed me and my mom we were going to New York on a vacation for spring break. The timing was perfect because it would allow us to visit Lower Merion before I started school in the fall, since Philadelphia was less than two hours from New York. I didn't know if I was more excited about Lower Merion or the chance to visit New York, a city I had only dreamed of seeing while watching movies and television shows. New York seemed like a world away from Rockwell. I was also very nervous about flying, because this would be my first time. I continued to have a fear of flying throughout my life even though I travel frequently for my career. Seeing the Statue of Liberty, the Empire State Building, the twin towers of the World Trade Center, Central Park, and other famous landmarks was helpful in getting me prepared to expand my world.

Finally, we were able to make it down to Ardmore to visit the Lower Merion ABC house. This was a great moment for me, Bob, and my mom. I'm sure others from the neighborhood saw nothing special about the home, but to me it was a mansion. The white three-story home had eight bedrooms, a basement with a washer and dryer, a large kitchen, and large backyard. I had never lived in a multi-level house before or had a basement and backyard. We were greeted by Jeanne, one of the resident directors for the program, who gave us a tour of the home. I walked through the home, envisioning myself in each room. I had never lived in a home with a washer and dryer inside the home. My mom always took our clothes to the laundromat, which was always a long, boring process. I never had a backyard with an enclosed fence which, to me at least, seemed like a football field-sized lot. I attempted to mask my emotions, but I'm sure my mom and Bob knew my excitement was increasing each time we entered another room inside the house. This was going to be my chance to live in a way our family had never experienced.

Jeanne gave us a detailed explanation of the program and daily routines. She explained that the program consisted of nine male students along with two resident directors and two tutors. Also included was Mrs. Taylor, who was the ABC cook and prepared meals Monday through Friday night. Dinner was served from 5:00 to 6:00 p.m., followed by a mandatory study hall from 6:00 to 9:00. Although the program had a rigid structure, I knew it was necessary to provide the students with a level of discipline needed to do well in school. I was confident that my academic self-discipline while living in Rockwell prepared me to adjust to ABC's routine.

I left the ABC house eager to start the school year and not thrilled to return back to the ghettos of Chicago. The experience forced me to count down towards my Grant School graduation. My ABC life couldn't come fast enough as I started realizing the dangerous lifestyle inside of Rockwell. I also started to treat my life as a precious commodity that needed to be protected in order to have the chance to succeed.

The last few weeks of school were a blur. Since I already knew I was going to be valedictorian, my focus was solely on attending Lower Merion and escaping the hell of Rockwell. I couldn't wait to move into the white mansion in Ardmore and meet the other students. Mr. Bottom constantly told me how proud he was that I was leaving home to attend Lower Merion. He reminded me how brave I had to be in order to make the decision to leave behind everything I had known up until that point in my life. His words of encouragement were necessary as I was still trying to overcome my fears of this new life. The closer my graduation date appeared, the closer I was to starting my new chapter in life. The foundation established in my youth would now be transformed and molded into something not yet known by anyone.

My graduating class selected "We Are the World" as our graduating song, which had a significant meaning to a kid living in the ghetto. The lyrics "We are the world, we are the children, we are the ones to make a brighter day, so let's start living" were a perfect complement to Mr. Bottom's phrase. Through these words I knew that I had to overcome any fears if I wanted to strive for success. Since there were limited examples in my family or surrounding community that I could solicit educational advice from, I had to leave everything in God's hands.

Finally, it was time to graduate. My graduation day was memorable. I wore a black 80's style tuxedo with a pink cummerbund and bow tie along with pink leather shoes with a hot pink suede stripe in the middle. My cousin James wore a white tux with a red tie and cummerbund with white shoes. My mom helped me with my speech and gave me confidence to address the assembly as the leading student for the class. I was also excited that Bob would attend the event as he was my first inspiration to strive for greatness.

I don't remember the exact words from the speech, but I do recall my attempt to inspire the other students to dream big and work hard to fulfill those lofty goals. My greatest achievement at that point was being able to survive Rockwell. I witnessed more in my first fourteen years than most adults would in their lifetime. However, instead of using this experience as an obstacle, I would turn it into a relentless driving force to succeed. I was even more anxious and determined to work hard for success because of the opportunity provided to me. I had to succeed not only for my family but for the neighborhood. I had to succeed for the ancestors that did not get the same opportunities I received. I had to succeed for the future generations of my family, giving them the blueprint that was not established when I was growing up. I was confident that my life was about to change in ways not previously discovered by anyone I knew.

Part II

TransformNation

Clockwise from top: ABC students and staff, 1989; me at Lake Forest College; me and Michelle with Malik and Jacqui; me and Michelle on our wedding day

Summer of 1986

AS I BEGAN MY MENTAL and physical transition from Rockwell, the summer of 1986 would become the most important period in my life. Not only would I be challenged in ways that could put my ABC future in jeopardy, I was also placed in life-threatening circumstances. That summer gave me the fortitude and maturity to be prepared for being away from home and provided great confirmation of why I needed to leave Chicago. The summer of 1986 was the turning point of my life; it was the period that would determine my potential success or adherence to the status quo of Rockwell. As with life, the closer you are to overcoming obstacles, the more obstacles appear before you. That summer featured many close encounters that each could have had a significant and severe impact on my life which, as a youth, I didn't realize at the time.

Often, my friends and I traveled on the bus and El to go to the movie theaters or visit neighborhoods on the far South or North sides. We were told about a neighborhood kid that rented cars during the weekend to anyone that needed them. Rob was the only one among us that had a driver's license, so he became the designated driver. We used to wonder why the car we rented was missing parts and pieces from its console. We also wondered why it was difficult to turn on the ignition in the normal manner it was intended. Eventually we found out that the "rented" car was actually a stolen car. Fortunately for us, we were never stopped by the police for any traffic violations or else all of us would have served time for stealing the car, which meant I most likely would not have been able to participate in the ABC program.

On one calm summer evening, I was hanging in front of my apartment with two friends, trying to squeeze the last few weeks of friendship before I started my new adventure in Pennsylvania. All of a sudden, police were everywhere in front of our apartment, frisking us against the cold brick wall and questioning where we spent the last few hours. After answering truthfully that we had been in front of our apartment all night, one of the policemen accused me of breaking into someone's car to steal the purse of the female passenger. The police then brought the male driver in front of me to ask for confirmation if I was the individual that robbed his family. I thought for sure I would be released until I heard the worst word of my life come from the accuser's lips: "Yes!"

Immediately, the police cuffed me and my friends and led us down the stairs to their parked patrol car. As we were being marched to the car in handcuffs, it seemed as if hundreds of Rockwell tenants rallied and were frantically screaming for the cops to release us. They knew the police had the wrong boy. My heart was racing as I knew a police record would take away my opportunity to attend the ABC program, dramatically changing the blueprint I was starting to draw for my future. I felt as if I were in a bad dream or movie that would eventually end. The closer I got to the car, the more I realized my future dreams were about to end for something I was not in control to fight against.

After my mom was told about the situation she rushed downstairs, still in her house robe, to plead on our behalf. The police were unmoved, as they were convinced we were the culprits and maybe motivated to lock up people who they assumed were worthless kids from the ghetto. However, one of those kids had big dreams to fulfill that were against the status quo and beyond those historically impenetrable physical and societal walls. I developed a great appreciation for those angrily repudiating the false accusations directed towards me and my friend. These were the same people that placed on my shoulders their hope that I would succeed. I was one of theirs who would break the cycle. They invested as much into my dreams as my own family had. Fortunately, I was able to establish my brand among them so that they knew I could never think about risking my future for a senseless crime. After at least thirty minutes of begging and pleading from my mom and others in the neighborhood, the police finally released us after either realizing they captured the wrong teens or desiring to stop the incessant pleas. I was so grateful for establishing a positive reputation in the eyes of my neighbors. Without my reputation and brand intact, my scholastic career would have ended inside that police car on that beautiful summer evening.

Just when I thought my experience with the Chicago police was over, I was proven wrong. On a sunny afternoon while playing basketball with a few friends in front of our apartment building, I noticed a speeding patrol car stopping abruptly in the adjacent parking lot. The sight of excited policemen was almost a daily occurrence in the ghetto. However, this time they were approaching me. Similar to the incident a few weeks before, the police threw me against their car, searching my pockets for anything that could incriminate me. After sensing their frustration for not finding treasures, I asked why I was being frisked. I quickly learned that the Chicago police didn't want to be questioned by a worthless kid from the ghetto. How dare I challenge their authority and not believe the supposed facts regarding their profile of me? The same storyline from the summer evening a few weeks earlier repeated itself on this sunny afternoon day. I was being accused for stealing someone's purse.

My mom made it downstairs after I was placed in the car and proceeded to beg AGAIN for them to release me. This time I was only held for about fifteen minutes before the cops gave up on debating with my mom. Again, I was one of the fortunate ghetto souls that was able to avoid entering the punitive system. It made me think of the large amount of unfortunate kids who populate jails across the country because they had no one to fight on their behalf. They either weren't able to establish their own brands among their community, or they didn't think too much of their future to fight against the injustice. I was deeply saddened thinking about all of the shattered dreams and damaged families that came as a result of false accusations. However, this was a time for me to count my blessings and pray that my time in Chicago would hopefully end very soon.

The Awesome Force strength was needed during our first encounter with racism. After winning Crane High School's talent show in the summer of 1986 while performing New Edition's "Lost in Love," our manager decided to treat the group to Showbiz Pizza (now called Chuck E. Cheese's). The restaurant was located at 5030 South Kedzie Avenue on the South Side of

Chicago in the area known as Gage Park. Unbeknownst to all of us, that area was one of the most racist in the country. When Dr. Martin Luther King, Jr. marched in nearby Marquette Park in 1966, he was struck on the head with a stone thrown by a racist protestor. The blow brought Dr. King to his knees and would later influence him to admit that even he had never witnessed the level of hostility and hatred he had seen at Marquette Park, regardless of the level of bigotry he witnessed in the racist South.

Since none of us were able to drive, we took the Western Avenue bus from Van Buren Boulevard to 50th Street. It was a beautiful Friday afternoon, so we decided to walk a mile on 51st from Western to Kedzie on our way to Showbiz. On our way to the restaurant, we noticed a group of teenaged white males staring at us before shouting towards us, "Niggers, get out of here! Go home!" Since we outnumbered them, we decided to not waste our time and allow them to ruin our special evening. We also felt they were trying to influence us to start a fight, which none of us were interested in that day, mostly because of the unknown neighborhood. While at Showbiz, we enjoyed pizza, played games, and reminisced about the talent show. We stayed at Showbiz for hours until darkness arrived. Since our walk was enjoyable earlier (with the exception of the idiot racist teenagers), we decided to try it again.

While walking, we noticed an eerie feeling in the air. Even though it was still early in the evening, Gage Park was like a ghost town. We stopped at a nearby restaurant to buy milkshakes, noticing the cold behavior displayed by the workers inside as if they knew something we didn't. After leaving the restaurant we proceeded to walk down 51st towards Western. We noticed the same group of racist teens standing in the same location from earlier that day. Just as before, the racist teens shouted similar threats towards our group. Again, we decided to not allow this behavior to destroy a great evening. We were also out of our comfort zone since we weren't familiar with the neighborhood. As we passed the group, we had no idea what to expect. Cook turned around and told the rest of our group, "Shit! Here they come!" As we briefly turned around, we noticed that the racist idiots were joined by at least twenty more of their closest friends, all shouting, "Run, niggers!" while running towards us.

Since I was the slowest in the group and lacked endurance, I was not confident in my ability to escape. However, my adrenaline helped me to run as fast as the rest of the group, even though I was wearing the slippery dress shoes I had worn during graduation. We ran past the neighborhood spectators as well as a set of policemen patrolling the area. Unfortunately, no one aided us in escaping this nightmare until we came across an older white gentleman, who was screaming, "Follow me! I'll lead you out!" After briefly vacillating between staying on our route or detouring for his suggested one, we made a hasty decision to follow him. Fortunately, his route led us towards an alley that provided a short cut to Western Avenue. Chicago's segregated neighborhoods are often separated by blocks and streets. In that neighborhood, Western was the border street between white and black residents, which is why the racist pursuers ended their chase.

Once we escaped, I was prompted to stop at a church along the way to briefly thank Heavenly Father for giving us the strength and intuition to get away. My heart was still racing while I recollected the horror of that evening. After arriving at our stop, Quamie's brother Red took out his anger towards whites by punching an innocent and unassuming white passenger before exiting the bus. I never told my family about our experience until years later. Rarely does anyone from Awesome Force recall that evening during our various reunions. We realized that we dodged a significant bullet that destroyed our youthful innocence regarding racism and could have brought harm to all of us.

I never understood the purpose of racism. Why would someone spend energy hating another person because of the color of their skin? I was exposed not only to racism in regards to whites versus blacks, but also blacks being racist towards whites. Often, family members or friends warned me to not trust whites, telling me that whites were always trying to find ways to harm or make blacks feel inferior. While this was true for those racist idiots on the South Side, I would not find out until later in life that there were many whites that genuinely loved all races.

The next night would be just as eventful. After a neighborhood party, my cousin Boone and I were walking our girlfriends to their nearby apartment building. After making sure the girls arrived safely, we started our journey back to our building. While walking past a darkened alley, we heard a loud gun shot, and then immediately saw the spark from the grazing bullet as it hit the fence in front of the house where we stood. Boone and I looked at each other with fear before splitting up to run back to our building. I believe there was another shot shortly after the first one as my mind ran through potential consequences of getting shot.

My heart felt like it was beating outside of my chest as I ran towards my building. The closer I approached the building, the more I realized how close I was again to seeing my dreams unfulfilled. Once I arrived, I met up with Boone as we tried to make sense of what just happened. We didn't know if we were mistakenly targeted by the Disciples because of our uncoordinated and coincidental red and black color combination that evening, which was the color combination of the rival gang. Regardless, that was the last time we walked in front of that area late at night.

I received my most severe life lessons that summer. I witnessed racism, rode in stolen cars, experienced false imprisonment, and suffered from gang violence directed towards me. I was fortunate to have escaped all of those obstacles, believing it was confirmation of why I needed to leave Chicago. I knew that I had to sacrifice my family relationships in order to strive for greatness. Nothing would be easy. I knew I would have to fight for every achievement and prepare myself for adversity every day of my life. I was entering a new world—one that was not met by anyone in my family before me. It was almost as if there was a force that would not allow me to escape. However, I knew that I was ready for whatever was in store thanks to that eventful summer of 1986.

A Better Chance

THE WEEKS LEADING UP TO my departure from Chicago were very stressful. I realized that I would be leaving home, which had been a place that, even with its own volatility, provided me my only comfort in the middle of chaos. I would also leave my mom, who was the one person who provided me with great strength during my early years. However, I also knew that my family understood the sacrifices we all had to make in order for me to change our history. My friends did not understand why I needed to leave the only world we knew in order to achieve success. Since none of us had ever left the neighborhood, we were all afraid of the challenges that came along with adapting to other cultures, religions, and races.

The day of my departure was painfully somber for all of us, which was helped by the drizzling rain and overcast. Bob came down from Waukegan to take the family to Chicago's Midway airport. On the way to the airport, the car was eerily quiet. I kept wishing the car would get a flat tire or that there would be another reason that would delay my flight. I was scared. I would not have the security blankets that surrounded me for the first fourteen years of my life. The closer we got to the airport, the faster my heart beat.

During those days, entire families could wait at the airport gate along with the passenger. As we arrived at the gate, we had the chance to talk about the excitement this new opportunity would bring. I struggled to convince myself that I made the right decision as I started to have flashbacks about various events, good and bad, that took place in apartment 603 of the 340 South Western building in Rockwell Gardens. I then tried to envision my life away from my nest in a new city, with new friends and a new beginning.

I waited to board until all of the passengers were on the plane. When it was time, we all stood up and hugged each other in a circle while saying a prayer. The prayer was for my safe travel (a tradition I continue to this day, occasionally with my mom), confidence to survive away from home, and my scholastic success. After the prayer there was not a dry eye in the circle. We sobbed openly and kept assuring each other that we could stay in touch. Finally, we broke the circle. Each step toward the ticketing agent was one step away from the life I grew to enjoy, regardless of how much it was infested with crime, drugs, infidelity, or other experiences too mature for children. After sitting in my seat, I was able to see my family waving at me from the large windows at the gate. I wiped my tears, waved back, hoping they'd see me, took a deep breath, then decided at that moment it was time for my transformation.

After arriving in Philadelphia I was greeted at the gate by Bill, one of ABC's resident directors. Bill was a young white male that studied at one of the nearby colleges. The ride to the ABC house was the first time I had ever been alone with a white person. I cannot remember our conversation but do recall how uncomfortable both of us seemed. When we arrived at the house, I realized I was the first student. Bill gave me a quick tour of the home, introduced me to the other staff members, and then directed me to my room. When Bill left, I closed the door, dropped my bags in the middle of the floor, and then started to cry relentlessly.

Within a few minutes, the other students started to arrive. I was able to meet all of the students, including my roommate Mark, by the end of the day. One by one I met Brian (the only other Chicago student), Danillo, Ralph, Everett, Nashid, Dave, and Alfredo. Mark, Danillo, Ralph, Nashid, Dave and Alfredo were all from New York, while Everett was the only one from Boston. Mark entered the program that year as a sophomore while Dave, Nashid and I were the freshmen. Brian and Ralph were seniors, Danillo the only junior, and Everett and Alfredo were the other sophomores.

Since I was also from Chicago, Brian instantly took me under his wing. He and Mark also developed a strong bond because of their athleticism. Mark and Brian were very popular with the females because of their engaging personalities and athleticism. Brian was the starting point guard for the varsity basketball team and an aspiring rapper. He and a local friend, Randy, rapped at parties and other events as a duo named Fire and Ice. The year was 1986 and the rap group Run-DMC controlled the radio airwaves as well as provided inspiration to Fire and Ice. Hip hop was still in its early years and I had not yet fully embraced it. However, I enjoyed listening to Fire and Ice and marveled at their ability to write poetic verses while performing over drum beats. Brian reminded me of DMC from Run-DMC because of his Gazelle glasses, Kangol hat and rhymes. Randy was a smooth rapper and a solid basketball player himself as the starting forward for the team.

The phrase "boys will be boys" held true in the ABC house. Upperclassmen of the ABC house enjoyed the tradition of roughhousing with the new class. Since I was one of the taller "rookies," I was targeted often. However, since most of us came from violent neighborhoods, the roughhousing was never seen as threatening behavior. During our "matches," the ABC staff cleared the living room and enjoyed the spectacle of upperclassmen hammering away at the rookies. I maintained a chip on my shoulder because I knew I came from the worst neighborhood of any of the other students. Since I had already been shot at, chased, and had experienced activities kids should not be exposed to during my Rockwell years, I wasn't going to allow someone to bully me in the suburbs of Philadelphia.

Even though the upperclassmen treated the incoming class with great disdain inside the house, they were extremely protective of us at school. I knew I didn't have to worry about bullies because of my ABC brothers and their friends from the neighborhood. I also maintained an edge because of my Rockwell upbringing. The Rockwell edge was needed in order to prepare for any potential racial challenges, which I never experienced while at Lower Merion. Since the school was mostly Jewish, blacks were easily welcomed. Because both races endured painful histories, Jews and blacks accepted and sympathized with each other more easily than with other races.

A few weeks into my ABC experience, I received a phone call from my mom delivering great news. She called to let me know that we moved out of the projects! My mom moved into a split level home on the West Side of Chicago, not far from the Mars Hill church. I was excited and scared at the same time, not knowing how our family would be impacted by the move. I was also worried about ways in which my relationship with friends from Rockwell would change. I was already viewed by some as trying to be white because of my decision to improve my future by leaving home, and knew I would lose more friends with a physical move from Rockwell. However, I was confident that the moves made by me and my mom were the right decisions. After receiving the news, I began my countdown to Thanksgiving so that I could see our new home.

I didn't realize I was extremely poor until I attended Lower Merion. As a Rockwell resident, my only exposure to luxurious cars was on television, attending car shows, or seeing the latest toys from the neighborhood drug dealers. At Lower Merion, many of the students arrived in the newest BMWs, Mercedes-Benzes, Audis, and other impressive vehicles. Having wealthy friends at Lower Merion was appealing because it gave us the means to enjoy various activities.

We were attracted to the Jewish and Caucasian female students, but dared not to date them for fear of being called a *sell-out* by our own race or not being accepted by theirs. Surprisingly, interracial relationships were openly accepted, even though some of the black males still kept them secret for fear of offending family or friends. Racism was nonexistent at Lower Merion. The only racial episode I encountered there occurred when a white student held up a black pen, then used it to compare to my skin. Even though I wanted to choke the living hell out of that idiot, for the most part, racism was non-existent. Blacks integrated very well with the majority population.

While Lower Merion was nestled in a wealthy community, Ardmore was a different world. Although far from resembling the violent Chicago landscape, it was populated by lower income, blue collar African Americans. I believe the economic and ethnic makeup of Ardmore assisted with my transition from Rockwell. I was able to communicate with others from the neighborhood that could at least understand my plight versus the students surrounding the wealthy Lower Merion communities that may strike someone from my background as an alien. Fellow ABC students tried earnestly to save our weekly $8 pittance of an allowance to eat at fast food restaurants like Roy Rogers and McDonald's while occasionally going to the movies. Luckily, our attempt to stretch our allowance was done in Ardmore.

Throughout school, I hid my financial situation from my mom, not wanting her to worry or sacrifice money she needed more just for my own convenience. Mom had to force me to accept money she'd voluntarily and surprisingly send, knowing I wasn't being honest when I told her I had enough funds. Even though I was excited to receive the additional financial support from my mom, it made me sad to think about the sacrifices she took to send it, which made me more careful how I spent the money.

One of the ways my fellow ABC students were able to connect with the local residents was through our legendary house parties. ABC house parties were always well attended. As the DJ spun records in one of the first floor bedrooms, the Ardmore residents and other guests danced and grinded mostly to popular rap records at that time such as Eric B & Rakim's "My Melody," MC Shan's "The Bridge," or Biz Markie's "Make the Music With Your Mouth, Biz." Fire and Ice often used these parties to perform their latest song. Unfortunately, the ABC parties would sometimes prematurely end in fights, ruining an otherwise good night. I never understood the purpose of fights at parties. I wondered why guys would be upset with anyone when there was a clear advantage in the ratio of girls to guys. Sometimes fights involved jealous girls, which always drew the biggest spectators. Even though none of us ABC students wanted fights to occur in our house, we felt safe because of the differences between Ardmore and our neighborhoods back home, where fights ended with gun shots.

I didn't make a lot of friends outside of the ABC house during my first two years at Lower Merion. I always felt like an outsider whether at school or in Ardmore. I found out later that some neighborhood kids thought ABC stood for "All Butter and Cheese," a derogatory term to denote the food received by welfare recipients, or "Abandoned Black Children," thinking we were delinquents left alone by our parents. I also knew that it would be difficult to date while attending the program because I would always reside temporarily in Chicago during major holidays and Ardmore during the school year. I envied the local kids because of their residential stability and the chance to live year-round away from violence. Many students at Lower Merion thought I was from the South because of my horrible grammar and southern twang. Kids growing up in Chicago were greatly influenced by our parents, who mostly migrated from the South for better jobs, bringing with them southern grammar, accents, foods, and cultures.

Because of the lack of being taught how to speak proper English while in Rockwell, my grammar was horrible. I didn't realize until then that Grant School students were roughly four years behind others in reading and math, mostly because of the limited resources such as book or even teachers. While there were good teachers like Mr. Bottom, Mr. Schuman, Ms. Schumpert and others, there were also ones who were less than adequate and will go unnamed. While we battled the classrooms during the day, we had to battle to survive the violent neighborhood at night. Even though education was important to me, I only knew what I was taught, which was very limited with the small budget provided to Grant.

At Lower Merion, my essays were often written in the same slang I unknowingly spoke while in Rockwell. I wrote phrases such as "I'm fixing to go..." instead of "I'm going to..." and didn't realize it was incorrect. Resident directors at the ABC house decided to hire an English tutor for me because of my low grades in English classes. Each afternoon after school, while the other students were enjoying Ardmore, I was stuck inside the ABC house trying to enunciate words I had never heard in my life. The sessions not only improved my writing ability, they also increased my confidence to communicate with others outside of the ABC house.

I counted down the days when I would be able to visit Chicago and see my family and new place during my Thanksgiving break. Even though I was gone only three months, I knew there would be a lot of noticeable changes among my family, friends and myself. When I arrived at the airport I was greeted by my mom, who hugged me as if she hadn't seen me in years. She had already lost her oldest son to the prisons, but she realized she needed to sacrifice her youngest to the educational system. When we arrived at our new place, I walked through the small apartment with great pride. I was happy that my mom found the courage to move from the place she called home for twenty-one years.

I felt strange in my new surroundings since Rockwell had been my only home for the first fourteen years of my life. Even though Rockwell was extremely violent, I still enjoyed a level of comfort. Moving into this new place would require a major adjustment. I didn't know any of my new neighbors. I had to now take the bus or El to visit my friends in Rockwell. *What would my friends think of me when they visited our new place, which was far from Rockwell?* I struggled with accepting the fact that my mom worked hard and gained enough courage to move us out of the ghetto. While I should have been excited to have our own scaled-down version of The Jeffersons' "moving on up," I was more worried about the perception among my friends.

My first visit to Rockwell felt even stranger than my arrival at our new home. When I was living in Rockwell, I was used to seeing the violence, drugs, and poverty, but living in Pennsylvania changed my mentality. My exposure to wealth and neighborhood peace had awakened something within me to strive for success, moving me farther away from any desire to accept poverty or a lack of hope. Returning to Rockwell opened my eyes to how horrible our living condition was. My mom provided great love inside our home, but our external exposure to the daily rituals of the ghetto placed our lives in danger on a daily basis. My expanded world removed my blinders and now placed a fear of the ghetto inside me that never existed before.

It was great to see my Awesome Force brothers. They were excited to hear about my new world and were able to see how East Coast hip hop had started to influence me. Hip hop in the middle to late 1980s was considered by many to be the Golden Era, and there was no better place to be than on the East coast. The East coast produced most of the successful rappers and dance moves during that period. Upon returning to Chicago I was able to show my Awesome Force friends East coast hip hop moves such as the Wop and Running Man. I was also able to display the fashion greatly influenced by the East coast such as Kangol hats, oversized sweat shirts, or my then signature look during the late 1980s and early 1990s… my 8-inch Cameo high top fade that I aggressively tried to mirror the style of my favorite rapper, Big Daddy Kane. I even parted my eyebrows and front of my hair to resemble Kane.

My travels back and forth between Lower Merion and Chicago were filled with conflicts. Eventually, I dreaded returning to Rockwell because of the violence, drug usage, and lack of hope. However, toward the end of my Chicago visits I didn't want to return to the level of wealth at Lower Merion that I didn't believe I could ever achieve in my life, or to the neighborhood kids whose perception of me was just another welfare recipient or abandoned by my family. The closer the time came for us to leave my Chicago home to return to the airport, the larger the knot inside my stomach grew. Even though I knew the ABC program was vital to my future success, I again had no desire to leave the comforts of mediocrity. While I actually debated my decision each time I traveled to the airport, the closer I got to the airport, the more I appreciated the blessings and escapism provided by the ABC program.

While I was trying to adjust to my life at Lower Merion, my world in Chicago was crumbling underneath me without me knowing it. While I was away, my mom and Bob were being followed by the FBI because of their involvement in illegal real estate activities. The concocted scheme was to illegally gain access to Waukegan property they'd purchase then sell back to the city. After my mom made various deposits for Bob, he then took the funds and split among other cohorts which also involved other city representatives. This explained why Bob always seemed to carry a wad of cash with him. With the excess funds, he bought my mom a new car and other material possessions. Eventually, the FBI got involved after noticing suspicious activities and purchases for a *supposedly* poor family living in the ghetto.

The FBI visited my mom while she was home and I was away attending school. The agent asked if she knew Bob, which she confirmed. He then invited her to go to the Dirksen Federal Building in downtown Chicago where he showed her records of every check received and cashed by her as well as receipts from hotels where Bob and Mom stayed on business trips, airline information, and other pertinent information to clearly implicate both of them. Knowing her world was about to come to a severe stop, my mom's life flashed ahead of her. She was a single mother with a son trying hard to obtain the education needed to escape poverty the *right* way.

As the trial began, my mom was questioned several times about her dealings with Bob. She was instructed to answer every question with "I refuse to answer on the grounds it may incriminate me." My mom was convinced by the judge and prosecutor to tell the truth or else she would have to go to federal prison, which was the obvious fate ahead for Bob because of his dominant role in the scheme. They also attempted to convince Mom that she was being used by Bob because she didn't receive luxury cars or other more expensive assets like Bob and his cohorts.

Bob's wife, Trudy, attended the proceedings and was forced to listen to detailed information about the long-standing affair while sitting a few feet away from my mom. Bob was indicted in June 1988 by the federal government. Even though other city officials were involved with the real estate activities along with Bob, he was forced to take the fall for everyone as a result of various threats made towards his family if he were uncooperative. Fortunately for my mom, she only received probation, narrowly avoiding a crushing blow to our family had we lost our leader.

When Bob went to prison, my mom lost not only someone she loved but also our financial contributor, which could have an extremely negative impact on the family. Since everyone was shielding me from the court proceedings, I never realized until I became an adult how close my mom was to going to prison along with Bob. While trying to keep me focused on school, my mom's world was becoming an internal hell. She was barely able to buy clothes, food or other necessities. She unsuccessfully attempted to borrow from family. She struggled so badly with buying clothes that she reached the point where she had to take back a pair of shoes she loaned to one of her sisters. Some family members who borrowed from Bob before he went to prison refused to pay my mom back the owed funds, even though Bob had instructed them to do so. The only person who consistently supported my mom during this time was her best friend, Lottie, who occasionally provided food in addition to money.

While my mom was living through her struggles, I continued to have my own types of struggles at Lower Merion. I continued to be very shy and laconic, especially with anyone outside of the ABC program. Rarely did I voluntarily strike up a conversation with any of the students. Each day in my school homeroom, I sat quietly waiting for the bell to ring, which seemed to take hours. I sat behind a kid named Jim, who was also the starting quarterback for the junior varsity football team and obviously a popular kid in school. We both knew of each other from being on the same bus to and from school. I also knew of him while unsuccessfully trying out for the basketball team each year. Even though I knew I was better than at least a handful of players on the team, I realized I was fighting against a political machine. Some of the players selected were from wealthy and historically prominent families in the community who spoke loudly if their sons didn't continue to obtain privileges they were used to receiving.

Jim also lived in Ardmore, but it seemed as if he, during my first two years, viewed me as a charity case since I was in the ABC program. I found out later that Jim was one of those neighborhood kids who assumed kids were sent to the ABC program because we had behavioral challenges or were abandoned by our families. Jim had frequent animated discussions with other classmates on broad topics ranging from sports to television shows. On one particular day, these discussions would pique my interest.

While sitting behind Jim, I overheard him mention my favorite R&B group, New Edition. Jim was commenting on the newly released New Edition album *Heartbreak*. After hearing his positive comments about the album and group, I inched closer to breaking out of my shyness, anxious to let him know how much I admired New Edition. Still reliving my Awesome Force days in Chicago, I often practiced the various New Edition dance routines inside my head. "I know all of those dance routines," I hesitantly stated to Jim. Surprised at my statement and the fact that I could speak, Jim incredulously replied, "Really!?" Knowing that I couldn't retreat now, I replied "Yes! If you came by the ABC house after school I'll show you the routine to 'Count Me Out.'" I am sure Jim was a little concerned with accepting my invitation, not knowing if I was luring him into a home of deviants.

After arriving at the ABC house after school, Jim and I went into my room. After I closed the door, I popped New Edition's *Count Me Out* cassette tape into my radio. Once I pressed the play button and the opening shout of "Count meeeee ouuuuut!!!" filled the room, I proceeded to go into the routine as if I had been a member of New Edition. My sharp, crisp synchronized moves validated my statement made earlier in class. From that moment on, Jim and I established a friendship that would continue throughout my life. We decided to form our own dance group and named it Ultimate. We recruited three others, including Mark (from the ABC program), Doug, and Andrew, both Lower Merion students.

Ultimate provided me with a way to become more outspoken at Lower Merion. We often performed in battles at parties against Lower Merion competitors such as The Boeskys and a female group from Ardmore. We harmonized to New Edition's "Leaving You Again" on the back of the school bus to prove that we weren't just dancers. As I hit the high notes of the song, others started to see my true personality escape from its shell with each performance. Our competitive desires influenced us to convince Lower Merion to have its first talent show in 1989, mostly so we could use the event as a platform to impress the girls. To prepare for the talent show, we often conducted secret practices inside Jim's basement. Mark and I snuck out of the ABC house during study hall in order to practice with no fear of being caught, even sometimes during the middle of board meetings. Escaping the board meetings was even riskier because we had to quietly and slowly walk past a window in direct sight of the meeting. We waited until it was completely dark to make it more difficult for them to see our escape. I think back now on how dangerous this could have been, but I found the risk exciting to take during that time.

Jim and I were responsible for Ultimate's choreography and performance routine, while Jim also served as our hype man. My additional responsibility was to put class into our performance. I achieved this by encouraging the group to purchase red roses, which we would use to tease and throw out to the ladies in the crowd. We also decided to purchase silky white shirts to go along with black MC Hammer baggy pants. I made sure we were very professional in our approach to the event and that we acted as if we were actual stars so that we performed like actual stars. Jim's political clout was very influential for us to execute most of our ideas.

We continued our clandestine preparations to increase the shock level among nonbelievers. On the day of the talent show, we decided to arrive in style. Our friend Anthony Caponigro drove us to the talent show in his luxurious Mercedes-Benz while we were dressed in non-performance, but professional, attire and donned shades, all processes for star performers. We took our rightful spots in the front row while we viewed the first part of the talent show. Ultimate was scheduled to perform right after the intermission, which was another idea we influenced the event coordinators to incorporate. We knew that we could build additional anticipation by waiting until after intermission to perform instead of going too early or too late. Also, since we were the ones that hyped the event through flyers and other marketing campaigns, we believed we earned the right to perform whenever we wanted to perform.

During the intermission, we went backstage for one last practice and to dress in our performance clothes. When we walked on stage while the curtain was closed, there was a rush of excitement once we saw the five microphone stands as Michael Jackson's "Man in the Mirror" played on the speakers. To ease our butterflies, Jim and I started dancing like the idol that influenced both of us to seek ways to entertain masses. The stands made us all truly believe we were a famous group and allowed me to flash back to my first talent show performance four years earlier as a member of Awesome Force. We placed the roses at the base of each stand while we provided the proper space in between each dancer. Once we were told that it was showtime, we went into our respective positions on the side of the curtains. When the curtains opened and New Edition's "Crucial" blasted from the speakers, we danced onto the stage to screams from the same girls that doubted our capabilities.

After our "Crucial" performance, we readjusted our lineup to prepare for our next song, New Edition's ballad "Can You Stand the Rain." During rehearsals I convinced the light crew to transition to a soft purple light that would set the mood for the ballad as well as visually announce we were slowing down the tempo. Once the light changed, the girls realized we had captured their hearts for that evening. I could vividly recall the looks of amazement on their faces as they rushed to the front of the stage and reached out for the roses that rested near our feet. Once we threw our roses into the crowd we witnessed physical battles between the girls for our broken roses. After our performance, we knew we had not only surprised the crowd but that we were going to win Lower Merion's first talent show.

At the end of the talent show, all of the acts were called onto the stage. When it was time for the winner to be announced, we all braced ourselves for the obvious victory celebration. "And the winner is…" To our surprise, the judges selected a competing rock band. *What?!?!? How could we have lost to a band? How could the judges not award us with first place since we were the reason why the auditorium was packed after our strategic marketing of the event? I'm sure this was a misprint!* After reality sunk in, we were all devastated. Mark and I slept in our sweaty outfits all night, refusing to believe we did not win the show. Rarely does a conversation take place today between Jim and me when we fail to mention how we were cheated from winning that talent show. I will let you be the judge for yourself as the performance is posted on YouTube under "Ultimate...performing New Edition at Lower Merion."

We performed (and lost) again the next year, after I made a big mistake of replacing Mark (who graduated the year before) with a strong neighborhood singer who was actually positioned to be the fifth member of Boyz II Men. I thought his singing ability would translate into a greater appeal with the crowd and judges, but the chemistry was destroyed. I knew the moment I walked off that stage in 1990 that we lost again and didn't deserve to win. We tried too hard to replicate the magic we had the previous year. We also didn't practice as hard and automatically assumed we would get better just because another year had passed.

The 1989 talent show will forever be etched in our minds because of our ability to surprise the doubters. And although we lost as a group, I gained individually from that experience. Before the talent show, I wasn't as popular, mostly because of my shy personality. However, after our surprisingly amazing performance, I quickly gained popularity among the Ardmore residents (males and females) while also gaining traction with some of the white students. They were able to see my alter ego on stage, which they didn't realize had been crafted for years while in Rockwell. I was finally able to show my entertaining personality without worrying about the perception of others. Our ABC house became more popular and school more enjoyable because of the increase in local friends. Music was again my saving grace, bridging together different ethnicities and, more importantly, allowing others to see what ABC truly meant.

When we weren't hanging with our neighborhood friends, ABC tried to assist with our transition from home environments through their host family program. Each student was assigned a family that would, in essence, adopt and host that student in their home while acting as a surrogate family. Students visited their host families formally one Sunday each month. The bonds between some of the students and their host families were so strong that host families became a very important entity in the lives of students even beyond Lower Merion.

In my freshman year, Brian's host parent was Patti LaBelle, which made the rest of us boys extremely jealous. We often heard about Patti's amazing culinary skills and his enjoyment in the LaBelles' indoor pool. Our jealousy dissipated, at least temporarily, the moment Patti gave us tickets to one of her Philly concerts. We saw Patti prove that she was even better live on stage, especially when she performed "Somewhere Over the Rainbow." She kicked off her shoes while she sang and made you feel as if you were inside her home listening to a private performance.

My first host parent was an obese, single, black, slothful woman who lived in downtown Philadelphia. Initially, she traveled on train from Philadelphia to Ardmore to pick me up and take me to her condominium. After a couple of visits, she instructed me to come to Philly on my own. She even arranged for the condominium staff to provide me with a key to her place. When I arrived at her apartment, I often found her sound asleep in her bedroom while I watched television all day. Knowing that I could have enjoyed solo television time back at the ABC house, but without the train travel, I became frustrated with my host parent. Because of my unfamiliarity with Philly, I often roamed lost, trying to find her building.

After constant complaints I made to the ABC staff regarding my host parent, I was given a new host family, the Scotts. Preston and Patricia Scott provided me with my first exposure of a minority married couple. They had no children of their own which allowed them to quickly embrace me. Unlike my previous host parent, the Scotts broadened my cultural experiences by taking me to museums, sporting events, movies, and various Philly restaurants. They also had a basketball hoop on their driveway, where I spent many moments pretending to be Dr. J. On the occasions when we did not go to restaurants, the Scotts prepared delicious dinners before returning me to the ABC house.

I considered the Scotts to be my second parents. Even though Preston and I often created tense moments (mostly because of my teenage rebellious period), he became my first completely positive father figure. I was very impressed with his career and professional demeanor while working for the Securities and Exchange Commission. Patricia was a schoolteacher and had one of the kindest hearts I had ever witnessed. She was always making sure I was doing well and would serve as my buffer during the occasional battles with Preston.

The Scotts provided one of my favorite and unfortunate moments in sports. In 1990, as a surprise, the Scotts took me to the Philadelphia 76ers and Chicago Bulls game on January 26 at the old Philadelphia Spectrum. Watching Charles Barkley and Michael Jordan dual in a competitive game was exciting. Even though fans in Philadelphia were known to be violent against opposing fans, I proudly cheered for my Bulls. Barkley outscored Jordan 37 to 31 in a game that was hotly contested until the end of the fourth quarter. Unfortunately, the Bulls lost 120 to 109, but my night would get much better after the game.

While waiting for the crowd to dissipate, the Scotts motioned me towards the locker room entrance. I nervously commented to Preston several times that we would need passes to enter that restricted area, but wondered why I was being ignored. Once we approached the guard in front of the entrance, he replied to Preston "Hey Preston!" Seeing Preston's smile gave me an indication that the Scotts had something up their sleeves. As we walked just outside of the Bulls locker room door, I saw some of my favorite Bulls players walk the hallway. I nervously posed for pictures with Craig Hodges, B.J. Armstrong and Scottie Pippen, who was from Arkansas like my mom. I also saw Coach Phil Jackson, Stacey King, Bill Cartwright, and others from that team. Scottie and I briefly talked about my mom's hometown, Brinkley, as well as my fascination with his game. Patricia snapped various pictures while knowing how excited I was to see my heroes.

I could tell by the increased gathering of media that Jordan was about to exit the Bulls locker room. Seeing the tall, athletically built Jordan enter the throng of media and fans gave me my first star-struck experience. Jordan's charisma was amazing. I wanted to be able to enter a room with such a strong presence like Mike. I gathered all of my internal courage to approach Jordan for a picture. "Mr. Jordan, would you mind taking a picture with me?" I asked. "Sure!" he replied. Jordan then put his arm over my shoulder as we took a picture in the middle of the chaos. After the picture was taken, we exited through the same area as the players. Because of my height and Bulls attire, one of the young fans thought I was a player and asked for my autograph. Not wanting to disappoint a fan, I promptly scribbled "Lamont Robinson." I'm sure he spent years trying to explain to his friends who "Lamont Robinson" was for that 1989–1990 Bulls team. As I sat in the car on my ride back to the ABC house, trying to recapture that night's memories, I continued to smell the residue of Jordan's cologne that seemed to permeate my hand.

After telling the ABC crew about my entire experience, some refused to believe me. I assured them that my experience would be validated after receiving the pictures taken by Patricia. The next day, however, provided extreme disappointment. Patricia called me that evening with sadness in her voice. She explained to me that she took the camera to a repair shop before the game to make sure every part was working appropriately. Unfortunately, after the film was initially removed, she forgot to put it back inside before using the camera that evening. Although devastated, I believe I received the news better than Patricia because I still had the memory of spending time with the Bulls that evening while she unfairly dealt with the guilt of not being able to capture an incredible moment in my life on film. I also had the memory of having a one-on-one moment with the greatest basketball player in the history of the game.

My experience with meeting the Bulls was amazing, especially as a young kid from the housing projects where your heroes were drug dealers, gang leaders, or athletes. Meeting Jordan gave me inspiration to have that same type of charisma to own a room. Although I still hadn't decided my career path, I knew that I enjoyed the feeling of being someone of importance; someone others were drawn to regardless of whether or not they knew me. This newfound goal wasn't an ego-boosting necessity as much as it was having the need to strive for greatness. Jordan was great at his profession. My competitive desires would push me to be the best at my chosen career path. I needed to be "Jordan" in comparison to my peers. Again, I needed music to comfort me during this emotional event.

Rap artists during the late '80s such as Kane, Run-DMC, LL, KRS-One, Rakim, A Tribe Called Quest, Kool G Rap, and others wrote rhymes that would become my own personal theme songs. I rushed home from school to blast my favorite rap songs from my enormous radio. My radio also allowed me to plug in a microphone, which I'd use to rap along with the greats. Of all artists, Kane influenced me the most. His laid-back style combined with his melodic and metaphorical rhymes were unprecedented during this period.

Kane had the ability to rap about his fascination with ladies while also able to switch it up with something regarding his reign as the king. "Rappers steppin' to me, they want to get some… but I'm the Kane, so 'yo, you know the outcome…" from his "Ain't No Half Steppin'" classic would be one of my favorite lines ever to open a song. Because of my laid-back style, sleepy eyes and Cameo fade, I thought I was the light-skinned version of Kane. Kane's lyrics influenced me to write rhymes of my own that were full of one-liners and metaphors. Although I wouldn't display my rhyming skills while attending Lower Merion, influences from the Golden Era would lead to a greater focus on the genre while in college.

The positive experiences I had while in the ABC program allowed me to focus less on the negativity surrounding my life back in Chicago. I was able to enjoy moments I could only dream of having while living in Rockwell. The more I went to Lower Merion, the more my mentality was changing for the better because of my expanded horizon. However, just when I thought life for me was approaching perfection, I would be brought back down to earth because of idiotic decisions.

3 Strikes?

WHILE MANY OF MY EXPERIENCES going back home were enjoyable, the summer of 1989 provided me with my first wakeup call. During this period I was dating the sister of a close Rockwell friend. Along with his girlfriend (who was also a friend of mine), we often double dated, which sometimes ended up with intimate nights for both couples. I had lost my virginity the previous summer at the tender age of 16, ironically enough to the girl that was accepted into Lane Tech instead of me and voted Grant School's salutatorian. Incorrectly believing that I was now a sexual stud, I allowed myself to have unprotected sex with my girlfriend. My sense of invincibility was extremely high during this time after I survived two years of Lower Merion and the violent Chicago summers.

Before returning to school in the fall of 1989, my girlfriend gave me disturbing news... she was pregnant!! Immediately, I started to formulate my future without an education and a good job to take care of my responsibilities as a father. Abortion never entered my mind after going fatherless. Although I knew having a baby would delay my educational progress, I became excited about the opportunity to raise a child and provide him or her with the type of love I wish I had received from my unknown father. I delayed telling my mom for fear of seeing her disappointment in me of having a similar fate as other neighborhood young men. Surprisingly, she supported and consoled me during this emotional period.

Shortly after returning to school, I received a phone call from my mom, who informed me about an encounter my sisters had with my girlfriend after finding out the baby was not actually mine. While my sisters were angry with my girlfriend for lying about the true father of her unborn child, I was extremely relieved that I could continue on my path to educational success without the burden of being a young father. My girlfriend's mother supposedly influenced her to falsely claim the child was mine because of my potential to succeed. Obviously, I ended the relationship with my girlfriend but privately thanked her for saving my life. The real father of her child actually matured into a great individual who took care of his biological child. I often wonder how my life would have changed if I allowed myself to believe I was the father of her child. I also hope that the child grew up with the same hopes and dreams I had of escaping poverty through education.

I wish I could say the wakeup call matured me, but that would be dishonest. Since the ABC resident directors and tutors were mostly college students and only a few years older than the youth in the house, I allowed my naturally flippant teenage mentality to influence disruptive behavior that could have impacted the opportunity of my lifetime. As a freshman, I attended a drinking party thrown by a Lower Merion student that was raided by the police, which was something I had never experienced in Chicago. In a drunken state and standing near the back of the home, I heard someone yell, "Police!" Because I was drunk, I was not able to escape over the fence in the backyard like most of the partygoers. After getting caught, I was taken to the Ardmore police station. The police called Jeanne, one of our resident directors, to pick me up and bring me back to the ABC house. During our ride home, while still intoxicated, I kept wondering why I would place myself in that situation. I knew there was a good chance I could get kicked out of the program. This would be strike one.

Mark, my sophomore-year ABC roommate, brought me a bottle of imported beer from New York after one of his weekend home visits. We were obviously too young to drink the beer and would have faced serious punishment if caught with alcohol in the house. Again, because of my desire to test authority, I decided to accept his gift. I hid the green bottle of beer on the floor inside my desk. Each Friday night while the students performed chores, the resident directors and tutors conducted room sweeps, mostly to determine if the cleanings were done satisfactorily but also to make sure the students were not hiding inappropriate objects inside the rooms. Unfortunately, I forgot about the bottle of beer while my room sweep was being conducted. Cindy, our resident director at that time, found the beer while searching around my desk. "What is this?!?" Cindy asked in an excruciating high pitch. Panicking and clearly understanding the magnitude of the situation, I replied "Mark gave it to me!" My heart dropped while flashes of my future quickly flickered through my head of returning to Chicago without a Lower Merion education.

Days after Cindy's discovery, Mark and I were summoned to plead our case in front of the board. Before this incident, Mark had been my best friend inside the ABC house. I knew this event would severely impact our friendship, and I would have sacrificed my ABC education if Mark was removed from the program. Although we were able to avoid the ultimate punishment, I suffered tremendously because of the now damaged relationship with Mark. He avoided speaking to me for weeks and never again displayed his warm personality towards me from that moment. I knew that I deserved this change in Mark's attitude but there was nothing I could do to change the situation. I was happy that Mark's education would not be impacted but always wondered if he had to face the wrath of his parents because of his punishment. This was strike two.

The reasons behind my next punishment have always been vague. As a senior and outspoken leader of the ABC students, I was continually urged by the staff to be more proactive in supporting the underclassmen. As I recalled the disdain shown towards me from the seniors and juniors while I was an underclassman in the program, I strongly believed the underclassmen needed to go through their own rites of passage. I emotionally and physically punished the smaller underclassmen as some sort of revenge for all of the abuse I received. Since I was the most vocal student at that time, I was able to negatively influence the underclassmen, occasionally staging chore boycotts because of my displeasure with the way we were treated by the staff. I allowed myself to believe that I was untouchable since I had made it to my senior year.

Reality stung hard in the spring of my senior year when the staff informed me that Nashid, another senior leader in the house, and I were to meet with the Lower Merion ABC Board to discuss disciplinary actions as a result of our belligerent behavior and overall negative influence on the younger students. Even during this process, I was overly confident that Nashid and I would be slapped on our wrists with a trivial punishment then allowed to finish out our senior year. Why would the Board throw away everything we had positively contributed to the ABC program over the past four years *now*?

We soon realized this process was very serious and could lead to one or both of us being removed from the program depending on our ability to *sell* our repentance. My fear of facing my mom and Chicago friends as a failure drove me to be contrite and reform rapidly. Unfortunately, Nashid remained rebellious and was not going to accept any level of punishment from the ABC Board. I decided quickly to show the board I was willing to accept the punishment and change my behavior. I also had a great supporter throughout my years at ABC in one of the board members. Lois Davis was a well educated black female lawyer and was my liaison at school. Her stern approach with me and the other boys she supervised was necessary to make sure we didn't deviate from the ultimate plan of graduating from the program. As I awaited my fate, horrible images of my potential future without the ABC program flashed before my eyes. Even though I thought I was liked by enough of the board members, I was convinced they had seen enough of my antics over the years to decide to terminate my participation in the program. For days, I prayed hard that I would be able to remain in the program. I had stopped attending church when I entered the program, but knew that I needed God more than ever at that moment. I was facing another life-changing event in my early life.

Finally, we were asked to enter the meeting room to receive the message about our ABC future. I was thrilled to find out that I could remain in the program but with severe restrictions. Our punishment consisted of being confined to our rooms immediately after returning home from school, then remaining there for the entire night with the exception of dinner and study hall. Unfortunately, because of Nashid's staunch refusal to reform, he was removed from the program with one remaining semester. Nashid was fortunate to have a strong relationship with his host family who allowed him to stay with them to finish out the school year.

My isolation allowed me to reflect on my purpose for being in the program. While I cannot recall the length of my punishment, it was much more feasible than facing my mom while trying to explain to her reasons for my failure. This should have been strike three, but I was fortunate to remain in the program mostly because of Jeanne, Lois, and others fighting on my behalf. While they knew I had great potential to succeed if I graduated, they had an even greater fear when thinking about the consequences I'd face had I returned home.

Graduation was soon approaching. The closer I got to graduation, the more fearful I became. *Would I be able to grow without the academic discipline provided by the ABC program? How would my Chicago friends accept me after my new education? Could I handle the pressures to succeed now that I was forced to work harder in life with this newfound education?* Some of the black seniors, including myself, decided to not attend prom mostly because there wouldn't be diversity in the music played by the DJ. I also couldn't afford to travel to Atlantic City, where a lot of the students decided to party. My occasional shyness manifested by me not asking any of the females to be my prom date. I found out later in life that some of the females I had crushes on were also interested in me. Had my confidence been established during my high school years, I would have enjoyed that period even more.

My mom drove from Chicago with Earnest to attend my graduation. I could tell that she was extremely proud I survived my second major test in life and was able to do it on my own. While she offered verbal support whenever it was needed, I had to find inner strength to succeed. I needed to overcome shyness, improper grammar, financial challenges, and teenage rebellion in order to walk across that graduation stage. I was thrilled that my mom could share this moment with me.

The ABC program truly provided me with a better chance in life. I was able to expand my world through the program, gaining exposure to other cultures, social classes, American cities, and religions. ABC also validated Mr. Bottom's motto that I could achieve any level of success as long as I worked hard. The four years I spent at Lower Merion were not without struggles. In order to obtain the level of education needed for future success, I had to sacrifice relationships with family and friends. I knew that I also had to establish my own identity. No longer would I find it acceptable to use slang in my vocabulary just to fit in.

I also knew that it would no longer be acceptable to allow my sacrifices to be wasted. There was a tremendous purpose for me in life, and I was determined to discover it. I also knew at this time that my sacrifices were made not only for myself but for my future offspring, whom I would bring into this world legitimately through marriage. I was confident that my desire to provide better chances in life for my future family increased significantly once I walked across that Lower Merion graduation stage.

Lake Forest College

Because I had been away from my family and friends, as well as my jealousy of the ABC students that were able to hop on weekend trains to visit home, I decided it would be best for me to return closer to Chicago for college. I applied to four colleges during my search: Lake Forest College, a small, private liberal arts college in Lake Forest, Illinois; Washington University, a large university located in St. Louis, Missouri; Knox College, a small college located in Galesburg, Illinois; and, Bradley University, a medium-sized college located in Peoria, Illinois. I was able to visit Lake Forest College during my senior year at Lower Merion, which also allowed me to visit my mom. While at Lake Forest, I fell in love with the small college and quaint, wealthy town of Lake Forest. At that time, my favorite football team, the Bears, practiced on the Lake Forest campus.

Fortunately, I received acceptance letters from all four schools to which I applied. While I believed my future desires to become an accountant would flourish sooner had I attended Washington University, I accepted Lake Forest College's offer because of its proximity to my mom and great reputation. Similar to Lower Merion, Lake Forest had a mixture of wealthy students as well as those of us needing financial aid. However, unlike Lower Merion, some of the black students at Lake Forest were also wealthy, which was a new dynamic for me. I allowed my early assumption that all blacks were poor to create an ignorance that had to be changed once I met others that came from families just as wealthy as many of the white Lake Forest students.

Lake Forest and the towns surrounding Lower Merion had other similarities. Both areas enjoyed wealthy residents who positively impacted the level of education provided at both schools. Both areas had students and young residents who had great access to materialistic possessions because of wealthy parents. Both areas also had a majority of "old money" residents who frowned upon those that flashed their wealth through outrageous parties or outlandish purchases (outside of homes and cars). When Mr. T moved into Lake Forest during his 80s peak, he caused an uproar among the residents after chopping down most of the century-old trees that lined his property. I'm also sure his gold chains, flashy cars and trademark mohawk didn't influence many friends in that extremely conservative town.

When my mom and I arrived at Lake Forest College, I realized soon that the academic discipline I developed at Lower Merion would be challenged because of the freedom I now enjoyed. I didn't have to worry about mandatory two and a half hour study halls, Friday chores, or restrictions on having female guests. My first roommates consisted of a wealthy hockey snob from the New England area, and Pete, my Jewish, Bob Marley-loving, acoustic guitar-playing friend from Cincinnati. Pete had such a great demeanor about him and welcomed anyone who was nice to him, which fit me perfectly. Although I didn't necessarily enjoy smelling or seeing Pete's gray-colored pancakes (which could have been laced with his favorite recreational medicine), I had great times getting to know him. Lower Merion allowed me to become colorblind, which was key at Lake Forest in helping Pete and I to become friends, even though we were from two distant worlds.

Even though I enjoyed rooming with Pete, I decided to move into another room in the middle of the semester with Lonny, who was a tall black sophomore also from Chicago. Because of my tendency to attach myself to older black males as I searched for role models, I looked up to Lonny. Even though he was only a year older than me, he seemed much older. He also seemed to have earned the respect of most of the black students on campus. As his roommate, I discovered that he was actually colorblind. Many times I helped him with his color coordination as he would attempt to leave the room with a purple MC Hammer baggy suit and lime green socks. I can't imagine how many cool points he would have lost had I not saved him from his uncoordinated attire.

Lonny was protective of me and treated me like his little brother. He became the big brother I never had, since June had been incarcerated most of my life. Lonny and I had great conversations about college life as he helped with my transition and attempts to balance education with the entertaining elements of Lake Forest. Since we weren't that far from each other in age, he seemed to understand my plight, even though we weren't from the same type of neighborhood. Hanging with Lonny was extremely helpful while I struggled with integrating into the popular salacious options around campus most of the students seemed to enjoy.

Because of the wealth associated with many of the Lake Forest students, I enjoyed attending the ubiquitous weekend parties. Instead of studying during my first semester, I often spent my free time watching television or sleeping. Many of my friends followed the same routine, so rarely could any of us positively influence each other to strive for greatness academically. In fact, students that preferred to study hard were sometimes playfully ridiculed by those opting for parties and sex.

Because of the costly tuition associated with the private institution, many of the Lake Forest students received financial aid through academic scholarships. In order to keep the scholarships, students were required to maintain at least a C- average. Since the ABC program at Lower Merion required a much stricter academic requirement, I was extremely confident that I could perform marginally in the classroom while enjoying the parties and other distractions offered to students.

Another distraction mostly among the black male students was the advent of the video game system Sega Genesis and its sports games. A group of us often held tournaments for the Madden NFL game, the NBA Live series, and various baseball titles. Being a die-hard Chicago fan, I only played against opponents as the Bulls, Bears, and Cubs. My passion in sports influenced me to lead efforts in organizing the tournaments. That same passion negatively impacted my attitude when I lost games because I took each loss personally. I was always the type to want to play my opponent again if I lost so that I wouldn't have a bad taste in my mouth from losing. I also wanted to play again if I won as I wanted to continue my domination. This approach would lead to hours of game play, often sacrificing classes and necessary studies, which obviously had a negative impact on my grades.

During my freshman year at Lake Forest, the Bulls began their basketball dominance. After failing to advance past the Detroit "Bad Boy" Pistons in the late '80s, the found the right formula during the 1990–1991 season. Jordan, Pippen, Grant, and the rest of the crew overcame all challenges to earn their first title, which brought a joy to the city similar to the '85 Bears. Unlike the Bears, the Bulls were a special team that was poised to win additional championships. Because they took place during the same time, I remember my Lake Forest years as much for the Bulls' three consecutive championships as I did for my education.

The paltry population of blacks at Lake Forest College was at times humorous. Including myself, there were only three black men in my freshman class when I started in 1990. One of the other black male students was Eric, a short and stocky boy from Maywood, a Chicago suburb. I was fascinated that Eric's parents were still married and actively engaged in his life. Even though he was short, he was a very good point guard for the college's basketball team. His parents leased a car for him, which added to his popularity among the other students.

In addition to Lonny and Eric, I quickly befriended Renee, who came to Lake Forest from Harlem. Because of her humorous and engaging personality, Renee's room became the hangout spot for many of my fellow black Lake Forest students. Like many of us, Renee struggled with the dichotomy of being smart and driven while occasionally being lazy. We engaged in deep conversations mostly because of our similar personalities. Renee became one of my closest friends and is considered to be family in my heart. I always appreciated not only her candor but her encouraging words of support.

Since the entire population of black students at Lake Forest was small, we hung out with each other often. Some of my fondest memories at Lake Forest involved animated but entertaining discussions among our group in the cafeteria. For the most part, we all got along because the majority of us were from humble households but had proven ourselves academically in predominantly white high schools.

As a result of our negative academic influences on each other, most of us struggled to maintain the grades necessary to stay at Lake Forest.

Since Lake Forest didn't provide meals during the weekend, many of us scrambled to eat. We bonded while finding ways to pitch in for ingredients to make meals we shared among each other instead of eating the ramen noodles that most of the students enjoyed. Many of us had campus jobs, but because of our focus on school, we couldn't work enough hours to build substantial paychecks.

To support our small paychecks, many of us obtained credit cards to acquire the items we felt we needed. Unfortunately, placing credit cards in the hands of immature college students is a disaster waiting to happen. Also, many of us didn't have examples of family members who did a great job of managing finances. Most of our purchases were impulse decisions and often didn't involve needs. Since many of us didn't make enough with our campus jobs to support the credit card bills, our debt accumulated while we continued to purchase on credit. Some of us had parents that bailed us out. Unfortunately for me, I knew that was not going to be an option. So, I purchased and purchased until the card reached its maximum limit with the goal of paying the minimum until enough funds were cleared on the card for another purchase.

Credit card companies preyed on us because they knew our increased debt and inability to pay would increase our financial burden and subsequent fees. The less we paid monthly, the more they were able to profit from the higher interest rates. Unfortunately, this debt followed us after college, placing many of us in a financial slavery system before we received our first "real world" paycheck. I didn't realize how much of a problem it was until I was with a college friend as he attempted to purchase an item from a Lake Forest store. After attempting to pay for the item with his credit card, he was informed that the card was declined because he reached his max. He then pulled out another card and was told the same thing. Embarrassingly, he provided a third card but was denied a third time. He then walked away and pretended as if it was a system error and not the result of his financial mismanagement. I'm sure his level of embarrassment wasn't as severe, since I was with him and he knew I was also from a humble background and most likely in the same financial situation. Our struggles forced all of us to bond as we were all struggling and trying to find our way, whether for financial, educational or emotional reasons.

We also bonded because of the dearth of black leaders within the college administration and faculty. We automatically clung to the ones that existed, often seeking their answers on how to survive as a black student on a white college campus. Many of us were first-generation college students and couldn't turn to our own families for advice, so any information received from the black leaders was of great benefit as long as we listened. Some of us, including myself, were drawn more towards the black male leaders as father figures since we were devoid of that in our own households. We were all one step closer to the real world and needed guidance to prepare us for what was ahead.

I spent a lot of time going back and forth between Chicago and Lake Forest, which didn't necessarily help to improve my academic performance. My weekend visits resulted in me doing just enough academically to pass classes instead of striving for greatness. My goal changed from wanting to make the dean's list to earning C's so that I could balance my academic and social lives. After realizing I couldn't survive at Lake Forest much longer with that mentality, I decided to force myself to stay on campus during the weekends. Initially, I felt alone because I was without my campus big brother and roommate. Eventually, I felt more comfortable around others on campus while trying to improve my grades.

The summer before I started at Lake Forest, I started dating Angie, who lived with her grandparents in a nearby Rockwell neighborhood. Angie was mixed with black and Mexican and was different than some of the other Rockwell females because she embraced education. Angie always found a way to make me believe in myself. The only challenge of being with Angie was that she was a little younger than me. We first started dating when I was seventeen. However, now that I was eighteen and in college, I started having reservations about dating the underage Angie.

The timing of Angie in my life was perfect. I had lost confidence in myself and stopped trusting women after my previous ordeal with my alleged, albeit false, impregnation of my friend's sister. Puberty also played a role in my insecurities as I had developed a severe case of acne. Traveling back and forth between school and home was enough for my mental plate, so having any level of romance was secondary. However, Angie allowed me to realize what true love was, even though we were both very young. She looked beyond my outer shell and always made me feel like she fell in love with my soul. We wrote letters to each other often, especially when I was at Lower Merion. She was in my life during a critical transition between high school and college as I was about to enter a world unknown among my family.

Angie's biggest fear regarding our relationship was that I would go to college and forget about her. She worried that I would prefer to be with older college women and push myself further from my Rockwell past. Unfortunately, her fears came true. While I didn't forget about her, I mentally removed myself as far away from Rockwell as I could. The women and campus parties were major distractions in my freshman year, which was a different experience for me. I was fascinated with the intellectual capacity of the women on campus and attracted to their commitment to finish school.

After my first semester, several of my friends, including Lonny, were not invited back to the school for academic reasons. Again, another black male was leaving my life, forcing me to learn life on my own. One of the biggest disappointments from my Lake Forest years was that my communication with Lonny was completely severed once he left. I thought for sure we would remain strong friends since he still lived in Chicago. While we connected a few times in Chicago, our relationship was never the same. I felt that he was somewhat embarrassed that he failed to remain at Lake Forest. I also believed Lonny thought my perception of him turned negative since he was discharged for academic reasons, which wasn't accurate. Although I was friends with others on campus, I was reluctant to get close to anyone else for fear that I would be disappointed again. I spent more time traveling home on weekends, opting to be around my old Rockwell friends instead of making new ones on campus.

For the first time in my life, I was placed on academic probation after my grades fell below the required threshold for my academic scholarship. I knew my Lake Forest career was in jeopardy the moment I took my first midterms. While getting ready to prepare for one of my classes, I realized I hadn't removed the plastic cover from the book and could only answer five of the 100 questions provided on the test. I had gone an entire semester without studying for most of my classes. I knew I would have the difficult task of explaining to my mom why I wasted four years at a prestigious high school to flunk out of college in my first semester.

Fortunately, I was given a chance to improve my grades while on academic probation. My old studying discipline returned as I worked hard to improve my grades. While my social life suffered somewhat, I was able to remain at Lake Forest College. After serving time on academic probation, my grades were never horrible in college, but I only worked hard enough to be a decent student. One of my biggest regrets in my academic career was that I never fully applied myself to be the best student at Lake Forest. I allowed the various normal college distractions to shift my priorities. While I should have been focused on working hard in school, I worked even harder to avoid being seen as an anti-social nerd.

Since Lake Forest wasn't necessarily catering to its black population, we often found solace by throwing our own parties. The parties thrown by the white fraternities and sororities were often focused on drinking alcohol and students falling over each other in drunken stupors while black parties were all about dancing. Waxmaster often came up to Lake Forest to deejay parties, accompanied by DJ Rated X (Rashied's new moniker) and the Awesome Force crew. It was fun dancing to the early '90s New Jack Swing hits while displaying the latest baggy pants and flat top haircuts.

Awesome Force enjoyed coming to our campus mostly because of the temporary companionships that a lot of the female students, black and white, were eager to provide. They would often battle among each other to see who could get the most phone numbers from the girls attending the parties. We typically crashed in my room that evening before they headed back down to the city. Having them on campus gave me the chance to witness my college and youthful worlds collide. I was excited to see my Rockwell friends receive a taste of a different world; a world that involved different cultures, religions, and ethnicities. Since I was exposed to those things during my Lower Merion years, I knew their worlds would expand as well.

The town of Lake Forest wasn't as kind to my Chicago visitors as the campus had been. My friends would often get pulled over by the profiling policemen of the town while driving through to drop me off or pick me up between Chicago visits or when returning to the campus. We often noticed police cars following us until we left the boundaries of the town, making sure we weren't breaking any laws. This was often frustrating to us, but we knew we couldn't be rebellious or else we would face the wrath of the town that didn't want us there in the first place. Again, I needed to turn to music to maintain my equanimity in dealing with this injustice.

The lack of R&B music on the campus influenced me to become a DJ for the campus radio station. Shortly after joining the station, I was put in charge of the station's rap music. My responsibilities included buying the latest rap albums and hosting a weekly radio show along with Eric. My mischievous behavior often led me to order duplicate albums so that Eric and I could keep one for ourselves to play at parties. Our show was popular on campus as we played rap music the first two hours and slow songs during our final hour. We often received phone calls from campus couples requesting various slow songs to help them make their evenings more special. Having a radio show and being in charge of the station's rap selection helped to influence my music path.

During this time, I honed my skill for writing raps. I constantly kept notebooks to jot down my latest rhymes. I was led to write because of different situations based on relationships, popular songs or other ideas. I developed my original stage name "Master L" and a persona that was laid back, quick-witted and metaphorically focused. While attending a party at a local college campus, I decided it was time to launch my rap career. As the DJ was spinning the records, I convinced him to allow me to grab the microphone and rap my new rhyme. As I was shouting my lyrics to the crowd, I realized then that I had a gift with words and stage presence. The Lake Forest crew that attended the party with me was surprised and influenced me to expand and display my gift more. Shortly thereafter, Eric decided to write rhymes himself under the name Enuff. We decided to form a group called 2 'Uva Kynd and performed at most of the black parties on campus, on our weekly radio show, and at local events.

To entertain ourselves as well as improve our rhyming skills, we often conducted freestyles while hanging out in someone's room or even while sitting in class. Freestyling is a method of improvisational rapping that typically centers on a theme started by the first performer. The subsequent freestylers attempt to continue the rhyme pattern while staying on the theme and keeping the rhyming intact. Because of its impromptu delivery, this was a great method of perfecting rap skills. Renee, Eric and I had many battles going back and forth while coming up with clever lines to joke about campus life or each other. No one ever got offended if a rhythmic joke was made about them because they had the ability and platform to respond with an even better joke than what was said about them. It was during these sessions that I received confirmation of my poetic gift.

My rap style continued to be heavily influenced by my favorite rapper, Big Daddy Kane. My style was very similar to my normal personality at that time: laid back, smooth and full of intelligent material. I focused on writing rhymes that had metaphors and memorable one-liners that made listeners think deeply about what they just heard. I pushed myself to be the best with Kane as my barometer. I often wrote rhymes to respond to popular rap songs with the hope of getting my chance to battle.

I became infatuated with writing rhymes and filled several notebooks with my lyrics. Once I started writing raps, I became more perceptive of my surroundings as I constantly sought to find my muse for the next song. The controversial gangsta rap, which focused on violence and misogyny, was popular during this period of the early '90s. Since I had grown up in a violent neighborhood and didn't want to focus on that dark past, I wrote songs that were about positive subjects and my love for women. I couldn't pretend to be someone I wasn't by rapping about guns and drugs. I was impacted by the violence while living in Rockwell but not *directly* involved, so anything written from me that glamorized those subjects would be a farce of the actual lifestyle.

Since, as students, Eric and I were practically too broke to have songs produced in a studio, I developed a skill with dubbing songs using a dual cassette recorder to make our instrumentals. After choosing a favorite break in an old school song, I recorded a few seconds of that part over and over until I was able to form a three to five minute instrumental. My favorite dubbed instrumental was taken from The Commodores song "Zoom." Usually, I wrote my lyrics and the song title after hearing the instrumental, inspired by the melody of that specific song.

We held an on-campus concert during my senior year at Lake Forest while being accompanied by a live band. I also used the concert to introduce the various talents from the Awesome Force crew such as Jay Rockwell and Rob. We led off the concert with a dubbed instrumental version of Shalamar's "A Night to Remember," which also served as our theme for the concert. Our group, 2 'Uva Kynd, was appropriately the last performer on our special night. As we tore up the stage with our carefully crafted rhymes backed with a combination of dubbed instrumentals and a live band, we both realized that we created something special.

Music was also my panacea for overcoming my lack of confidence with women. One Lake Forest female who had an early influence on me was Shelia. She and I started dating in my freshman year while she was a sophomore. She was very intelligent and would often correct my grammar whenever I relaxed my speech and allowed my slang to be released. Our relationship strengthened in my junior year after she graduated and decided to move to the Rogers Park neighborhood in Chicago. During the summer after my junior year, I accepted an internship at a local credit union. During the week I hopped on the Metra train to travel from Lake Forest to Shelia's apartment in Rogers Park.

Shelia's Caucasian roommates never seemed to welcome me, but I wasn't necessarily warm to them either. I would often arrive at their apartment dressed in my baggy, thuggish attire, with an earring in my left ear and an intimidating stare caused by the unnecessary hatred of whites created by the movie *Malcolm X* and the pro-black movement during that time. I stopped eating pork and listened to violent raps about police brutality that added to my hatred. I always had a stare that appeared as if I was mad at the world, but I especially worked on the stare during that period.

Shelia was often a calming influence on my tumultuous world. I was attracted to her intelligence and maturity. She seemed completely different than most of the other females I dated. Her mannerisms and network of friends gave me a different perspective of myself. I realized that I focused too much on my blackness and not the reality of surviving in a white world. Shelia and I would have many debates about my future plans. I believe it was during those conversations that she realized there was no future for us. I was very immature and couldn't see the world she was trying to expose me to. As a result, she ended our relationship during my senior year after finding someone who was on a similar path as her in regards to maturity and career aspirations. Although I was heartbroken, I soon understood that my focus needed to be redirected.

While I was attending Lake Forest, it was extremely difficult for my mom to maintain the tuition payments because of Bob's incarceration. Because of her lack of funds, she turned to the only people she knew that could help: the drug-dealing boyfriends of Renee. If I had known drug-dealing money was used, I would have done everything I could to find ways to earn money for my tuition. After all, this was the same money that was used in the type of transactions that destroyed the lives of my sisters. How could my mom ignore this fact while accepting this dirty money? However, as I got older I was able to place myself in her shoes. She did *everything* she could do to keep me in school. While this was not the right thing ethically or legally to do, she sacrificed everything to provide for me the education I needed to achieve what hadn't been done in our family before.

My mom is a very strong woman. Most women would have been driven to insanity had they experienced what she was dealing with during the late '80s and early '90s: a son who was serving a lengthy prison term; daughters who were hooked on drugs and suffering abuse; her baby son, who had to travel a thousand miles away from her to obtain a better education; a boyfriend who was married and now in prison for something that could have sent her to prison as well; a family that turned their backs on her when she needed them the most; her daughter's children, who were practically raising themselves because of their mother's drug problem; and, the need to beg for money from people who sold the same products that were destroying her daughters. Although I wish I could have been able to provide comfort to my mom during this period, I love and admire her for shielding me from her turmoil. Had I known about the tumultuous life she was living, I probably would have decided to return home, which could have had an adverse impact on my life since education would not have been as much of a priority.

While my mom was going through her own living hell, she decided to go through the legal system to remove Ronetta's kids so that they could be raised properly. Ronetta's child neglect and abuse had become worse, which led my mom to take severe action. Ronetta continued to struggle with her drug usage while my mom raised her kids. Visiting her was always mentally painful for me because of the uncertainty of what I would discover. I always felt great sorrow for her kids because they never had the joy of seeing their mom when she was clean and happy in a relationship. They also did not understand the impact of the murders of their fathers on Ronetta's life. My life was in constant chaos dealing with the struggles of home while trying to succeed at Lake Forest. Fortunately, I had a keen focus on finishing college, mostly because of my desire to bring positivity to my mom's crumbling world.

While Bob was in prison, he worked hard to obtain a college degree while understanding the latest technology. He and I wrote each other numerous letters about our rapidly changing lives. In Bob's letters, he apologized for not being in my life during such a critical period. He also apologized for the wrongdoing that sent him to prison. I admired the way he took full responsibility for his actions. Through my letters, I was able to tell Bob how eager I was to establish the father-and-son relationship I needed in my life, as I now needed a father figure more than ever as I was about to enter the real world. Bob was finally released from prison during my senior year at Lake Forest, just in time to attend my graduation.

As I prepared myself academically and mentally to graduate from Lake Forest, I started to feel an even heavier burden. I knew that my graduation meant more than just walking across the stage to receive my degree. My graduation stood for a blueprint for others to hopefully follow. I hoped that my example would pave the way and inspire other family members to overcome their fears and seek education as a way to succeed. I also felt a burden to show my mom that her hard work would lead to a successful career for me. I wanted to obtain the level of success that would allow me to take care of my mom financially. I didn't want her to work hard another day of her life. I wanted her to experience the same joys that other women her age enjoyed without worrying about the lack of funds in her bank account.

On Saturday, May 7, 1994, I was preparing to graduate from Lake Forest College. The unpredictable Chicago weather, which produced a wintry mix of rain and snow along with mid-40s temperatures, forced us to hold the ceremony indoors. Many family and friends were able to attend my graduation, enjoying the journey I was embarking upon as if all of us were succeeding. It was their encouragement and strength that allowed me to have confidence to work hard and be able to walk across that stage as our family's first college graduate. My mom became so emotional that day that she developed a migraine which forced her to go to the local hospital and miss the entire ceremony. Shortly after graduating I rushed to visit her instead of celebrating with the rest of my classmates, which included Nate Berkus, Oprah Winfrey's famous interior designer.

On one hand, I was excited when thinking about the prospects of entering the real world. I believed I prepared myself well since my time at Lower Merion; however, I was still fearful of failing. I knew that I couldn't throw away all of my hard work to obtain an education by failing in my profession. I realized that I had to find a job that was going to position me to reach the level of success others had already pinned on me since I lived in Rockwell. The weight of the world was on my shoulders. While externally my face expressed confidence, internally I was an emotional wreck. I couldn't disappoint my mom, Bob, sisters, brother, cousins, aunts, uncle, grandparents, Rockwell tenants, ABC students and faculty, and anyone else who expected my future successes. I have always wanted options ahead of me for success, which was provided to me through our excitement about 2 'Uva Kynd as well as obtaining my college degree.

2 'Uva Kynd gave me and Eric the chance to strive for musical aspirations that were within our passion and love for music. After graduating from Lake Forest, we attempted to continue our passion by recording five songs with a local producer with the goal of succeeding in the music industry. I changed my stage name to Da Masta and we were able to record some of the penned colorful campus classics such as "Come Here Byatch" and "Da Luvas and Da Playas." Although we received many compliments about our type of music and style, we weren't able to continue with our dreams. Shortly after graduating from Lake Forest, Eric accepted a job that moved him to New York. I had no desire to pursue a solo career and thought I should focus on corporate America to pay my bills which, in essence, ended 2 'Uva Kynd before it even started.

In order to regain the confidence needed to proceed into the next phase of my life, I had to revert back to my favorite quote, "If it is to be, it is up to me." My success had to be driven by my own determination. I never believed entirely in luck being the primary driver for success. I believe we are all provided with key moments in our lives during which, with hard work, we can plan our own successful journey. Those who wait for success to serendipitously find them are the same ones who continue to wait today while finding excuses for why they are not successful. Since I was not given the same chances in life that a lot of my classmates were provided through private education, eye-opening trips around the world, or parent connections that led to job opportunities, I knew that I had to outwork everyone else. My differentiator had to derive from a level of dedication to succeed, derived mostly because of the pressures from my early years.

The Real World

After graduating from Lake Forest, I was able to reconnect with Bob, since my Lower Merion years and his prison sentence took us away from each other for years. Our relationship was obviously different as we both had changed from before he went into prison. I was entering the real world and starting to become even more independent in my approach to life, while he was trying to get reacquainted with that same world.

Instead of a father-and-son relationship, Bob and I started to develop more of a friendship with mutual respect. Since his Chicago visits during my Rockwell years were typically only overnight, I never got the chance to bond with him as the primary father figure in my life the way I desired. My early intimidation of him also prevented me from proactively seeking ways to strengthen our relationship. Bob started to see the fruits of his seeds harvest as I started my professional career. I asked him various questions to prepare for corporate America. My life came full circle as I was now able to pick the brain of the man I emulated and the one who inspired me to become a businessman.

I moved into Bob's home briefly before settling into an apartment he owned next door to his house. Living next door to him gave me an opportunity to strengthen my relationship with Trudy. I'm sure she was still struggling with the pain from knowing about his relationship with my mom, but she showed extreme maturity and forgiveness by never making me feel uncomfortable. She always embraced me like I was one of her children. She went out of her way to make me feel as if their home was mine as well. My time spent around Trudy gave me greater sympathy for her and an even greater appreciation for how she treated me versus the way most women in the same situation would have. Trudy knew I had genuine love for Bob and wasn't in his life to seek financial rewards. Since we were never able to see each other during my childhood visits to Waukegan, Trudy finally was able to witness my personality and the impetus for my drive towards success.

As I waited to get cable installed in my apartment, I decided to return to Lake Forest to watch the Bulls play the Knicks in their heated, epic rivalry. Jordan had retired at the start of the season after winning his third straight championship, mostly because of his emotional dealings with finding out his father was murdered. The Bulls were left without their leader but still had key pieces such as Pippen, Horace Grant, and coach Phil Jackson. Phil prepared them physically and mentally to deal with the sudden retirement of arguably the greatest player to ever play the game. They were joined that year by Tony Kukoc, a Croatian star who was drafted a few years earlier but had to wait to play in the NBA. Kukoc teamed with Pippen to continue to be a strong team that used its emotional fortitude to stay relevant after Jordan's departure.

While heading to LFC to watch Game 2 on the Wednesday following graduation, I decided to make a visit to the local grocery store in Lake Forest. As I walked across the street after parking my car, my lack of focus almost caused me to be struck by a car driven by a young female. I was probably walking in a daze while thinking about the life ahead of me and wearing my Bill Cosby-like thick sweater while it was muggy and humid.

After arriving at the dorm to watch the game, I noticed Michelle, who was a girlfriend of a former Lake Forest colleague, sitting on one of the couches prepared to watch the game as well. Her father was Caucasian and her mother, who died while Michelle was a young teenager, was Filipino, which created an exotic and attractive combination. I always thought she was arrogant and generally not happy, which is why I mostly avoided her.

I decided that I would continue to ignore Michelle, not wanting her negativity to ruin my entertainment from the game. I also didn't think she was interested in sports. However, I noticed her glancing at me occasionally during the game. She finally asked me about my day, after which I opened up with "Maaaannnn…let me tell you… I was almost struck by a car today while crossing the street. I was also not able to get cable installed on time, and I need to find a job." As it turned out, Michelle was the young female driver who almost hit me with her car. After admitting that she was the driver, she stated that she was shocked I spoke to her. She told me later that she perceived me as a big man on campus, mostly because of my 2 'Uva Kynd concerts, and had automatically assumed I was too arrogant to talk to anyone that I didn't feel was important enough.

After both of us overcame our initial misperceptions of the other, we enjoyed a great conversation. We both realized we enjoyed all of the Chicago sports teams (except the White Sox) and thought it would be fun to go to a Cubs game. After that night, Michelle was able to purchase two tickets for an afternoon Cubs and San Francisco Giants game ten days later, on May 24. While neither wanted to call this an official "date," we were very excited to spend time getting to know each other even more.

Upon arriving at the game, Michelle informed me that our seats were not next to each other because of the few seat selections for the popular Saturday game against the superstar Barry Bonds and his Giants. Her ticket placed her a few rows behind me. She revealed later that she didn't want to wait too long to connect with me, and had assumed that once we arrived at the game someone would be kind enough to allow us to sit next to each other. Luckily for us, we were able to find two unoccupied seats that would allow us to use the game as a way to get to know each other.

The Cubs beat the Giants that day during a 12-10 slugfest which featured home runs from juiced-up stars Bonds and Sammy Sosa. Since Michelle purchased the tickets for the game, I decided to plan our activities after the game. We went to see the Meg Ryan and Andy Garcia drama *When a Man Loves a Woman* then headed to Buckingham Fountain downtown. While at Buckingham, we realized it was fireworks night, which gave us a great ending to our "date." After I returned to my apartment that evening, I knew that I wanted to have Michelle in my life while overcoming the racial differences.

Michelle and I spent a lot of time together that summer. We attended concerts, other sporting events and movies. I struggled to find the right time to introduce her to my family. This was uncharted territory for me as I had never introduced my family to a girlfriend who wasn't black, or at least partially black. I worried that this would be another reason for my family to think I was trying to be white. I thought they would make Michelle so uncomfortable that it would be impossible for us to have a successful relationship.

My fears were eased after seeing my mom and sisters fully embracing Michelle, making her feel as if she had been a part of the family all along. One of our funniest moments took place during our first Thanksgiving, when Michelle was offered chitterlings by Renee. While obviously not knowing chitterlings were actually pig intestines, Michelle accepted Renee's invitation but was stopped after I finally told her the truth.

My family's love for me was manifested in the way they looked beyond Michelle's race to accept her completely because of my feelings for her. While there could have been criticisms behind my back, I've never felt embarrassed to be in an interracial relationship around my family. Michelle's immediate family also accepted race differences. She was the oldest of three kids from her biological father and mother. Her father, who retired from the Navy, had remarried to another Caucasian after the death of Michelle's Filipino mother and proceeded to have five additional Caucasian children.

Dating someone outside my race was risky outside of my immediate family. I knew some would use this as a way of claiming I was "trying to be white" and a "sell out." Outside of the encouraging words for my educational success, I never allowed opinions others had about me shape me into someone I wasn't. Interracial marriages have increased significantly in the United States over the past forty years, from 310,000 in 1970 to 4.8 million in 2012. The rise has led to an increase in the number of mixed children and contributed to almost half of children aged six and under today that are considered minorities. The continued increase in interracial marriages and children will drive minorities to eventually become the majority group over the next twenty years.

Because of the abundance of interracial relationships, it has become more acceptable to date outside of your own race. Unfortunately, there are still people from all races with closed minds that believe everyone should remain with their own race in regards to relationships. My mentality was consistent with this myopic way of thinking until I was exposed to many cultures, religions, and ethnicities while attending Lower Merion and Lake Forest College. The longer I dated Michelle the more I forgot she was of a different race.

Too often in our society we allow ourselves to be influenced by others when it comes to matters of the heart. Race is irrelevant in regards to relationship success. I have experienced successful *and* failed relationships with black women, just as I could have experienced good and bad relationships with women from other races. My openness was shaped by the fact that I had always allowed my heart, and not society's rules, to dictate my decisions. Also, my experience leaving home at such an early age provided me with the confidence and maturity needed to follow my heart.

Having a supportive family made my decision much easier—my mom always taught us to be kind to everyone, regardless of race. I'm grateful to have been raised with this understanding, as this isn't the normal case for those growing up in financially underserved communities where you're taught to distrust those outside of your race. I'm also grateful for the foundation established by my mom which allowed me to avoid any bigoted perspectives even after getting chased by the racist idiots on the South Side of Chicago in 1986. To allow anyone to dictate relationships based on race would be a disservice to the independence I worked very hard to obtain since leaving home.

Outside of her appearance and personality, I was attracted to Michelle because she reminded me of what I didn't witness while growing up in Rockwell. She was adamant to maintain her sexual purity, which wasn't something I was used to in Rockwell. Premarital sex wasn't even a phrase used in Rockwell because it was widely accepted. It was rare to hear parents encourage their children to practice abstinence versus protection. Kids were teased if they were virgins instead of being praised for saving themselves for their future spouses. Parents willingly accepted their children's sexual explorations by providing them with contraceptives, worrying more about pregnancy and disease instead of the loss of their sexual purity and innocence.

Even though Michelle wasn't wealthy herself, she was exposed to individuals that were of the economic status I was interested in attaining. Michelle was a nanny for a wealthy family in Lake Forest. Her primary responsibility for the family was to care for Michael, the couple's mentally and physically handicapped son. I was attracted to the way Michelle passionately and genuinely cared for Michael. She never displayed any frustrations when he had occasional breakdowns. She was always very protective of him and defensive when she thought others were mocking or treating him unfairly. Michelle's behavior towards Michael gave me confidence that she would be a tremendous mother and future wife for someone. Just as Shelia had a great impact on my need to focus on education and a future career, Michelle's influence on me to become a better person and future family leader was vital to my future.

Michelle's foundation was strongly influenced by her religion, which was the Church of Jesus Christ of Latter Day Saints, better known as Mormons. I knew very little about the church except that it lacked a large African-American population. However, the church members were always genuinely nice to me. They also had a strong focus on fellowship as well as family values, which was a concept desired by members of my childhood religion but rarely practiced. Mormons seemed to work very hard on various service opportunities in and outside the church. The most impactful aspect of the church to me was the way tithing was handled. Members privately paid ten percent of their earnings. Unlike some churches, Mormons were not mandated to pay tithes and offerings in front of the entire church as they believed this was a sacred and discreet process between the member and God through leaders of the church.

As a kid, I was often embarrassed on Sundays when I didn't have money to contribute to the offerings basket that circulated among the members or to stand up to drop my tithing envelope inside the box in front of the church. I also didn't appreciate the approach of the minister as he purposely embarrassed members into paying more than they were prepared to pay. I seethed when seeing his new luxury car parked in the lot while his members struggled with paying for utilities, rent, and other necessities. I knew there was something the church was missing, and knew that once I left home I wasn't going to continue to go to that type of church. As an adult, I was starting to feel the urge to attend church consistently, which I hadn't done for eight years until Michelle introduced me to her church.

I was curious about the church, attending many services while contemplating if I should join. I was very impressed with the men in the church. These men did a great job balancing their church callings, family obligations, and career aspirations. I received great advice from many of these men. They were the closest to ideal men I had ever been around, not because they were white but because they followed a religion that taught many principles I yearned for but hadn't found in any of my previous churches. For the most part, Mormons weren't the cheating, drug-using, and abusing husbands and fathers I was accustomed to being around as a kid. I often had deep conversations about the church with these men and grew to see them as models of how I wanted to pattern my life.

My mom is a God-fearing woman who rarely misses church. She often shed many tears while thinking about the various struggles happening in her life as well as the struggles of her children. To deal with her pain, she typically received strength from going to church. When I informed her that I was attending the Mormon church, she worried that I was joining a cult based on what she heard from others. I assured her that I could never join a cult because I could never allow anyone to manipulate me. After she was exposed to members of the church, her fears were eased and she received her own spiritual confirmation that the church still focused on God and Christ.

A primary difference between Mormonism and other churches was the Mormons' belief that the Gospel was restored on Earth through their prophet Joseph Smith, who helped to translate records provided to him into the Book of Mormon. The Book of Mormon contains records from prophets as well as historical information regarding inhabitants of the Middle East and the Americas. To an outsider, Mormonism seemed strange and blasphemous. Most Christians believed God's communication with His children ended with His words from the Bible, and that there would be no other forms of communication until Christ returned to Earth in the fullness of His glory. For a religion to claim that Christ continued to fellowship and teach on Earth after His ascension was reason for most to view it as strange and a cult. However, the foundation of the church continued to intrigue me, regardless of what I was hearing from others. I pondered reasons why would God stop communication with His children just because we didn't live during the days of the Bible. I knew His plan was for us was to return to live with Him, and I thought the Mormon church provided me with the best plan to make that happen in my life, regardless of the lack of diversity within the church.

As our relationship grew, Michelle and I decided to attend the 1996 Olympics in Atlanta. While we were in Atlanta, Michelle thought it would be a good idea for us to visit one of the local wards, or individual Mormon church buildings. Upon entering the Atlanta ward, I was shocked to see that the majority of members were black, including the bishop. I was able to talk to some of the black members about their experience as a true minority in the church. After leaving, I knew that I should seriously consider joining the church, especially since I enjoyed the way families were valued by members. The church believes the family is the basic organization in time and in eternity, and it is a cornerstone for God's plan. Until that time in my life, I was never taught how important family success was to my eternal salvation. The church's emphasis on the roles of fathers, mothers, and children is something all religions could emulate. I truly believed I discovered a gold mine regarding the religion and the values it emphasized.

Shortly after returning to Illinois from the Olympics, I received a knock at my door. I noticed two young Caucasian men in suits which, in Chicago, usually meant they were detectives. Automatically, I started to assume that something happened to a relative of mine or that I was being framed again for something I didn't do. Reluctantly, I answered the door. After finding out they were missionaries sent by Michelle, I refused to allow them to enter as I didn't want to receive their messages until I was sure it was my decision and not Michelle's.

After receiving my own personal revelation that I should learn more about the church, I finally decided to receive discussions from the church's missionaries. I wanted to make sure the church was true and the one I should join. My mentality was that even if the church wasn't true, I would be a better person if I practiced principles from the religion. I started asking friends who were members more direct questions about the church. I would often ask questions I believed would confirm the church was a cult, only to find myself enjoying another element about the church. I knew that my conversion was taking place and it was only a matter of time before I would become a member. I also knew I needed religion in my life to prepare me for the mental battles I'd face in corporate America.

Entering the workforce after college was very difficult. I felt pressured to find the greatest opportunity that had the perfect salary and most ideal career path. I settled on a job as an accounts payable clerk with the Lake County Forest Preserve. Shortly after coming to the Forest Preserve, I moved out of Bob's apartment into a home owned by the Forest Preserve and located next to the office where I worked. I paid an extremely discounted rent for the small two bedroom ranch home while committing to taking care of the landscaping needs for the property. The one-acre property was often difficult to maintain as I used my manual lawn mower to cut the grass. All my life I have dealt with a major fear of snakes. Each time I cut the lawn, I looked for snakes, knowing that some were often lurking around the property since we were in a forest preserve with a nearby creek. While living in the home for over six years, I encountered at least five snakes in the basement. I also had an invasion of frogs in the damp basement, which was infrequently visited by anyone in the house.

While I was adjusting to my new job and life with Michelle, her father and stepmom decided to move from Illinois to Indiana, which forced her to make a decision on whether or not to move with them or stay in Illinois to build our relationship. Luckily for me, she decided against an Indiana relocation to move in with me. However, living with me was a difficult decision for Michelle to make because of the belief among church members that we were fornicating since we were living together as an unmarried couple. Michelle struggled with the moral element of her decision to take a chance on me. I wasn't as sensitive to Michelle's decision because if I was in Rockwell, this decision would have been made without anyone viewing it negatively. Instead, it would have been praised as a step towards committing to the relationship. Even though it was great being under the same roof as Michelle, our decision to live together exacerbated our relationship struggles.

Temporarily, we moved in Michelle's younger sister, Merry Jean, who was then a senior in high school. This occasionally caused tension in the home because Michelle and I were trying to be the responsible adults, which led to attempts to discipline Merry Jean, who was still enjoying life as a teenager. Michelle was working during this time, so Merry Jean and I spent a lot of time together. We formed a brother/sister bond that is still strong today. She became the little sister I never had and frequently asks for advice with events going on in her life.

As Michelle and I continued to work on building our future lives together, I focused on improving my career at the Forest Preserve. My primary job as an accounts payable clerk was to process payments for the suppliers we used for goods and services. Since my desire at that time was to become an accountant, I forced myself to enjoy the opportunity even though the mundane functions of the job made it hard to get excited to come to work. The saving grace was the great relationships I was able to establish with my co-workers. However, I knew there was something else that I should have been doing at that stage of my life that was more impactful to society. I strongly believed I was wasting my acquired college and ABC knowledge as long as I stayed in that job. This mentality wasn't meant to offend any of my co-workers as much as it was to remind myself why the sacrifices were made while in the ABC program and attending Lake Forest College. I knew that in order for me to succeed beyond my then-current situation, I had to be more aggressive in managing my career.

I often asked the leaders at the Forest Preserve for greater responsibilities outside of my then-current role. I was anxious to display my intelligence through projects that were more important to the organization. Unfortunately, most of the leaders pigeonholed me into clerical roles, not seeing me as a strategic asset. I then allowed my displeasure for the job to impact my performance. My attention to details worsened the more I convinced myself that I was traveling fast on a dead-end career path. I started to make mistakes that normally would have been caught and corrected early. I also stayed up late during the week, coming into work half asleep and often nodding at my desk. My boss decided to place me on probation after realizing I was not showing interest in the job.

While my career was stalling, my personal life was blossoming. Michelle and I were becoming very serious in our relationship. I decided it was time for us to take the next step and get married. She was unaware of my feelings while I struggled to think of ways I could financially support the purchase of an engagement ring. I knew that having Michelle in my life as my wife would bring blessings because of her spiritual foundation. As I worried about how I could afford to provide her with a ring she would be proud to display, I was blessed with a tremendous gift.

The Bulls were in the middle of their dominance during this time, winning their fourth title the previous year and working on their fifth. While Michelle and I were watching a playoff game at my mom's apartment with the family, I was pulled to the side by my mom into her bedroom. My mom knew my feelings had grown strong for Michelle and decided to give me her wedding ring to present to Michelle. Not wanting to waste time or risk changing my mind, I decided during halftime I would propose to Michelle, which completely caught her by surprise.

My mom, Renee, and Ronetta were witnesses of my commitment to marry Michelle and were very happy for me, knowing that I would be the first within the siblings to make that step in matrimony. While it wasn't the most romantic way of proposing, I was hoping that Michelle would look beyond the delivery and focus on the future. Fortunately, she said yes which pleased everyone in the apartment. Finally, someone from the family was going to get married! After my proposal, Michelle and I spent a lot of time preparing for our upcoming wedding, which would take place on May 3, 1997.

Experiences while growing up in my family exposed me to mostly negative perspectives on marriage. The odds were definitely stacked against us based on my family history. Bob and my mom were involved even though he was married. Renee had fallen for Ray-Ray, who was married. The same situation existed for Ronetta and Boo. Only a handful of my childhood friends had fathers in their households. There were only a few married relationships on my maternal side of the family. No one in my family considered marriage as a prerequisite to have kids. I even thought about the impact of marrying someone outside of my race. *What would our children look like? How would they be treated by others because of their mixed race? Could I stay committed to the same woman for the rest of my life since I never had great examples around me?*

I had to overcome these fears before finally deciding to make the next logical step by marrying the person I was deeply in love with. My competitive juices convinced me I should try to break the cycle of marriage failures in our family. However, I worried about my background and how it would impact our relationship. Michelle wasn't exposed to the same experiences I encountered and often became jaded to her surroundings. Even though I knew a life with Michelle and the church could improve me as a person, I was concerned about the impact my past would have on both.

The Church

THE CLOSER MICHELLE AND I got to our wedding date, the more we fought. We allowed small issues become major arguments. Michelle is a very outwardly emotional person, which made it difficult for me to have meaningful discussions since I was the opposite. I usually prefer to calmly approach challenges, mostly because of my chaotic childhood. Although I was exposed to constant calamity as a child, I wanted to work hard to have serenity in my adult life.

On our wedding day, Michelle and I separated into our own groups. As her bridesmaids took her to purchase last-minute items and get beauty touch-ups before the big event, my groomsmen relaxed with me, putting my mind at ease before our very stressful day. My groomsman lineup allowed me to fuse together my Rockwell, Lower Merion and Lake Forest years. Included were my cousin (and best man) James, Jim Pollard from Ardmore, Rob from Rockwell and Eric from Lake Forest. Our ring bearer was Renee's son, Germaine. Merry Jean had flown in from Florida, where she moved after graduating from high school. The Scotts flew in from Philadelphia to witness our special day. Many family, friends, and co-workers from the Forest Preserve were there to enjoy the day. However, the differences in our cultures became extremely obvious on that special day.

As the groomsmen and I waited inside the church for the wedding to start, we were told Michelle and her crew hadn't arrived yet from Michelle's pampering sessions. The packed church became restless while waiting for the wedding to begin. In the Mormon chapel, cameras are not allowed so as to maintain the sanctity of the building. Hearing this news infuriated an already agitated group of family members who refused to understand or comply. Some of my family members even decided to smoke on the church grounds, even though members do not smoke and it wasn't allowed on the property. Many family members decided to bring and drink alcohol in their cars in the church parking lot, even though members of the church do not drink and, again, it wasn't allowed on the property.

Finally, Michelle and her crew arrived at the church, which delayed the start of the wedding by an hour. As we were directed to enter the chapel, I noticed many of our family, friends, co-workers and other associates inside. The church seemed to be divided by my family and friends, who were predominantly black, while the other side consisted of Michelle's mostly white loved ones. After reaching the front of the chapel, I waited for Michelle to enter. As she walked inside, I was excited to see her in such a beautiful state. Her gown looked amazing on her and she seemed to glow with such a tremendous smile on her face. The closer she got to me, the more I realized I had made the right decision to marry her, regardless of any social, racial, or religious barriers.

After the wedding, our reception would provide a severe turn. Before the wedding, Michelle had strongly urged me to not succumb to the traditional cake-smearing moment. I thought for sure her nerves were causing her to turn this fun and traditional moment into a stressful situation. I knew for sure that once we were able to get beyond the wedding ceremony, she would relax and enjoy the rest of the evening. As the cake-cutting moment approached us, I was urged by mostly family and friends to smash the cake on her face. After contemplating for a few seconds and being urged by Michelle to not do what I wanted to do with the cake, I decided I would fall to the pressure and smash the cake on her face. The moment I released my hand from painting her face with the cake, she immediately began to cry and scream towards me *"Lamont!!!! I told you to NOT do this!!! Why did you do that?!"*

I became embarrassed after noticing the awkward looks from family and friends and realizing her screams would continue as long as I stood there. I decided the only way to stop her screams was to walk away and outside of the reception. My sisters were incensed and wanted to fight Michelle or anyone else that supported her actions, not understanding that I should have respected her wishes. However, I believed Michelle could have done a better job of masking her emotions, opting to maximize the positive feelings from the day.

As I sat in an area outside the reception, I contemplated the events that led up to my decision to ignore Michelle's wishes. I also thought about how this incident scarred an extremely important and special day for both of us. Even though I went against her wishes, I knew Michelle's reaction was a warning flag that something else was wrong. I had never seen anyone have a public breakdown with no regard to the audience or circumstance. I've always been taught to avoid discussing problems in public, instead seeking to resolve them in the privacy of your home. I couldn't believe Michelle's decision to react the way she did in front of everyone. I immediately started to feel more embarrassed for my mom, who was surrounded by close friends at the wedding. Knowing she had waited decades to see at least one of her children get married, I hated that the image of this incident would potentially ruin my mom's positive feelings about this special day. I also didn't like the thought of the gossip that would follow among family as some would see this as a blemish on the golden child's reputation and image.

After being convinced to re-enter the reception to prevent a civil war, I decided to make the best of the rest of our stressful evening and luckily Michelle and I were able to move beyond this negative moment, at least during this night. Although, it's difficult to not be reminded of this incident each time we witness a cake cutting moment at future receptions. I felt the eyes upon us while I walked back into the reception. But, as I was always taught by my mom, I lifted my head and showed the confidence I developed as a result of my life experiences. I wasn't going to allow this situation to define me or my marriage, and I definitely wouldn't allow my family to be hurt in the process.

The reception was, unfortunately, the beginning of my marriage woes. Settling in as husband and wife was difficult for both of us. Neither of us wanted to follow the numerous and negatively impactful examples of dysfunctional marriages in our families. Unfortunately, neither one of us had enough positive marriage experiences in our lives to equip us with methods for having a successful marriage. The only examples either one of us could use were from church members. We both received a plethora of advice from members concerned about the future of our marriage, knowing that our childhood experiences would make it extremely challenging to have a successful marriage.

During our times of tumult, Michelle gave me the greatest news of my life... we were going to have a baby! I was going to be a father and be given the chance to do many things other father figures in my childhood were not able to do. I knew that I would become more mature with a child in my life. Even though I often worried about financially supporting a child, I was excited about the opportunity. I also believed that one of the reasons Michelle and I fought often was that I hadn't yet accepted the Gospel in my life. I knew that I had to join the church and accept God in my life before my child would be born into this world. I wanted my child to have a great example of a father, which was unlike what I had experienced.

Toward the end of 1997, I contemplated the timing of my announcement that I would join the church. I chose to make the announcement during a fast and testimony meeting. Most Sundays, the church is divided into three services that are roughly an hour each. The first hour consists of the Sacrament, which is when members renew their commitment towards living a Christ-like life by taking the bread and water. The bread symbolizes Christ's body, which was sacrificed for us, while the water represents His blood, which was shed for us.

During Sacrament, members are assigned topics to prepare talks to present in front of the congregation. The second hour is Sunday school, during which adults and youth are separated to receive lessons appropriate to their age group. During the last hour, the men and women are separated to receive pertinent and appropriate lessons. Fast and testimony Sunday, which typically occurs the first Sunday of every month, is a service that allows any member or non-member to share their testimonies to the rest of the congregation. I decided it was appropriate for me to announce to everyone during a fast and testimony Sunday as I would be able to provide my conversion story to others that had similar struggles.

During fast and testimony, my heart pounded as I knew I needed to strike up the courage to walk to the podium. When I convinced myself to proceed, I stood up and walked towards the pulpit while feeling eyes watching me, wondering what was going to come out of my mouth. Michelle looked at me with eyes that hinted unbelief and fear of not knowing what testimony I was going to bare. When it was my time to talk, I walked up to the podium and shared my gratitude on the genuine love and support felt by members towards me, even though I was not of their faith or ethnicity. After expressing my love, I then asked the congregation to accept me into their Church. In my youth, in order to join our church you typically walked in front as the minister called out to anyone that wanted to accept God in his or her life. Not knowing the Mormon process, I thought I should follow a similar procedure. While most understood I was basically asking to be baptized into the church, Michelle was unsure until someone else congratulated her on me accepting the Gospel and desiring to be baptized.

Becoming a Mormon would have its own set of challenges for me. While I never smoked and had already weaned myself off of drinking, I knew I wouldn't have a problem with obeying the Mormon "Word of Wisdom," which prohibits drugs, drinking alcohol or coffee, using tobacco, or anything that is harmful or addictive to the body. The Word of Wisdom emphasizes that our bodies are our temples, and we should take care of them in as reverent a manner as we would God's home. I also knew that I would not have a problem serving, as I always enjoyed the feeling of helping others. Tithing would not be problem either since I started doing that even before I thought of joining the church because of the private manner in which it was handled. I also knew the funds were going to help those in need versus those in greed, which had been my experience as a youth. However, I knew my biggest obstacle as a member of the church would be avoiding pornography.

Pornography had been a powerful influence on my life because of the openness and availability of it in my household as a kid. Growing up, I was never warned about the negative impact caused by pornography, mostly because my culture didn't view it as a problem. Not even in church did we discuss the pernicious root of pornography. Friends frequently shared magazines with each other. We hid our magazines from our parents not because of our fear in them telling us it was wrong but more about the awkwardness and embarrassment of them knowing we enjoyed it. The Mormon faith warns about the destruction that pornography has on families. Husbands, wives, sons, and daughters that view pornography allow sensual desensitizing images to influence them into lusting after others. Spouses then proceed from lust to pursuit, which usually ends with inappropriate relationships outside of marriages. Children progress from lust to premarital sex, which was a topic actually encouraged in the ghetto.

While being interviewed by the bishop of my church's ward, I decided to not disclose my challenge with pornography, which had grown into an addiction. I thought once I was baptized the destructive images and thoughts would dissipate, especially knowing that I had a beautiful wife by my side each night. I believed that the baptismal waters would wash away not only any sins committed but also the strong temptations I had on a daily basis to view pornography.

In addition to the church laws pertaining to alcohol, tobacco, premarital sex, tithing, and pornography, being one of a few blacks in the church was another emotional hurdle I would have to jump. There is a misperception of Mormonism within black Americans, which isn't helped by the fact that blacks weren't allowed to hold the priesthood until 1978, which I admittedly still struggle with understanding. As I researched the Church, I discovered there were other famous black members such as the legendary soul singer Gladys Knight and the late LeRoy Eldridge Cleaver (formerly of the Black Panthers). Even now there is an up-and-coming basketball star, Jabari Parker, who is a member of the church. Many black ministers joined the church after 1978. Also, what isn't widely known outside of the church is the fact that the founder and first president of the church, Joseph Smith, was an abolitionist.

When Smith ran for president of the United States in 1844, his anti-slavery platform called for a gradual end to slavery by 1850. When Mormons migrated to Missouri, they faced tremendous persecution from the pro-slavery Missourians, which continued until Smith was killed in 1844 (which some believe was partly due to his anti-slavery stance). Subsequent presidents of the church didn't necessarily share the same anti-slavery beliefs. One even conjured up a phrase known as the "Curse of Cain" which used Biblical references for how Cain's seed was cursed by God with blackness after he had slain his brother Abel.

I am honestly not as concerned about the origin of the priesthood ban. I am more concerned about moving forward and seeing more blacks receive the priesthood while diversifying the church. As long as I believe in the foundation of the church, I will not allow others' opinions to change my feelings about the religion. Unfortunately, some ministers use this history as support for their own hypotheses that the church is racist and not open to other races, which couldn't be further from the truth.

Most churches have negative and embarrassing elements of their histories that would discourage others from joining if extensive research was conducted. The Ku Klux Klan was founded by Southern Baptists. Numerous accounts of children being molested by Catholic priests or other leaders surface each year. We are all familiar with the attempts to link Islam with terrorism. However, all three of those religions, among others, have contributed greatly to the growth of this nation regardless of their histories or the character of their leaders. My faith in the fundamental beliefs of the church remained strong regardless of its history because I chose to place more faith in the church itself than the people leading it.

I was drawn to the church's emphasis on family and fellowshipping, which is something that's spoken but rarely seen in practice at other churches I attended. Also, members of other churches complain often about ministers who profit financially from their congregations, yet continue to support him each Sunday. It sickens me to hear about ministers who use funds from hard-working church members to finance luxury automobiles or private jets so that he or she is not inconvenienced with commercial travel.

Materialistic greed displayed by some ministers was definitely one of the main drivers in my decision to not continue as a member of my previous religion. I was always against paying someone to preach the Gospel, especially within poor congregations. In the Mormon faith, tithing and fast offerings are used to build church temples and meeting places (avoiding the use of debt) and to assist families that are in need, not to fill the coffers of a greedy minister. Members are assigned callings which provide them with responsibilities to assist with building God's kingdom here on Earth.

I knew that my decision to join the church would provide additional fodder for some of my family and friends who already thought I had an elitist perspective towards everyone else. Although I knew that there was a greater purpose for me in life, I also knew that I would constantly have an internal battle brewing between my natural desires and my spiritual needs. But, in order for me to become a stronger husband and father, I knew I had to establish a spiritual foundation. The Church of Jesus Christ of Latter Day Saints was the perfect church for me to become the person I had always wanted to become. It gave me specific instructions on how to be a better husband and eventual father.

My baptism in January 1998 was a beautiful ceremony. My mom attended as well as other family members. They saw how happy I was to accept the church in my life. I was prepared to use Christ as an example and was excited about my future life with Michelle and our future children in the Gospel. Being a member and living the standards of most members would give me that Cosby-like life that I had always dreamed about. The church itself gave me the peace I had been searching for my entire life. There was always a sense of reverence I felt in the members' homes that I didn't feel while a member of my previous church. There is a constant focus surrounding Jesus Christ that wasn't as emphasized at those churches beyond occasional pictures of Jesus along with Dr. King and President John F. Kennedy. Once and for all, I needed my home to be a place of refuge, a place where I could escape from the perils of life.

As I came out of the baptismal font, I felt renewed. I felt as if the weight of the world was lifted from my shoulders. As a new member of the church, I could now be used as a conduit for other family members and blacks to join the church, providing them with lives we had only seen in movies. I knew my road as one of the few blacks in the church would not be easy, but I would be needed to help others open their eyes to the blessings of the church.

The purpose of becoming a member of the church was not to make me more "white;" I knew that as a member I would have a tremendous responsibility to educate others about the religion and the values that we emphasize. I knew that premarital sex was wrong even though everyone around me encouraged it through conversation or their own actions. Even though I wasn't warned about the dangers of alcohol and drugs, I saw firsthand examples within my own family. Even though pornography was not frowned upon by others, I knew that I felt such a strong negativity surrounding me while enjoying the lustful pages and videos. I was blessed to have been introduced to the church and excited to see how it would transform me into a true leader.

Part III

Maturation

Clockwise from top: my mentor, Mr. Earl Reubel (RIP); me and my dad, Preston LaRue, Jr.; at a work function with Deborah Williams and Eric Troillot; my kids, Malik, Payton, Jacqui and Antonio; me, Mom, Renee, June and Ronetta at a family reunion in 2008

The Turnaround

I AM CONVINCED IT WASN'T a coincidence that shortly after joining the church, my career path began to improve. Being placed on probation at work served as a wakeup call, as I had never been fired before and needed the money to pay for my family's necessities. My performance changed drastically after I decided to strive to be the best accounts payable clerk. I discovered it was better for my mental and spiritual state to approach the job as if it was the greatest opportunity for me. I had to stop comparing myself to others, understanding that what was best for someone else at that moment wasn't necessarily best for me and my situation. My turnaround also provided greater exposure to the senior leaders and led to various internal awards and recognition.

After serving in this position for a couple of years, I knew I had to make a change. My passion for accounting had shifted drastically. I realized that one of my strengths was my ability to connect more with others inside and outside the organization. I knew that a role that could help me utilize that strength would maximize my capabilities and show my true value. I approached one of our senior leaders to let him know I believed it was time to find other opportunities outside of the company. Not wanting me to leave, he offered for the Forest Preserve to pay for me to become a certified public accountant or to pursue my MBA. Since I knew my desire to remain in accounting was waning, I was confident that going after the MBA would be more beneficial to my future, which would have an even greater impact on my budding family. I enrolled in the graduate program offered by Keller Graduate School of Management. I wanted to attend Lake Forest's graduate school program, but it was more expensive than what the

Forest Preserve desired to pay. Regardless, I was excited to get the chance to pursue my MBA, which would be another achievement not yet realized by anyone in the family, establishing an even greater benchmark for future generations.

While contemplating my next career move, a co-worker and friend in purchasing decided to leave the company. During his going-away celebration, he strongly urged me to pursue his former job as a buyer because of my background and personality. Unfortunately, at that time, I didn't have the confidence to transition from my mundane role to one that would have involved more responsibility. I was persuaded by someone else to not pursue the job, and I watched as the company hired an outside individual for the position. Fortunately for me, the person hired was in the role only a few months before it was mutually decided that he wasn't a good fit for the company. I knew this was more than just coincidence. I had to pursue the job even though I didn't know where the new career path would lead. I sought after and was hired for the buyer position in February 1998. The promotion came at a great time as we knew our new child was due to enter this world the next month.

Being a buyer provided me with the opportunity to display knowledge learned in school and the personality that had been hidden during my time as an accounts payable clerk. Once I overcame my shyness in high school, I realized how much I enjoyed being around other people. As a buyer I was able to communicate with all of the departments within the company, negotiate price points with suppliers, and use analytical and strategic skills that had been taught to me since I attended Lower Merion. Skills acquired from my accounting background would also be beneficial when seeking success as a buyer.

As Michelle got closer to her due date in March, her contractions increased. On the evening of March 15, the contractions persisted every five minutes. Instead of calling her doctor, she decided to ignore the physical alerts and attempted to sleep. After being awakened to sharp and consistent contractions that came exactly three minutes apart, I convinced her to contact her doctor. After the doctor was told about her situation, we were urged to rush to the hospital. My mind was racing and my heart was pounding as I knew what was imminent.

The Turnaround

I knew that our lives were about to change and we would welcome our new bundle of joy soon. After hastily entering and turning on the car to head to the hospital, almost on exact cue, Sam Cooke's 1964 hit song "A Change Is Gonna Come" started to play on the radio. The hairs on my arms began to rise because of the message within the song. A change was coming in the form of a new bundle of joy that Michelle and I would be blessed with.

Being a father was something I had always dreamed of mostly to rectify the wrongs that had existed in my life by not being around my own father. My main fear was caused by the uncertainty of the impact of our first child on our marriage. Michelle and I already struggled with our relationship. Our differences were very pronounced while we adapted to each other under the same roof. Michelle was from a Navy family while my family never served. She was raised mostly in a Caucasian household while mine was all black. She grew up in the church, which taught her to avoid pornography, while my family's household embraced it. She was able to experience living in different places in the U.S. while my childhood was spent solely in the insular world of the Rockwell Gardens ghetto before heading to Lower Merion. We were from more polar opposites than most couples. Having a child in our lives could either bring us closer together or exacerbate the challenges we were already facing.

After arriving at the hospital we realized that having a child was closer to reality. We barely entered the labor and delivery unit before being told our baby would be delivered within the hour. As Michelle's contractions and pain increased in consistency, my heart raced faster, not knowing the outcome of our imminent delivery. When the time came to deliver our child, I became more nervous and I wished we had taken the classes offered to prepare us for the labor. Finally, after a few hard pushes, deep breaths, and no epidural, our new baby entered this world. As the doctor yelled out "you have a brand new baby…girl," I was overtaken with emotions. I was now a proud father of a beautiful daughter, whom we called Jacquilyn Markelle Robinson.

Jacqui looked like an angel with her dimpled cheeks and curly hair. Her amazing lungs captured our attention, alerting us that she was hungry, tired, or just wanted attention. I truly believe it was no coincidence that she was born with a birthmark that resembled a perfect five-pointed star on her shoulder. She was *my* star and I would work hard to be one in her eyes. Her name, "Jacqui Robinson," was already full of stardom and one that was chosen carefully as Michelle and I were breaking our own color line in both families as a result of our interracial relationship. I believe there is a reason most mixed children are beautiful: when races combine, physical beauty is the manifestation of the synergy formed by the diversity in God's children.

My preparation for parenthood was different than Michelle's. While she was constantly around babies as the oldest of ten, as the baby myself I did not gain experience raising kids. During the first week of caring for Jacqui, I used latex gloves while changing her diapers. I had never seen newborn baby feces, which didn't look the same as "normal" poop. Eventually, I went down to one glove before finally eliminating gloves entirely. I then became an expert at changing diapers, preparing bottles, and putting her to sleep. Fatherhood was challenging but extremely rewarding, and I enjoyed the new experience.

My life was now changing for the better. In addition to fatherhood, I had greater responsibilities at work. I knew that every decision I would now make personally and professionally would impact an entire family. My preparation for fatherhood began as a child, although during that time I learned more about the negative behavior I would *avoid* as father. As a member of the Church of Jesus Christ of Latter Day Saints, I learned more about the *positive* influences a father could have on his child's life. Through many examples of strong men in the church, I was able to understand that my role as a father and priesthood leader of our household should not be taken lightly. I understood that God has a major plan for me and that my purpose in life had not yet been fulfilled.

Unfortunately, the demons that haunted me from childhood began to rear their ugly heads. Not fully understanding or appreciating the blessings provided to me by God in the form of my beautiful wife, adorable child, and professional progress, I continued to indulge in pornography. I allowed myself to be fooled into thinking it was more fun or cool to follow the examples of society. I wasn't living up to the "if it was to be, it was up to me" mantra as I discovered it was easier to follow society. What we read in books and magazines or watch on television and movies could influence us in unimaginable ways. We allow ourselves to see images in media that

The Turnaround

society views as beautiful instead of appreciating the beauty in the godlike beings surrounding us.

I constantly attempted to conceal my struggles with pornography, especially from Michelle. Her strong views against it, mostly driven by the standards set by members of the church, were consistently driven into our home. Whenever a television program, movie or commercial became too racy, she would either leave the room or ask me to turn the channel. While I thought this behavior was Pollyanna-ish, I understood the impact of those images. However, I strongly believed pornography was not as destructive as Michelle and the church emphasized, since it hadn't impacted me yet from all of those years of indulging. What I didn't realize was that those pornographic images embedded in my mind from years of pleasure allowed me to be desensitized towards God's true beauties in life.

While I was dealing with my internal struggles, ironically, my career was starting to shape itself. As I worked toward the completion of my MBA program, I started to visualize a future that would involve the level of success I sought after as a student attending Lower Merion. I knew those years of sacrificing while being away from home had to start shaping into professional achievements. In order for me to realize this success, I had to be willing to take risks. Going after the position as a buyer was my first test to take chances. I knew that there would be bigger risks to take in my near future. Unfortunately, there was no one in my family who could relate with that phase of my life. I then decided to seek advice from some of the successful members of the church, developing informal mentor/protégé relationships. I felt that the more I was around successful people, the greater the chance for success through referrals or shared knowledge.

While Jacqui was still an infant, Michelle and I received shocking but pleasant news: we were pregnant again. Having one child while barely surviving financially made the reality of a second child an ominous thought, but I knew I wanted a large family, mostly to correct all of the wrongs of my childhood by leading my own successful unit. I secretly hoped to have my first son, whom I could teach all of the things I wished my father could have taught me when I was a kid, such as shaving, playing sports, or being a father himself. I wanted to break the cycle and raise a strong, intelligent man who would fulfill all of his responsibilities in life as a father and husband.

Balancing work, school, marriage, and parenthood was difficult. My hectic life included working full-time, coming home briefly before heading off to school, sitting in class for four hours, coming back home after school, eating late dinners, studying into the early hours, awakening to a screaming and hungry child, then waking up to repeat the process after obtaining an inadequate amount of sleep. But, these were all sacrifices I had to make in order to realize my dreams. The daunting thought of bringing another child into this world quickly subsided when I reminded myself of the sacrifices I had already taken in life to get to that point. Even though I hadn't achieved the level of success I knew was in my future, I knew that I had been blessed to have escaped the ghettos and the cyclical negative mentality that had plagued my family for years.

Michelle was due to deliver our second child shortly after my birthday in April of 1999. The closer we got to the due date, the more I hoped we wouldn't deliver on April 4. I wanted my child to have its own unique birthday. I also selfishly wanted to continue to have my own special day. However, God has a plan for all of us. On my birthday, which fell on Easter Sunday in 1999, our son Malik Julius was born. Malik was the greatest birthday present I could ever receive. My preference for having unique birthdays for us was quickly overshadowed by the excitement of being able to raise a son. We would also be able to share a special day where we would always have the chance to create memories with shared birthday parties and father/son events.

Raising a son would be completely different than a daughter. Jacqui was my princess. She could convince me to buy whatever she wanted just by having me look into her beautiful brown eyes. A boy could surely challenge my parental skills. I believe most fathers are naturally harder on their sons because they don't want their seeds to acquire their negative traits. I wanted Malik to avoid the same problems that plagued me as a child that, ironically, directly resulted from me not having a father in the house. Most fathers want their sons to be the man they've always wanted to be themselves.

Malik's name itself had great meaning in a couple of ways. Malik in Arabic means "king." I desired for my son to have king-like qualities that could cause others to be drawn to him for positive reasons. The decision to name him Malik was agreed upon by me and Michelle after watching one of our favorite television shows from the early 1990s, *New York Undercover*. One of the main characters was portrayed by an actor named Malik Yoba. *New York Undercover* was not only entertaining, it also reminded Michelle and me of our dating years, which were, for the most part, without tumult. Malik's middle name, Julius, was homage paid to my childhood hero and the figure who influenced me to come to Philly, Julius "Doctor J" Erving of the 76ers.

While most of our family and friends worried about the impact of having two young children early in our marriage and career, Michelle and I both had a vision. We were both from broken homes and wanted to break the cycle by establishing our own version of *The Cosby Show*. We both knew that we were in uncharted territory by striving to have a successful family and career without many around us who could offer guidance on doing so. It was extremely rare on my side of the family to see married couples stay together for their lifetimes without major struggles along the way. I was also personally determined to put an end to the stereotype that black men were not good fathers or husbands.

Michelle and I decided to get sealed in the church's temple in September 1999. To be sealed as a couple in the Church of Jesus Christ of Latter Day Saints meant you were joined in union for all eternity, not just until death as practiced in most religions. The day of our sealing added to the suddenly building challenges in our lives. Michelle and I had an argument that resulted in neither of us wanting to attend the ceremony, even though we knew our friends and family were waiting for us. We argued vehemently until receiving a visit from a mutual family friend, Sherrie Labrum. Her warm personality always turned negative situations into a great day. I also received a phone call during this time from Sherrie's husband Ron, who was also a great friend and a leader within our ward. While Sherrie used biblical and practical reasons for why we were going through these obstacles on the day of our sealing, Ron bluntly threatened that he would come and force us to go to the sealing if we didn't show up on our own. Finally, Michelle and I were convinced that our sealing was essential for an eternity of happiness. Ron and Sherrie maintained their strong influences on our family until Sherrie's death in 2013 as a result of complications from an unfortunate accident.

I was excited to see my mom at the temple even though she knew that she couldn't witness the actual ceremony. Only righteous church members are able to enter the sacred services inside the temple. However, my mom walked the serene grounds while Michelle and I enjoyed the ceremony with our church friends and two young children. I prayed that the sealing would improve our marriage as we were now committed for an eternal life and responsible for our children being a part of an eternal family.

Struggling through my constant cycle of work, school, kids, and occasional sleep would take great tolls on our marriage. I became emotionally and physically distant from Michelle and the church. My desire to be comforted through pornography grew even greater as I sought childhood comforts, ignoring the greatness that was ahead of me. However, as long as neither Michelle nor the church knew about my behavior, I fooled myself into thinking I could manage my addiction. Addictive behavior causes the addict to seek solace in a pattern that works to control that person's way of life. And, the more the addict experiences success in various phases of life, he or she continues to be drawn in to the addiction, falsely believing that the addiction has no impact on them or their behavior.

Although the end was nearing for school, my worldly vision of our future often dissipated as a result of our financial struggles. Working at the Forest Preserve was not allowing me to see a clear career path. I knew that I needed a change in my career landscape in order to properly provide for my family. I started inquiring about various job opportunities before obtaining my MBA, realizing that having an MBA at the Forest Preserve would be wasted. I was advised by several successful men from the church during my job search. Not only did many of them distribute my résumé to their respective companies, they offered me valuable information regarding ways to conduct myself during this vital time in my career.

Finally, I approached the end of my MBA program. I graduated in June 2000 on a beautiful sunny Saturday at Navy Pier in Chicago. I prayed that my mom would be able to witness my graduation this time after not being able to see the Lake Forest College ceremony because of her sudden illness. After persistently checking on my mom's health I was assured that all would be well. I knew that the day would be extremely emotional since I would be the first member of my maternal side of the family to receive a master's degree. I hope I will influence future generations, including my children, to strive for greatness by obtaining an MBA. No longer would receiving a bachelor's be the goal for our family, which I hoped would provide a positive impact on the lives of future generations.

After graduation, I focused entirely on finding a greater opportunity in the workforce. My blessing would come in the form of being hired as a purchasing agent for Abbott Laboratories in October 2000. Abbott would provide many career firsts for me. It was the first global company I would work for and one that would stretch my capabilities. I would finally be able to proudly describe my employment to others, knowing that a global organization could offer the future opportunities I didn't have as an employee of the Forest Preserve. It was the first time I would have my own office, which is something I've always desired once I entered the workforce after graduating from Lake Forest College. Abbott was the first company that would allow me opportunities to travel, which is something I wanted, even though I still had a fear of flying.

My first business trip was to Key Biscayne, Florida, where I stayed at the Ritz Carlton. Upon entering my room and realizing my window view was of the Atlantic Ocean, I quickly opened the patio doors and slept while listening to the crashing waves. I knew at that moment that my sacrifices of leaving my home to pursue my dreams were done for moments like that. I was amazed that a kid from the housing projects on the west side of Chicago could be enjoying a plush bed inside the Ritz Carlton while being mesmerized by the sounds and sights of the ocean. While most of the other attendees at the conference took the scenery for granted, I knew better. I knew that my life had changed, and that I was quickly moving into uncharted territory while trying to overcome any fears of the unknown. However, my fears were constantly dissolved after I reminded myself of the impact I could have on those who grew up in similar environments and did not have the same opportunities.

2001

Shortly after starting my career at Abbott, Michelle and I found out that we were expecting our third child. Even though my salary increased at Abbott, I knew that a third child would make our living arrangements more stressful. In addition to the pending birth of our child, 2001 would be another memorable year for various reasons. In August of that year I received news that would finally complete my family tree. In the early months of 2001, I often spoke with my aunt Dorothy about the need to find my father, who at the time I thought was Leroy. Knowing that this wasn't accurate and not wanting me to go too far down a path to find someone who was not responsible for bringing me into this world, Dorothy pressured my mom to reveal the true identity of my father.

Dorothy gave my mom an ultimatum: tell me the true identity of my father the very next day or Aunt Dorothy would tell me herself. The feelings of guilt that developed from keeping this thirty-year-old secret and having a child out of wedlock with a married man weighed too heavily on my mom. She decided to have Bob break the news to me. After being summoned to Bob's house on a late Friday evening in August, I was finally able to hear information that would complete my life and answer many questions I had throughout. Bob hesitantly informed me that Leroy was not my real father, which I had always doubted after seeing previous pictures of him. A child should be able to see old pictures of either parent, especially the one of the same sex, and automatically see features they had inherited.

Back in 1971, while my mother was working at the Automatic Electric Company along with Dorothy, she met Preston LaRue, a married father of two girls. My mom was separated from Ronald during this time and was starting to enjoy the life she didn't have while she was being mentally and physically abused by him. Preston was then struggling through a marriage that was a tremendous burden on both partners. My mom became pregnant during her affair with Preston. Not wanting to destroy his family, my mother never informed him. She left Automatic Electric in early 1972 before her pregnancy became obvious, while my dad relocated to Houston, completely severing any communications. I was born to a single mother and an uninformed father. My mom then decided to raise her four kids as a single parent in Rockwell with the intention of keeping the true identity of my father a secret for the rest of her life.

Upon hearing of the potential inclusion of a father in my life, I became excited. Since Bob had been my father figure for my entire life, I felt awkward receiving the news from him. I worried that he would feel threatened that someone else had the chance to fill that void in my life. The main threat to Bob in this situation was that it was my biological father. However, because of Bob's contribution to my life, including his role as my main influence for obtaining an education and following a career path, I will always have love for him, regardless of my situation with my potential father. But this wasn't about my relationship with Bob; I had to find a way to bring closure to my life. I knew that I would forever go through life wondering what could have happened if I had met my biological father if I didn't act on the curiosity of finding him.

I woke up early the next day after my meeting with Bob, determined to find Preston. I searched the internet and found two men with the name Preston LaRue. The first Preston was an 80 year old Caucasian male who lived in North Carolina. I confidently assumed he couldn't be my father. The second was a black male around the same age as my mother and who lived in a Houston suburb. Remembering that Bob told me Preston was either in Chicago or potentially somewhere in Texas, I was confident he was my target. I gained the courage to contact him after saying a silent prayer that the situation would turn out the way God intended it to.

As the phone rang, my heart beat rapidly as I waited for him to pick up the call. I knew I couldn't leave a message with him and this would need to be delivered live over the phone. As Preston answered the phone, I wished him good morning and asked him the following screening questions:

[Me] "Are you Preston LaRue?"

[Preston] "Yes, I am."

[Me] "Did you live in Chicago around 1971?"

[Preston] "Yes."

[Me] "Did you know Lula Adams, my mother?"

[Preston] "Yes."

[Me] "Well, before you say anything, I don't need anything from you. I just needed closure. But, there is a chance you may be my father."

Preston immediately became silent—this must have been startling news to receive so early on a Saturday morning. He had worked the late shift the night before and was still trying to adjust to the morning call.

Fortunately, after going through our mutual screening process, we were able to realize that there was a great probability that he was my father. We were both the same height (6'3"), the same build (slender), the same prominent facial features (big eyes and ears) and both enjoyed the same love for baseball. Preston's magical words to me were "I don't even need to see a picture to know that you're my son." I didn't know how to react to this encounter as I never thought I would ever hear the voice of my biological father.

Throughout my life, I only knew of features and mannerisms I received from my maternal side. I knew that I was different, but without my paternal side I was unaware of the exact differences. We talked for at least an hour as if we had been in each other's lives from the moment I was born. The Spirit inside of me confirmed in my heart that Preston was my true father, even though I hadn't seen a picture yet. After our picture exchange, it was obvious to everyone on both ends that we belonged to each other.

Going fatherless for the first twenty-nine years of my life negatively impacted my perception of fathers. For this entire duration, I had a significant disdain for fathers since mine wasn't in my life. Since the majority of my friends in Rockwell also didn't live with or know of their fathers, I was able to mask my hurt feelings. My impact came when I attended Lower Merion and eventually Lake Forest, where I would see students enjoying their fathers and looking at them as positive examples. I dreaded being asked where my father lived, because I honestly didn't know. I often wanted to create stories that my father was a federal agent or killed in Vietnam but was afraid the lies would confuse me. Even though most of the kids in Rockwell didn't live with their fathers, they at least knew where they lived. I had absolutely no clue and hated to have to confess.

The *positive* impact of not having a father in my life is that it made me commit to being a great father once I was able to have my own children. I knew that, regardless of my situation with their mother, I would always be in their lives. I knew that I would lay down my life to be with them, sacrificing everything I had and dedicating my life to making sure their childhood was much better than mine.

My conversation with my mom shortly followed my first encounter with my father. Nervously, she wondered about my perception of her knowing that I was conceived as a result of her affair with a married man. I believe if I had a relationship with Leroy who, up until that time, I thought was my father, I would have been upset. However, I was excited that the "mistake" made between the two adults resulted in this bastard coming into this world, which confirmed within me that there was a purpose for me to be here. This confirmation was strengthened after my mom admitted to me that she would have gotten an abortion if she knew earlier in her pregnancy that she was bearing a child. She was already a single mother of three and was barely able to support my siblings financially. It had been almost eight years since she had a child. She was also excited to start enjoying life after her tumultuous relationship with Ronald ended, but a baby would obviously hamper her plans. She sought my forgiveness, which automatically came because I was caught up in the euphoria surrounding the chance to meet my biological father.

The excitement about finally connecting with my dad temporarily lost a little of its luster on September 11, 2001. That day will forever be remembered around the world. For me, it gave me a new look on life and how I needed to shape my family and career goals. Because of my employment change to Abbott from the Lake County Forest Preserve in October 2000, I was forced to move out of the small home I had occupied for the majority of my employment. We moved into an apartment complex directly across the street from Abbott. I often enjoyed my walks which gave me time to ponder home and work situations.

On that beautiful Tuesday morning of September 11, I remember walking and thinking about how blessed I was to have a job I enjoyed that had a true career path. I was also happy to have a great family unit, which now included my dad. Shortly after arriving at work I was informed that a small plane flew into one of the World Trade Center towers in New York City. Thinking this was an accident and hoping no one was seriously injured outside of the pilot, I turned my attention elsewhere until someone else told us about another plane that flew into the Pentagon in D.C. I knew then that this wasn't an accident. After searching the Internet for additional sources, it was confirmed that the accidents were connected to terrorists. When I overheard the rumors that the Sears Tower in Chicago was potentially a target, I immediately called Michelle and the kids to make sure they were OK and to confirm that I was fine as well. Michelle knew nothing about the incidents until I called.

As I remained on the phone I asked her to turn the television on and activate the speaker phone so that the Abbott crew gathered around my desk could listen to the live events. While speaking with a calm Michelle, I suddenly heard her emit a loud, piercing scream: "Noooooooooo!!!!! Oh my goodness!!!" Screaming, Michelle explained to us that another plane had flown into the second tower. She described the surreal scene as if it were an action movie. My thoughts then turned to the safety of my family around the country, friends that were in New York and D.C., and co-workers that may have been traveling near New York or D.C. My heart sank into my stomach while thinking of the workers in the attacked buildings. These were fathers, mothers, sons, and daughters who went to work, in a manner similar to me, thinking it would be an average day. Children and other family members were left behind at home not knowing it would be the last day they'd see their loved ones alive. I also thought about the unrealized dreams of those who perished, which is a tragedy in itself not only for the deceased but for those of us who never witnessed the genius from their minds.

As we stayed on the phone, Michelle released an even louder scream "Ohhhhhhhhh my!!!!!!!" The second tower struck crumbled down to the ground with thousands of lives obviously lost inside the burning tower. Work wasn't to be done on this day. It was impossible for me to want to be anywhere outside of my home to make sure my family was protected in case there were any additional attacks near our home. The total destruction of the other tower shortly followed. I couldn't believe two landmarks I've grown to associate with New York were gone. I remembered watching the '70s movie *Superman* and seeing the Man of Steel flying with Lois Lane between the towers. I remembered various television programs that featured the New York skyline prominently displaying the twin towers. My sadness turned to anger. Why would someone destroy lives because of their hatred toward man? My life would now focus on making sure I left a positive legacy for my children after I left this Earth. The event also made me hug my kids a little tighter since tomorrow wasn't promised to any of us.

Later that evening, while sitting in our living room, Michelle and I reflected on the sadness of the most tragic moment, outside of family events, in either of our lives. We knew that this day would change our mentality or that of millions of others in the U.S. Not knowing if the attacks would continue, I worried about the future for my children. I thought about our unborn child and whether he or she would live in a world where the innocence of youth would be replaced by a constant tension surrounding public events we used to take for granted as safe. We also grew closer during that moment as the importance of family became even greater for both of us.

Life wasn't normal for days for anyone until I saw and heard the greatest sight and sound I could ever witness... a commercial plane flying in the skies. Planes had been grounded after September 11 for days. It was eerie to not see the sky cluttered with planes going to various places all around the world. While I used to dream of quiet days and evenings free of the roaring engines of planes, I needed to hear that sound again to go back to some level of normalcy. Finally seeing that first plane inspired me to believe in America again. I knew that America's fortitude was proudly displayed by going back to our normal, pre-September 11 events. Although we would never forget, we were able to move forward as a united country, regardless of the evil that existed in those who tried to destroy us.

After life returned back to normal, I told the story of reconnecting with my father to Sarah, the leader of our procurement group at Abbott and my mentor. Sarah had already been fascinated with my story of leaving home at an early age to pursue my dreams. She became ecstatic for me once I told her about contacting my father. Sarah always had great passion for helping others, especially those who were not from privileged backgrounds. She would often teach me basic rules of etiquette that I never learned as a child, such as the proper utensils to use and specific foods to order during business meals. I didn't know there was a proper way to enjoy a meal, realizing that the bread plate is on the left and the drinks go on the right.

After listening to me talk about my situation, Sarah decided to invite me to accompany her on an upcoming visit to an Austin, Texas, Abbott plant. I would then travel from Austin to Houston after the meetings to finally get the chance to meet my father. While in Austin, my anticipation level grew greater than I could have imagined. Even if I was able to overcome my angst in meeting my biological father, I knew I had to also focus on how the rest of his family would react to me. If there were any differences in my appearance versus the Houston contingent, I worried that they would never accept me as their own and see me as someone trying to force a relationship with Preston just to have a father in my life. Fortunately, my career path had started to improve, so any thoughts of me entering his life for any financial gain during that time should have been quickly dismissed as ridiculous banter.

When I arrived in Houston, I took a shuttle from the airport to a location suggested by my father. While on the shuttle, I wrote down my thoughts regarding the momentous encounter, not knowing if it was going to be successful. I wondered if my father would accept me from the moment he saw me or if it was going to take time. I wondered if I would embrace my father as if we had been in each other's lives since my birth. I also wondered what my mom was thinking about this occasion, knowing that she was directly responsible for removing both of us from enjoying all of the trials, tribulations, celebrations, and accomplishments that have happened to us over the previous twenty-nine years.

As the shuttle entered the parking lot where I was to exit, my eyes hurriedly searched around for a tall, slender male that resembled me. While searching, I heard a deep voice say to me "Hey, Son!" I turned around and saw myself thirty years into the future in the form of my dad. We embraced as if I was the prodigal son that had returned home. When we arrived at his home, we had the chance to talk about our lives. My dad was very impressed with my successes. He was especially emotional knowing that my mom hid her pregnancy from him to avoid destroying his family.

To introduce me to the rest of my Houston relatives, my dad decided to have a party at his home the next evening, inviting all family and friends. The party was reminiscent of a scene at the end of the movie *Antwone Fisher* in which the main character meets his paternal family for an emotional first time. At the party, I saw all of the physical characteristics and traits that existed on the other side of my family tree. Men on my maternal side were average or below average in height, but my paternal cousins were 6'4", 6'5", and even 6'10". My sleepy and bulging eyes were featured on an uncle, aunts, and cousins. My fat earlobes were also shared by many that evening.

The highlight of the night came when I met my last living grandparent, my paternal grandmother. She immediately introduced herself as my grandmother and gave me the biggest hug that a frail, older woman could give. I knew that she had a great heart the way she showed great interest in hearing about my life. My Houston family allowed me to believe that any reason for why I wasn't in my dad's life was irrelevant at that particular moment. I was accepted as part of the family, and the focus now shifted on making sure that I'd be involved in any family events for the future.

I always wondered about the differences in the scientific theories of nature versus nurture. However, my Houston visit confirmed my belief in nature as what shapes our individual characteristics. One particular situation helped me with this confirmation. I always enjoyed arranging my favorite songs from the '70s, '80s and '90s on cassette tapes or CDs for my enjoyment. While sitting in my dad's living room, I was listening and enjoying the music being played through his speakers. After realizing that all of the songs played were on my selection, I commented to my dad that I didn't realize he borrowed my mix tape. Surprisingly, he replied that the songs were on a CD he arranged himself. We had an identical taste in music! My dad also shared with me that he told his wife that if they ever had a son he would name him LaMont because he liked the way LaMont LaRue sounded. Since my mom had never told my dad she was pregnant with me, it was impossible for him to know her name intentions which created a fascinating coincidence.

My Houston visit provided me with a great understanding of how my dad's life shaped him into who he is today. My dad grew up in Fort Worth, Texas, as the second oldest of five children to Preston, Sr. and Iris, who lost two children at early ages. The LaRue height came from my grandfather, who was rumored to be at least 6'6". The LaRue temper also came from my grandfather, whose alcoholism often led to him abusing my grandmother as well as my dad when he was trying to defend his mother. One of my dad's earliest childhood memories was his father entering their home and attacking his mother while she was bathing my dad. His father's anger was usually a result of his constant false accusations that his mother was having affairs. My dad admitted that his childhood abuse led to him repeating that same behavior with his wife.

My dad was an athlete in high school, participating on basketball and baseball teams. His style in basketball was identical to mine today, which focused more on rebounding than shooting from the outside. After not receiving the sports scholarships he desired, he decided to enlist in the Air Force after graduating from high school in 1961. Before he enlisted, his parents separated, which gave him a feeling of being free from his father's constant verbal, physical, and mental assaults. He also felt happy for his mom, who wouldn't have to endure the abuse, especially since he knew he wasn't going to be in her home to protect her.

My dad continued to play basketball and baseball while in the Air Force after receiving a top-secret clearance. During his stint in the military, he was able to travel around Europe, serving in places such as Greece, the island of Crete, France, Spain, Athens, Istanbul, and other places. During his tour in Turkey, he found out that President John F. Kennedy was assassinated. Tension in Turkey escalated after President Kennedy's death because of its close proximity to Russia (it was originally thought by some that Russians were responsible for the assassination after the previous potential escalation of the Cuban Missile Crisis). While he was stationed in Greece, he received a letter from the U.S. government stating he had been inducted into the Army, which would have sent him to Vietnam. Since he was already in the Air Force, he didn't have to adhere to the demands of the letter. It was in the military where he met and married Sue, whose father was also serving in the Air Force.

My dad and Sue had two girls, Sheila and Shanee. My dad's alcoholism and abusive behavior surfaced during his marriage to Sue which had a negative impact on their household. While struggling in their marriage, they moved to Chicago after my dad's term with the Air Force ended in the mid-1960s. Chicago in the early 1960s was thriving with promised manufacturing jobs, which led to a great migration of blacks from southern states, which were bereft of jobs. The job as well as societal and family unrest added to the stress in the LaRue home, which led to more alcohol and physical abuse. Fortunately, my dad was able to find employment with Automatic Electric, where he met and worked with my mom and Aunt Dorothy.

My dad was a very jealous man when he and my mom were together. He often didn't want my mom to talk to other men, even if there was absolutely no way my mom had any interest in them. He frequently accused my mom of having affairs with the men, which was ironic in itself because of the nature of their adulterous relationship. Accusations increased as well as his vitriol towards the accused men as his alcohol usage increased.

My dad was a violent drunk during those times, leading to various assaults directed towards the accused men, my mom, and Sue. Admittedly, he repeated the violent behavior displayed by his father towards his mother. Sue's mental abuse towards him exacerbated his abuse. Whenever he felt unappreciated by his wife, he would often express his anger by lashing out towards Sue, even in front of the girls. Because the girls often witnessed this disturbing behavior, they grew up resenting my dad, not fully understanding the full story.

While abuse should *never* be condoned, I knew of victims that purposely agitated their aggressors to reach a violent point of no return. Unfortunately, during most of their confrontations, the aggressor had no self-control to prevent the inevitable. Instead of walking away from a physical and/or verbal clash, the aggressor's pride prevented them from avoiding an escalating confrontation. If alcohol or other impediments are impairing the abuser's actions, a violent ending is unavoidably created. Unfortunately, my dad used alcohol as his comforter during tumultuous times, which made it impossible to have an amicable resolution.

During the economic downturn of the early '80s, my dad lost his job at Automatic Electric. That, coupled with his struggling marriage, caused his decision to return to Houston to look for employment in the booming oil industry, while Sue and the girls would move to Alabama to be near Sue's family. My dad eventually landed a job at a Goodyear chemical plant. The girls often went back and forth between Alabama and Houston before eventually settling with Sue.

My sisters Sheila and Shanee have both accepted me as their brother. Sheila, the oldest and more outspoken one, accepted me immediately. She told me several times that she always wanted a brother. In many ways, Sheila reminded me of my sister Renee. Both are very outgoing and always go out of their way to make even outsiders feel like family. Shanee and Ronetta are similar in that both have more quiet and reserved personalities in comparison to Sheila and Renee. It took a little longer for Shanee to accept me, but she also appreciated having a brother.

Sheila's oldest son, Pierre, then a budding 6'4" high school sports star in Georgia, was about to graduate and invited me and the family to the ceremony in Georgia. I would finally get the chance to meet my sisters, niece, nephews and Sue. While unpacking the car after arriving at the motel, I heard a familiar voice calling for her brother. As I turned around, I noticed Sheila walking towards me. Instantly, I had a comforting feeling that I was in the presence of family. When I met Shanee, she also welcomed me like a long-lost brother. I was also able to meet my nieces and nephews as well as friends of the family before my anticipated meeting with Sue.

I was nervous before meeting Sue. I didn't know if she'd blame me for the affair between my dad and mom since I was physical proof of the relationship—no one could deny I was Preston's son after meeting me. I didn't want a fight between my dad and Sue to put a damper on Pierre's graduation celebration. I also didn't want Michelle and the kids to feel awkward being around my *new* family because of potential resentment by Sue or the girls.

When I first met Sue that weekend, understandably, she didn't automatically greet me with open arms. However, when she saw my personality and genuine love for my new family, she warmed up and treated me as if I had been in the family my entire life. Sue's reaction allowed me to enjoy the weekend while visually completing the other half of my family tree.

It was only fitting for such a monumental year as 2001 to finish with the birth of our third child and second son, Antonio Cornell Robinson, who was born on December 18. While Michelle and I debate the origins of his name, I believe I insisted on Antonio to pay homage to my favorite childhood rapper, Antonio "Big Daddy Kane" Hardy. Cornell was the middle name of Michelle's deceased mother. Our early Christmas present would present a great opportunity for me and Michelle to continue to improve as parents.

Having two boys and a girl gave us the feeling of having a complete family. However, many family and friends questioned us for having a third child as if we were two reckless adults having sex without thinking of the circumstances. While we were in the hospital after Michelle gave birth to Antonio, we were visited by a close friend who was also a nurse. After I privately asked our friend for advice on my self-analyzed postpartum depression in my spouse, she abruptly led me to the front desk presumably to seek guidance and mental health brochures. To my chagrin and anger she asked the nurses surrounding the reception area for information on contraceptives, not once mentioning my concerns about Michelle's mental state. I was highly offended that she took it upon herself to criticize us for having three young children, not understanding that this was God's plan.

I knew that Michelle and I were being blessed by being able to have children. We also knew that more children were waiting in Heaven for us to conceive. Since Michelle is the oldest of ten and I am the baby of four on my maternal side (with two additional on my paternal), both of us preferred to have a full home. Since I was the youngest of my siblings by almost eight years, I grew up without a close relationship with any of my siblings at an early age. I admired the way the Huxtables from *The Cosby Show* interacted with each other while the parents remained a stabilizing force for their family. I also knew that more children would mean a greater opportunity for me to dedicate my life to providing everything my children would need as well as being the strong male figure in their lives, which I didn't have in mine on a consistent basis.

More kids also meant a greater strain on our financial environment. Our income was greatly reduced after the increased but necessary expenses. I figured the only way to escape this persistent financial crunch was to either make more money or dramatically decrease expenses. Since decreasing expenses would require mutual agreement, I thought I should focus more on increasing our income. I increased my focus at work, delivering on goals and developing innovative solutions. It was during this time that I would finally uncover my career aspirations which would catapult my success and self-assurance that there was a purpose for my existence.

Supplier Diversity

WHILE INTERNALLY DEBATING MY NEXT career move, I was approached by Will, an older black co-worker who would become another early mentor in my career. Will led our supplier diversity program at Abbott, which focused on assisting mostly small companies owned, operated, and controlled by minorities, women and veterans. Will was the only one at Abbott responsible for supplier diversity, so he operated on his own schedule. His office was perfectly positioned near the stairwell, which allowed him to escape whenever his golf tee time was approaching. He had a small television in his office that he'd watch sometimes during the day to keep himself awake. Even though we knew that supplier diversity was important to Abbott, no one really understood its business case as a result of Will having a greater focus on the external joys of the initiative, such as travel, golf outings, magazine articles, and independence in the middle of a corporate setting.

Will had seen me present during an Abbott procurement team meeting. My presentation skills had been developed from an early age while performing in front of crowds, mimicking the moves of Elvis Presley, Michael Jackson, Prince, and New Edition, as well as from my Lake Forest College days on stage as a rapper. I was extremely comfortable in front of crowds and truly saw those moments as a performance. I always had an image during my rap days of leaving the stage with a microphone that was literally on fire because of the lyrics I had just poured into that device. I wanted anyone that heard my words or watched my performance to leave after being completely entertained. My competitive streak pushed me to constantly strive for that perfect performance; the person who made it impossible for anyone following my performance to capture the same level of enthusiasm from the crowd. While I presented, my true personality was displayed in front of my peers and superiors.

As I presented, I clearly remembered the smiles Will sent my way as if he were a proud parent watching his child fly away from the nest. After the meeting, Will asked me to speak with him in his office, where he congratulated me on my presentation. He also informed me that he was going to retire soon and would like me to be his successor to oversee Abbott's supplier diversity program. Like most of the Abbott employees, I wasn't aware of the purpose for our supplier diversity program. After Will explained to me that supplier diversity's overall goal was to bring jobs into the communities, I knew that this would be my life mission.

As a child in Rockwell Gardens, I never saw business owners who resembled me. Most of the business owners were Indians, Middle Easterners, Jewish or Caucasian. The lack of any black business owners intrinsically led me to doubt that it was possible. I didn't think about the countless number of products or services produced that were developed by black-owned business. I didn't think about *Jet* or *Ebony* magazines being written about blacks mostly because they were owned by us also. I didn't think about the historic and iconic run Berry Gordy had at Motown, producing legendary acts and songs while making decisions as a black man in the racially challenging 1960s. It was hard to focus on those external factors while visibly black business owners were nonexistent in my own neighborhood, even though our population was 100 percent black.

My discussion with Will was the single greatest meeting in my professional life. Our discussion led me to pursue a new career that would allow me to impact companies, individuals, and underserved communities that were similar to Rockwell. Supplier diversity could allow me to incorporate various areas of interest such as procurement, marketing, public affairs, legal, sales, operations, finance, and project management. As with any subject that piques my interest, I immediately began to develop a plan. I wrote down current strengths and weaknesses of Abbott's supplier diversity program as well as my plans to improve each area of need. I always enjoyed opportunities to improve processes that were broken, which is how I viewed Abbott's program, though to no fault of Will. I believe Abbott allowed its program to be unsuccessful because the company wasn't yet ready to embrace diversity. Will fought many internal battles but was often discouraged because of the misperception of the value that diversity added to the corporation.

In 2003, Will invited me to attend a national conference held in Chicago for the National Minority Supplier Development Council. At the event, I was able to network with effective supplier diversity professionals and see how other large organizations led successful supplier diversity programs. I wrote copious notes while listening to the presentations regarding this new concept of supplier diversity. As I recaptured the comments made from the presenters, I often incorporated my own thoughts regarding ways to improve Abbott's supplier diversity program. Also, seeing all of the successful minority business owners gave me a tremendous sense of pride.

I was drawn to the camaraderie that was obvious among the supplier diversity community. Everyone seemed as if they were there to help each other, from the supplier diversity professionals to the diverse suppliers to the advocates supporting the movement. I knew that I could be successful in this profession because of my passion to help others and my drive to increase the number of successful minority business owners that could provide inspiration to future generations of kids that grew up in neighborhoods similar to Rockwell.

As I returned to Abbott, it was difficult for me to concentrate on my job as a purchasing agent since I only desired to replace Will. Eagerly, I asked Will several questions about the various departments' interaction with diverse suppliers. I wanted to know who my internal champions would be and who were the ones that I needed to win over. I wanted to understand the areas he would have focused on to improve the program if he were to lead the program beyond his retirement. I needed to know Abbott's true commitment towards supporting the program. I knew I would need to change the perception of the program among the Abbott purchasing agents, because they only thought Will traveled, played golf and occasionally reported our diversity metrics to upper management. While some of the perceptions were accurate, I knew the value I could bring to Abbott's untapped supplier diversity efforts.

While my life was increasing in clarity, a couple of incidents brought me back to the reality that my childhood demons needed to be conquered, or else I could place my Abbott career and my family in jeopardy. I had always been an open person to people that I know in regards to answering questions about my life. My curiosity had also placed me in awkward situations since I often asked questions that may not have been appropriate to ask in corporate America. I wasn't shy to have conversations on forbidden subjects such as religion or sex. The more I knew someone, regardless of their gender, the more likely I would end up having these conversations. It was as if the more that was revealed by both parties the more my curiosity increased.

Abbott was contracted with a supplier for which I managed the relationship. Because of the importance of the relationship between both companies, the partner supplied us with Allison, an on-site representative who was a young blonde. While working with her to manage the account, we got to know each other more. The more we worked together, the deeper our conversations became about education. As I had done with other friends, I successfully convinced Allison to obtain her MBA. We also talked about our families. She was married with no kids while I often talked about my family situation, even discussing my struggles with Michelle.

The more we got to know each other, the more inappropriate the conversations became. One evening after work, Allison offered to drive me to a work function at a nearby restaurant. At that time, Michelle and I only had one vehicle since I mostly walked to work. During the ride to the restaurant our conversation awkwardly shifted to our mutual sex lives with our spouses. We both asked specific questions about the intimacy with our spouses. Although she was as engaged in the conversation as I was, we both knew we were playing with fire. Being in the car alone with her was inappropriate in itself, regardless of what was being discussed inside. We arrived at the event and proceeded to enjoy our night with coworkers and friends. She then dropped me off at home with no additional inappropriate sexual conversations.

A few weeks after the event, I received a call from a man who introduced himself as the chief human resource officer of Allison's company. He informed me that she proactively contacted him to talk about the inappropriate conversation she and I had in the car. She informed him that the conversation made her feel awkward and intimidated since I was a very important customer. I was shocked to hear about her feelings regarding the conversation since it was mutually engaging. I felt betrayed because I thought our relationship was open enough that she would have approached me about her feelings without having to report it to her leaders.

I knew then that I needed to discuss the situation with Sarah before it became an even greater concern for Abbott. Ironically, we were in the middle of renegotiating our contract with Allison's company. I pondered if this was an intimidation tactic they were employing to influence me to give them favorable terms on their contract. Nonetheless, I voluntarily placed myself in the wrong place at the wrong time. As I discussed the situation with Sarah, her disappointment in me was strongly felt. However, her support for me was unwavering. She offered to have a conversation with the HR chief so that we could avoid any potential liabilities. This was my first lesson about the politics of corporate America. It was also my wakeup call about the consequences of inappropriate conversations with the opposite sex.

The incident was resolved simply through a conversation between Sarah and the HR chief. However, escaping without penalty unfortunately provided me with a false sense of security that I could continue having inappropriate conversations. On another occasion, I was invited to lunch by another female on-site representative whom I will call Mary. On our way to the restaurant, Mary asked how Michelle and I were doing in our relationship. As I proceeded to tell her about our struggles, again I found myself talking about our sexual relationship as well as asking about hers with her fiancé. We openly provided great detail without any obvious sense of awkward feelings. Even though my previous incident was still in the back of my mind, I allowed myself to push the boundaries further by detailing the intimacy of my relationship which shouldn't have been discussed with anyone outside of my home.

As we entered the Abbott parking lot after returning from lunch, Mary invited me to her nearby home for future lunch dates. Since neither of us seemed awkward, I felt more confident that this conversation would be without consequences. Unfortunately, she arrived at my desk in tears an hour after our return, asking if I was contacted by my HR staff. She consistently apologized before finally admitting that she had a casual conversation about our lunch discussion with a female Abbott employee. The employee felt so uncomfortable that an Abbott employee would have such an inappropriate conversation with a supplier that she approached her supervisor to complain, even though Mary was completely comfortable with our lunch conversation. Her supervisor then contacted HR, who urgently invited me to a meeting.

At the meeting, I was given a formal Abbott letter that accused me of sexual harassment, not only with Mary but Allison as well. As I read the letter, it was clear that Abbott was trying to establish a pattern of harassment and inappropriate behavior, preparing for a way to eventually release me. The letter stated that another incident would be grounds for immediate termination. I refused to show Michelle the letter or talk about either situation, knowing that she wouldn't believe that I did not harass either woman. However, Michelle discovered the letter while cleaning the house. Our tense conversation centered on her disappointment that I was not being a righteous member of the church, which I truly agreed with. I was not being a good example by discussing sacred items about our intimacy with a member of the opposite sex. Even though I had no desire to further either relationship sexually, I made a significant error of judgment by having those inappropriate conversations.

I often questioned why I placed myself in both situations with Mary and Allison. I wondered why was I willing to push the boundaries without going completely across through a physical sexual encounter with either woman. As I'm sure is the case with many who engage in physical and/or emotional affairs, I believe I was seeking to fill in the gaps of the holes developed in my relationship with Michelle. Both women listened to me in ways I didn't believe Michelle did. Another reason I believe I didn't go all the way with either woman is that I worried about the consequences of not having the church in my life as a result from a discovered affair. And ultimately, neither woman necessarily expressed a desire to take our friendship further outside of an occasional flirt or Mary's invitation to watch games at her home.

Instead of receiving professional counseling during this time to deal with my pornography addiction and marital challenges, I allowed my behavior to continue to spiral in the opposite way of a successful marriage. I had no one in my family to seek guidance from because of my family's marital history, and I didn't feel comfortable discussing this with anyone from the church for fear of the consequences. I thought I could handle the situation alone because no one was getting hurt. I fooled myself into thinking that since it was harmless chatter with no physical engagements with either of the females, I had everything under control.

Without the church in my life, I would not have seen these two examples as forms of infidelity. Affairs don't necessarily have to be physical: lusting for another is an affair of the heart. Each time I viewed pornography was a commitment of adultery. It took a while for me to finally see that my marriage struggles were impacted by my refusal to believe the seriousness of my addiction. Each time I flirted with a physical or emotional affair, I was a step closer to not only being shackled by the immoral decisions made but a loss of membership in the church and the loss of the family Michelle and I worked so hard to build.

I fooled myself into thinking that my addiction was different than my siblings'. As I often chastised my siblings for their struggles, I ignored my own. Just as my siblings thought they were hiding their addictions from me and the rest of the family, I erroneously assumed Michelle wasn't aware of mine. I also incorrectly believed that she was ignoring my struggles because of a desire to keep the family together. As with any addiction, I was allowing my struggles to worsen because of my pride, which caused me to downplay the seriousness of my situation.

During this time, Abbott had divested itself of its hospital products division, which is called Hospira today. The new company needed to establish its own purchasing department, so individuals from Abbott's purchasing team were assigned to Hospira. I was surprised to find out that I was selected to go to the new company. I believe I was selected mostly because of the recent harassment claims. However, as with most negative situations, I looked positively at going to the new company to leave behind the blemishes on my Abbott record and hoped to establish Hospira's supplier diversity program.

I was told before moving to Hospira that I was going to be responsible mostly for supplier diversity, with only a small percentage of my time used to assist with purchasing agreements. After arriving at the new company,

I realized that the majority of my time would be spent on negotiating purchasing agreements instead of establishing the supplier diversity program, which had quickly developed into my passion. Also creating an obstacle for my Hospira success was Pat, a director who often displayed racist and chauvinistic behavior with rough managerial skills.

Pat had an old school, good-ole-boy style when managing his department. He refused to show any confidence in the abilities of his subordinates by not allowing any of us to apply for open managerial positions. In a one-on-one meeting with him, he boldly told me that he didn't see me as a manager, even though my MBA education provided me with the skills to lead. In a staff meeting, he ignorantly made disparaging remarks directed towards women, even though there were women present.

I knew that I had to leave Hospira in order to succeed in supplier diversity. Diversity in general didn't seem to generate much interest among the senior leaders for the new company. The combination of the lack of diversity commitment and my boss could quickly lead me to the unemployment line. I became depressed during this period, often arriving in the Hospira parking in the morning afraid to leave the car. I felt as if my career was back to the stalemate position similar to my years at the Forest Preserve. Each day added to my stress level and anger. Seeing our director on a daily basis exacerbated my negativity towards Hospira. In order for me to regain my mental health, I knew that I had to leave the company.

After an evening church meeting, I was prompted to have a conversation with Ron Labrum about opportunities at his employer, Cardinal Health. Ron was a senior executive at Cardinal and often assisted members of the church with finding employment at the company. In the past, I resisted asking Ron for assistance, wanting to achieve success on my own. However, I quickly realized that in order to achieve success, it would be vital to seek help.

During our conversation, Ron asked about my area of focus for Cardinal. Initially, my thoughts geared around procurement, but I was prompted to mention supplier diversity. Fortunately, there was a supplier diversity director position open for which interviews were being conducted. Ron provided me contact information for Kathy, who was the hiring manager for the position. As a vice president, Kathy led the supplier diversity team for Cardinal. She was Caucasian, middle-aged and often brutally honest. Before meeting with Kathy, I knew that I had to overly prepare for the position because of its importance to my career. I wanted Kathy to see that I could earn the job without Ron's influence. I prepared pages of questions while conducting extensive research on Cardinal and supplier diversity.

My interview with Kathy went very well. As she drilled me with questions about supplier diversity, she became very impressed with my responses. She could tell that supplier diversity wasn't just a job for me; it was a lifestyle that I would eternally pursue. Preparing for the interview also allowed me to tap into my strategic thinking that went unused during my Abbott and Hospira years. I prayed every night for the job, knowing that it could be the career breakthrough I needed. The job had the desired level, a salary range beneficial to support our growing family, travel to expand my world, and prestige to give me great exposure. I had to have this job!

While sitting at my Hospira desk, I received a phone call from Kathy. She stated that she was very impressed with me and would like to make an offer to work at Cardinal. Trying to control my emotions, I excitedly accepted. After the call with Kathy, I called my mom to let her know that her son's career was finally heading in the right direction. All of those sacrificed years during high school, college and my master's program would finally show rewards. After the call with my mom, I happily approached Pat. I told him that although I also didn't see myself as a manager of a $4 billion company (Hospira), a $100 billion company (Cardinal) saw me as a director. His smirk and reddish complexion validated my gratifying feeling that others would now see the value I knew was inside of me.

Before starting with Cardinal, I agreed to allow my nephew LaMonte to move in with us. LaMonte needed guidance from a positive male role model as well as a change of scenery from the West Side of Chicago. I strongly believed that giving him a chance to see a different way of life would compel him to change his own. On my first day at Cardinal, I received a phone call that changed my mentality: my nephew was detained for shoplifting at a nearby clothing store. I was now conflicted; should I continue to be my nephew's mentor, or should I send him back to his old environment to maintain peace within my home?

I made a hasty and difficult decision to send my nephew back to his unstable habitat. LaMonte's brief stay with us added stress to an already suffering marriage. I knew I had to make a choice between my nephew and family, and obviously the family was going to come first. However, I felt guilty that I failed him as a positive role model. I believed I let him down in the same way the older men in my life let me down as a kid. I wanted to see him succeed, but the more I debated my decision the more I felt as if I was involved in an experiment like Randolph and Mortimer Duke in the movie *Trading Places*. Was it possible to change someone's approach towards life by simply removing them from their neighborhood? Is this what happened with me? The only difference between me and my nephew at that time was that I *wanted* to change. I knew the consequences if I didn't change my environment, whereas my nephew was completely comfortable in that situation. Finally I convinced myself that the only way I could help change someone's life is for them to *want* that change as well. A person would need to have their own strategic plan and see my assistance only as an element of their change process, not a panacea for a successful life.

While overcoming the guilt from sending LaMonte back home, I was finally starting to see a clear path towards success in supplier diversity at Cardinal Health. Kathy gave me the flexibility to develop innovative ways of improving our supplier diversity program. My peer, Martha, was like a big sister who provided great career advice, spiritual guidance, and moral support. Martha had a comforting approach with those she loved. She would caution me when she thought I was moving too fast, which allowed me to strategically plan through the innovative ideas I enjoyed developing. Kathy's ability to persuade others to believe in supplier diversity had a great impression on me. The way she was able to *sell* diversity was the style I followed the rest of my career.

Because of my flexibility, I was able to expand my job into areas that impacted sales, marketing, procurement, operations, public affairs, and legal. I often traveled with the sales team to present to prospective and current customers, which were mostly hospitals and academic medical centers. Kathy and Martha's supportive words provided me with the confidence needed to be successful. I traveled often to team up with sales, attend conferences, or meet with customers or suppliers. The job provided great challenges and I was able to learn more about the healthcare supply chain. Another tremendous element of the job was the ability I'd have to give more presentations.

My role at Cardinal allowed me to have occasional speaking engagements that were high profile. One night in particular took place at the Chicago Theater for an organization called In Search of Genius. I was asked to represent Cardinal and allowed to invite others to the event, for which I asked Michelle and my mom to be my guests. The theater was packed as the various speakers lined to provide their brief speeches about the importance of providing educational opportunities to youth in underserved communities in the areas of science and engineering.

As we got closer to my turn, I looked around the theater and realized this was the same place I sat in to watch movies as a poor kid from the projects. This was also the same theater that witnessed iconic performers such as Michael Jackson, Marvin Gaye, James Brown, and others. I was excited that my mom and Michelle would be able to share this special night with me, but I'm sure neither fully understood what I was thinking at that moment.

On stage, I made sure to let everyone know that I was a product of the Chicago Public Schools system and a former resident of the Rockwell housing projects. I thought it was important to mention this in case there was another child in the audience that was in a similar situation and needed to hear that one drop of hope that anything is possible. I also mentioned my mom during my speech, acknowledging the hard work and dedication she had by raising me to have the mentality that even though I lived in the projects, my life would not end there.

My mom was finding her own epiphanies during this time. She had allowed my sisters, their children, and sometimes boyfriends move into her apartment above Aunt Sam on Ridgeway Avenue in Chicago. As she left for work each day, she had to step over sleeping adults who weren't proactively supporting their stay either financially or by doing chores around the house. My sisters were deep into their drug addictions, which led them to steal from others, including their own mother. My mom locked her bedroom door at all times to prevent thefts, even when getting up in the middle of the night to use the bathroom. The stress from seeing her daughters struggle with their addictions and realizing she was supporting a house full of non-working adults consumed her on a daily basis. Her stress level was so high that her minister warned that the situation would kill her if she didn't leave it soon.

Even though Ronetta was under the same roof as her kids, my mom was the one who continued to raise them. Renee struggled to parent Germaine, who was being bounced from relative to relative, searching for stability. She often hung out with Jerry, a paraplegic addict who also sold drugs, and other non-positive friends from the Ridgeway neighborhood. One night while hanging with Jerry outside, they were robbed at gunpoint for their drugs and money. When Jerry saw the robbers pull out their guns, he shot and fatally wounded one of them while the other shot Renee in the hand and another female nearby in the stomach. Renee fell while bleeding from the wound and immediately pretended to act as if she was dead, praying that the gunman wouldn't shoot additionally to ensure she was deceased. Fortunately, the gunman walked over Renee while running from the scene.

As Renee recovered from her wounds, my mom realized she needed to adhere to her minister's advice. She couldn't handle the emotional and financial tolls that drained her while living in that Ridgeway apartment. My mom decided to move into a senior citizens' home on Damen Avenue near downtown without any warning to Aunt Sam, who owned the building, or her children and grandchildren inside her home. She decided to leave behind not only the residents but also the furniture. She didn't want any remembrance of her life's struggles, which included her children and past relationships. My mom knew it would be hard to leave her children behind, but she knew it would be the only way for them to learn how to survive. Her unwavering love for them had turned into a crutch that prevented them from wanting to change their lifestyles. Leaving them became not just a desire but a necessity for everyone.

My mom moved in to her new apartment without any furniture. She slept on the floor for the first two weeks, excited to finally be free. Her best friend Lottie purchased a microwave for her while providing emotional support during this time. Mom and Lottie have always supported each other during tumultuous periods in both of their lives. Their unbreakable bond is a story in itself of a key element to survival. As much as my siblings' struggles emanated from being around the wrong people, my mom's friendship with Lottie was sometimes the only beacon of hope during their dark journeys.

As my mom was enjoying her newfound freedom, I continued to find success in my role at Cardinal. Kathy was very effective in grooming me to be a leader. She seemed to always find ways to allow me to represent Cardinal in front of the right audience. The more I represented our group, the more confidence I gained, which increased the amount of success I achieved. One of the greatest challenges she gave me came in the form of Mr. Corris Boyd. Corris led the supplier diversity program for one of our biggest customers, the HealthTrust Purchasing Group (HPG). Kathy thought it would be more effective for our team if I was the one responsible for building the relationship with him.

We invited Corris to be our keynote speaker at a supplier diversity conference we held near our Cardinal headquarters in Dublin, Ohio. My first time meeting him came after picking him up from the airport to drive him to the hotel. Before my meeting with Corris, I was given many warnings from our team that he enjoyed his reputation as an intimidating force. However, one of the benefits of growing up in violent Rockwell was that it was impossible for me to be intimidated by another man. Corris was a short, muscular black man from Louisiana. He had a heavy southern drawl and wasn't afraid to say "We are all about *bidness*" in front of the mostly white executives from the companies supporting HPG.

I was determined to find that common ground with Corris in order to impress him. As we were in the car, I could tell Corris was trying to test me out by asking me questions about Kathy and others from Cardinal. I continued to provide generic answers while trying to find out more about him. This chess match continued until we arrived at the hotel where the conference was held. Corris did a great job articulating his vision of supplier diversity as well as his passion for helping others. I knew that our mutual passion for helping others would be the common ground I sought.

After our conference, I was able to connect more with Corris. He was able to see my genuine passion for supplier diversity. Corris provided me with great advice, mostly regarding ways to involve Cardinal's top executives in meetings about supplier diversity. Since Ron was the one responsible for bringing me to Cardinal, I thought he would be the perfect person to assist with this request. I arranged a meeting between Corris, Ron, Kathy, and representatives from Kerma Medical Products, a minority-owned manufacturer based out of Virginia. One of the representatives from Kerma was Earl Reubel, an older black man with a resounding deep voice, who instantly demanded respect from others because of his intelligence and innovative ways to find opportunities for minority businesses. Earl eventually became one of my important mentors and a father figure. The meeting was successful and improved Corris's perception of Cardinal's support of supplier diversity, which wasn't a small task.

As we continued to build success between Cardinal and HPG, my world was rocked after receiving news that Corris was diagnosed with leukemia. How could a perfectly, healthy-looking man be stricken with such a dreaded disease? The news affected me in many ways. I knew that as a black male I needed to be more conscious of my health, because we had a shorter life span than most ethnic groups. I was also disappointed that another male mentor and role model would potentially leave this earth. Not having a father in my life forced me to search for others that could fill the needed gaps. Will, my Abbott mentor, had passed away around this time from cancer, and now Corris could potentially have the same fate.

While Corris was battling his disease, I reached out to let him know that my family was praying for him. During the call he gave me a compliment on how impressed he was with our success at Cardinal. He also gave me a personal compliment regarding my passion to genuinely support diverse businesses. Since Corris didn't provide many compliments, hearing those words from him had great meaning, especially since I knew he was in the middle of an extremely serious fight for his life. Unfortunately, shortly after our call I was informed that he had passed away at the tender age of 45. I attended his funeral and couldn't stop sobbing after thinking about what he meant to my life.

Although others viewed him as unnecessarily difficult, my relationship with Corris was different. He forced me to reach deep inside to think differently than other supplier diversity professionals to develop solutions that weren't status quo. He taught me that in order to build trust among the diverse suppliers, I had to always show my true passion to assist. Unfortunately, many supplier diversity professionals have an arrogance that gives them a God-complex—that they control the success of the diverse businesses striving to get connected with their companies. Because of this, I don't often congregate with other supplier diversity professionals unless I know they share the same passion to help.

At Corris's funeral, the saddest moment was watching his young son and only child walk alone to his casket. It was hard for me to imagine what was going on inside of his son's head at the moment, seeing his father's body resting in the wooden box. Watching this scene led me to take the torch that Corris held so boldly to support companies that are at a societal disadvantage. I would then have to teach the future supplier diversity leaders the winning formula taught to me by Corris and Will: allow passion to influence internal and external constituents to support diverse businesses while focusing on educating diverse businesses, making them stronger and more viable companies. As I strived for success, I knew it was vital for me to have others from which I could seek advice. Life is cruel at times and we sometimes don't understand why horrible events happen to good people, but our faith is what keeps us grounded.

Transition

My success at Cardinal was starting to get noticed by others outside of HPG. For the first time, Cardinal won an award for our diversity efforts from one of our top customers, Premier. Our team was featured in various diversity-focused magazines. I had a great opportunity to provide a quote for an article in the *Wall Street Journal*, which was an amazing accomplishment. Excitedly, I informed my mom and Bob about the quote. Bob immediately went around Waukegan trying to purchase every copy he saw of the *Wall Street Journal*. My mom proudly told her friends about her son being featured in the iconic newspaper. Kathy also realized that her student was quickly learning and needed to oversee a program of his own soon.

During this time, executives at Cardinal decided to transition more than 700 jobs from our Illinois facilities to the headquarters in Dublin. I knew that many of the friends I made at Cardinal wouldn't follow the transition. I also knew Kathy wouldn't be interested in leaving Chicago for Ohio, which would give me an opportunity to lead my first team. Another key figure who wouldn't make the move was Ron. While Ron was reluctantly prepared to move to Ohio, he had recently become a stake president in our Buffalo Grove, Illinois, region for the church. A stake is made up of various wards, which are typically the individual church buildings of worship. In order for Ron to accept his new calling, he would have to remain in Illinois. While many outside of the church couldn't understand why he would turn down this very important job transition, Ron clearly displayed his strong faith by accepting the church leaders' invitation to stay in Illinois and lead the stake.

I grappled with my decision of whether or not I should leave Illinois. I had never relocated for a job and never lived in another state as an adult.

However, I was excited about the potential chance to lead Cardinal's supplier diversity program. I knew that I was ready to lead after receiving knowledge from Kathy, Corris, and Will. My family wasn't as excited about the potential move, since it would create a disruption in their lives. However, the thought of not having a job wasn't an option since we weren't yet stable financially.

While going through the Cardinal transition, I was approached by VHA, a healthcare alliance in the Dallas, Texas, area, regarding a position to create their supplier diversity program. The job had tremendous appeal to me, knowing that my Dad was in Houston, and I could have the chance to lead and create a brand-new program. I knew that in order to take my career to the next step, it was time for me to lead. And my creative spirit was very excited about developing a new program that would always have my impact on it forever. After flying down to interview with VHA, it was obvious to me that Dallas was an area where I could see our family grow in many ways. I was also excited about living closer to my dad, which could help us to build the relationship we never had a chance to build over the previous three decades. Shortly after interviewing with VHA, I was offered the position. Unfortunately, Cardinal's decision wasn't made yet regarding their choice to lead their program. I informed VHA that I wanted to wait until I received the Cardinal decision, which would eventually happen after several weeks.

Although I thought it was impossible for Cardinal to choose someone else to lead their program since I had been an important driver of our success, I was shocked to hear otherwise. Cardinal hired a leader based in Columbus then offered me the opportunity to join her team in my same role. Cardinal's decision didn't appeal to me for various reasons, one being I would basically be responsible for training my future boss on how to do her job successfully while using the formula taught to me by my mentors. My dilemma was now forcing me to make a decision based on the following options: accept Cardinal's offer to relocate for the same job I was doing while training my boss to do her job; stay in Chicago without a job and hope the three-month severance Cardinal offered would last during my job search; or, accept the VHA offer and start building a new life for my family while creating a program from the ground up.

The positive side of me allowed me to see that the VHA position offered many more benefits than Cardinal: I would be able to see my father more; I would finally get the chance to lead my own supplier diversity team; and, I would be able to create a supplier diversity program with all of the facets I knew would lead to success. Another appeal of Texas was that the housing market was better in Dallas than in most major U.S. cities. Most Fortune 1000 companies were located in Texas. There is no state income tax in Texas. The relocation could potentially improve our family relationship. It took VHA to remind me who had the greater interest in my potential, and since it clearly wasn't my current employer I decided to make it official: I was going to accept VHA's offer and, for the first time, relocate my family to Texas!

During my house hunting visits I quickly realized the difference between Texas and Illinois. We could get three times the space for the same amount, which would be a necessity for our growing family. During the VHA courting process, Michelle and I delivered our fourth child and second daughter, Payton LaRue. The name Payton was homage paid to our favorite Chicago athlete, Walter Payton. LaRue was a tribute to my dad's last name. Payton was born on September 17 and balanced our family now with two boys and two girls. As a joke, the VHA team sent us a Dallas Cowboys bib and pacifier (which were never opened). Payton was an identical version of Jacqui but without the dimples. She had hazel eyes, which was a first for our children.

The timing of Payton coming into our family was perfect. Michelle and I had been struggling, especially because of the stress from the job change and the move to Texas, as well as my own internal demons resurfacing. We were at a crossroads with our relationship and it wasn't a guarantee that Michelle would ever make it to Texas. As the breadwinner of the family, I knew that I had to choose the best option, even if it wasn't the most popular one. I also knew that if Michelle decided against joining me in Texas, we would have to make an important decision that could impact the rest of our family for the rest of their lives.

For my first two months in Texas, VHA allowed me to travel back and forth to Illinois. During my home search, I physically looked at over twenty homes before settling on a 4,000 square foot house in Frisco, one of the fastest growing suburbs in the U.S. To go from a 1,200-square-foot townhome for a family of six to more space was a welcome change. I felt that I had finally achieved the American Dream I'd been seeking since attending the Lower Merion ABC program. We could place my entire Rockwell apartment inside my Texas living room. The house had a media room that would allow me to enjoy one of my favorite childhood hobbies, watching movies. On separate occasions, I was able to complete my media room by purchasing a 130-inch projector screen, a surround-sound speaker system, an HD projector, a Blu-ray PlayStation 3 console and a six-ounce popcorn machine. I envisioned many family movie nights inside that media room, hopefully drawing our family closer. The home had a see-through fireplace that could be turned on by a switch, and a spacious kitchen that had granite countertops with an impressive island in the middle. There were three showers, which were a necessity for a family of six. The home had a beautiful spiral staircase that made me dream of Christmas mornings with the kids leaving their bedrooms to see the stack of presents under the tree at the foot of the stairs.

The home also allowed me to live my life vicariously through my kids. I'd be able to provide them with a life I could only dream of when I was their age. Fortunately, they would never understand the struggles I had as a kid. I wanted them to get the very best education without worrying about having to leave home or the environment around their home. Their lives would already start out ahead of mine but with an expectation that they'd work harder for even greater success. I also knew that it would be a struggle to find a balance between providing for their every need while at the same time trying to instill a work ethic that would constantly push them to do their best. I believe it's impossible for them to have the same level of hunger I have, since they didn't grow up in similar dire situations. However, they could still have a great need to fulfill their dreams.

While I got caught up in the euphoria of the new home and job, it was difficult to convince Michelle to move. Since we had been dealing with our own emotional and marital challenges, she was unsure if she wanted to take the chance to move to an unknown area only to be left alone if I decided to get a divorce. Unfortunately, this caused even greater stress between us. It was difficult to be alone while trying to build a successful program at VHA. I found myself constantly making excuses for why my family hadn't joined me yet in Texas. Since all of our furniture was still in our Illinois home, the empty house was often embarrassing to display when others came to visit.

Going back to visit the family in Illinois was very difficult. While I enjoyed the space and modern luxuries of our Texas home, I was quickly grounded when seeing the living environment for my kids in Illinois. Shortly after purchasing my Texas home, Michelle independently decided to conduct an extensive remodel project for our townhome. Almost simultaneously, she ripped up the bathrooms, kitchen and living room. Her goal was to remodel everything herself, even though she had no previous training in remodeling. I would often visit and find the family eating their dinners out of a toaster oven, which was extremely painful to endure.

As I was enjoying everything in Texas, my children were struggling with life in Illinois. The looks of despair in their eyes were hard to accept each time I had to leave. I knew that the harder I tried to force a move, the harder Michelle would combat my attempts because of her strong-willed personality. I knew that I had to be extremely patient and pray that my plan would eventually fall into place. However, this wasn't going to be an easy process. For the first time in my life, I felt completely helpless and guilty that I wasn't providing my children with the life I wanted them to have at that point. I felt like a failure. Even though I was exactly where I needed to be in my career, my personal life regressed. I knew that I had to get my kids into our new home as soon as possible in order to maintain my sanity.

A key benefit of managing my lonely living situation was that I was able to focus on building a successful supplier diversity program at VHA. Because of my early success, I was promoted in February 2009 to Senior Director of Supplier Diversity, overseeing the efforts of VHA, Novation (the contracting company for VHA), UHC (Novation's parent company), and Provista (Novation's sister company). I was able to prove to everyone, including myself, that I could successfully lead a program. My success brought great publicity to Novation, which was enjoyed by the employees, especially the senior leaders. My credibility in the industry also increased significantly in a short period of time.

Transition

Shortly after starting my Novation career, Barack Obama was elected as the first black president of the United States of America. Witnessing Obama's inauguration brought great pride to me as an African-American male. Often, black males are given the smallest chance among most groups to succeed. Unfortunately, we are the ones mostly creating the lack of confidence in our success because of our impact on murder rates, jail occupancy, gang lives, fatherless kids and drug-related crimes. Because of our negative impact, typically there aren't a lot of positive black male role models to lend emotional support to the future generation of black males, which perpetuates a cyclical process.

Witnessing Obama become president gave me the confidence in myself to continue to shoot for greatness. I studied his approach as a leader and orator as I sought to establish my own brand at Novation. Regardless of his political party, he is a polarizing authority with a tremendous ability to conjure passion, whether positive or negative.

Another area of influence Obama had on me was the ability to develop a strategic plan. As I watched the inauguration, I strategized on ways to build a successful supplier diversity program at Novation. My plan involved short- and long-term goals, identified all key constituents, defined ways to market the success for the program, established timelines for each goal and the desired outcome after implementing all objectives. The Novation opportunity provided me with my first chance to become the leader I knew I could be, even though others at the Forest Preserve, Abbott, Hospira, and Cardinal never wanted to give me the chance. I saw the greatness within me and I knew that the Novation opportunity would be the conduit to fulfilling those achievements.

As I continued with my achievements at Novation, my sons decided on their own to move down to Texas to live with me. While I was extremely excited that I'd be joined by my sons, I worried about the level of caregiving I'd be able to provide to them with my busy travel schedule. While lamenting to my mom about my situation, she demanded me to stop feeling sorry for myself since she was able to succeed as a single parent herself. I didn't receive the verbal support from her that I sought. Instead, she gave me the confidence that I could juggle my career and parental responsibilities because of my mental strength, which had been growing since living in

Rockwell. Also, members of the church volunteered to watch my boys while I traveled, which gave me even greater confidence.

Having my sons in Texas allowed me to grow as a father. We spent a lot of time with each other in and out of the house. I saw their happiness and confidence increase because they were both great students and were able to make friends in Frisco. Since the weather in Texas is better year-round versus Illinois, they spent a lot of time outside playing with friends. Although it was difficult juggling my work/life balance, it was well worth it. I also realized that, if needed, I could be a successful single parent like my mom while maintaining a promising career. I was also able to enjoy the pleasure of cooking again, knowing it was essential and more economically feasible for us to eat at home rather than enjoying fast food restaurants.

During many periods of duress, I was often able to flash back to moments of my mom handling all of her responsibilities not with complaints but instead with a joy that is usually reserved for the faces of mothers. My strength and support from friends eased my chaotic living situation. As much as I was excited to have my boys in Texas, I still worried about my daughters back in Illinois and wanted them to also join us soon.

While fatherhood became more relevant in my life, my brother was enjoying his freedom. He had been released from prison earlier in the year and was able to finally experience life. He often explored Chicago in ways he was never able to as a youth or an inmate. He enjoyed a solid romantic relationship and spent a lot of time with my mom and sisters. He also called me occasionally to tell me how proud he was of me. Finally he understood why I made the sacrifice to leave home to pursue a greater level of education. June was a definitely a different and happier person from whom I remembered. I hoped and prayed this newfound happiness would be permanent. However, as I've learned throughout my life, good things don't always last.

November 5, 2009, was an unforgettable day. I celebrated my two-year anniversary at VHA/Novation while leading our biannual meeting with our supplier diversity advisory group. I always enjoyed the strategic discussions regarding our program and the opportunities to brainstorm future innovations with the group, which consisted of supplier diversity leaders for some of the largest healthcare systems and academic medical centers in the country. As always, the first evening was spent entertaining the group at a dinner. While were enjoying our dinner, I received a phone call from my mom. I ignored the call, thinking she was merely seeing how I was doing since I hadn't called her recently.

As the evening continued, I received a text from my cousin James ordering me to "call ASAP!" I then knew that my mom's call wasn't typical and that I had to connect with my family immediately. After asking to be excused from the dinner, I returned James's call. I knew something serious had happened after he asked if I was sitting. Since I knew at that time harm had fallen onto one of my family members, I demanded for James to tell me which one of my siblings was hurt without caring about what caused the harm. James then informed me that my *only* brother, June, was found dead that day while alone in his girlfriend's bed. The news was totally devastating and sent me to my knees. The pain in my heart was severe and one I hadn't realized after any of the previous deaths in the family. My only brother would not live to see another day and we wouldn't get the chance to build on the brotherly relationship we've always wanted but couldn't because of our own divergent paths.

Rumors started immediately about reasons for June's death. Not knowing the reason for June's death added to my pain. I was told that he had a deadly asthma attack. I also heard rumors that he died from being suffocated by the boyfriends of his girlfriend's daughters, whom he frequently feuded with. Another rumor was that he overdosed from drugs, which isn't something I could ever believe since I had never seen drugs as his vice. Actually, he often threatened my sisters to stop using drugs, or threatened their friends who made the drugs accessible. My mom noticed a gash in the back of his head when she went to view his body. He had always told Mom that if something ever happened to him, she would need to investigate because someone would have to attack him from behind instead of head-on. Regardless of the actual reason, the fact remained that my brother was dead.

I received assistance to regain my composure from three of my advisory group friends in order to drive home. During the ride, I tried hard to convince myself that I was living a bad dream and would soon awaken to find my brother still alive. After unsuccessfully convincing myself, I then worked on preparing to tell my sons and the rest of my family. My emotions fluctuated from feeling the pain of my loss to being angry that life cheated my brother from enjoying more of his earned freedom. I also felt cheated that I was not able to get to know him since he had been in and out of prison while I was very young, and his last year of freedom occurred after I had already moved to Texas. I thought for sure news of June's death would force Michelle to move to Texas as she knew I needed support during this difficult time in my life. Unfortunately, my assumptions were incorrect regarding her relocation, which added to our difficulties.

My brother's death was also a reminder of choices. The church teaches us that we all have free agency to choose our paths: for some of us, our paths are scarred with consistently bad choices, while others are able to lead lives closer to the purity we all wish to achieve. June's path was marred with struggles that mostly developed from the violent environment of Rockwell. Because of his violent life and the drug-infested ones of my sisters, I knew that my life wouldn't involve either choice. However, I was fooling myself to think my path was unscathed. Instead of violence or drugs, my path was negatively impacted by sex.

I strongly believe that we are all born with addictive behavior and spend the rest of our lives not knowing the things we are addicted to or working hard to temper those addictions. I also believe, fortunately, that we can overcome our addictions by not fooling ourselves into believing that we can heal ourselves. We have to maintain faith that God can help us overcome any obstacles while understanding the humbling reality that once an addict is always an addict.

I spent the week after June's death at home in seclusion. I didn't want to speak to anyone because I would frequently be reminded of the pain shortly into the conversation. As many family and friends called to see if I was feeling better, internally I wished I could be left alone. I kept thinking about the lost times with June and all of the things I wanted to do with my brother once he was a free man. I yearned to travel with him, to show him the world I was starting to explore. I wanted to show him my basketball skills since we often challenged each other to games while he was in prison. I wanted to take him to exquisite restaurants and other places that his lack of freedom deprived him of visiting. June had a full life ahead of him out of which he was cheated. All of us were cheated out of seeing his true potential as someone who didn't want the violent life anymore. He was my only brother and one that saw *me* as the older, more mature one. His spirit will forever push me towards greatness and I will miss hearing his encouraging words every day of my life.

Returning to Chicago for June's funeral was difficult. I knew the moment I saw my mom it would be extremely emotional for both of us since I was now her only son. It would also be emotional for my sisters because I was now their only brother. However, in a twisted way, I didn't think they were feeling the same pain I was feeling because my sisters *still* had a brother and my mom *still* had a son. I didn't have a brother anymore. I became very selfish with my grieving while trying to console my mom and sisters.

As we gathered in the family car to attend the funeral, the silence was deafening. I'm sure we were all going through our own memories of June. I'm also sure we were reflecting on our own lives since this was the first funeral that directly impacted our immediate family. June's death also brought all of us back to the way it mostly was in the home that I knew: my mom, sisters, and me. We had a tightly knit family and knew that we had to stick together in order to overcome the many challenges in our lives. Now, more than ever, we needed to rekindle that bond.

After pulling up to the front of the church we immediately saw the impact June had not only on our lives but on the lives of others. The amount of love shown to us was unforgettable. We composed ourselves inside the car to prepare for the emotional day. I worried a lot about my already emotional mom, not knowing if she could handle seeing her son lying in the casket. No parent should ever have to go through the tragedy of losing a child. My mom probably had feelings of guilt for June's life of crime for various reasons, but she should have been assured that we all have free agency.

Regardless of our choices in life, we all had a tremendous unconditional love for our mom because we all knew she would do anything for us. This is also the reason that it will always be difficult for anyone else, except for my children, to come between me and my mom. I have seen her struggle just to make a better life for her children. I have seen her shed tears alone just to keep her pain away from us. The amount of love I will always have for her will never be duplicated. Regardless of the love for a spouse, there is a special love for my mom that I will always treasure because of her sacrifices and the pain associated with her love for me and my siblings that no one else could ever know or understand.

When it was time to exit the car, we all hugged each other tightly. We knew that we needed to support each other for this emotional day. Renee and Ronetta went ahead of my mom and me. I hugged my mom tightly as we made our way up the stairs of the church and inside the chapel. I don't remember seeing any faces as I struggled mightily to keep my outward emotions at a minimum. I thought that my mom needed *my* strength, but as I neared closer to seeing my brother's body lying motionless in the casket the more I knew that I needed *hers*. Even as I write this section of the book I struggle with my composure while vividly recollecting the amazing strength my mom displayed while dealing with the pain of seeing her oldest son's lifeless body in the casket.

Before the funeral started, a video was played on a continuous loop that displayed various pictures of June's life with his family and friends. As the pictures rotated, playing in the background was one of our shared favorite songs, Sam Cooke's "A Change Is Gonna Come." My emotional breakdown occurred each time they came to the part in the song which says "then I go to my brother... and I tell him, brother help me please..." During this part of the song they displayed a picture of me and my brother together, enjoying a moment during the Thanksgiving dinner at my mom's house the year before he died. That night was very memorable because it was the first time I could ever remember all of the siblings sitting down and eating dinner together. I didn't know it would be the last time I would enjoy a meal with my brother or the last time we were all able to stand in our traditional prayer circle and not have to send a prayer that June would be able to enjoy a special meal away from the family while in prison.

Initially, plans were for me to sing the song during the funeral. However, I knew that I would not have been able to muster enough strength to get beyond the "brother" part. During that part of the song, I could hear my brother pleading for me to help him overcome the struggles of his life. I also could hear me pleading with him to help me with my own fears and obstacles. June and I used to playfully battle during our karaoke evenings to be the first one to sing that song, which had always been a staple in my karaoke selections. However, from the moment of his funeral I haven't been able to sing that song again publicly. The same song I enjoyed listening to when my first-born was brought into this world was now one that was somberly memorialized and forever untouched by my voice publicly. This was the least I could do for the memory of my brother.

After the funeral, I knew that a change was coming to my life. Although I had already realized some level of success, I knew that I had to mercilessly drive myself to strive towards all of my goals in life. I also knew that I would not allow anyone to keep me from reaching my goals. One of my goals was becoming a vice president either at Novation or somewhere else. Another goal was to finish a business plan I had toyed around with regarding the development of my own television channel. I also had a goal of reaching financial independence so that the family could have more options to enjoy life. And finally, I didn't know where my relationship with Michelle was going, but knew I had to push myself to become a better father for my kids. When I die, I want my kids to see me realize all of my potential. I want them to see the impact I made on others and the legacy I would leave behind for them to continue. More importantly, I want them to see that I would do anything to provide a better life for them. I would walk through fire to build a life for them that was far away from the one I had to endure.

When I returned to Texas, I sat down and wrote my goals to remind myself of the need to succeed on a daily basis. At Novation, mentally I behaved as if I was already an executive, which allowed me to achieve even greater success. In 2011, my hard work led me to be considered for a tremendous honor from the Federation of American Hospitals, which presented an annual Corris Boyd Leadership and Diversity award, named after my mentor Corris because of his tremendous impact on diversity in healthcare. The award recognizes an individual or company that has made an outstanding contribution in fostering leadership and workplace diversity in the healthcare industry. The 2010 award would be presented during the Federation's annual conference held in Washington, D.C., in March 2011.

As the attendees waited patiently for the event to start, I was a nervous wreck. There were roughly 4,000 attendees at the event, which was filmed and displayed on enormous screens across the room. As I sat among the Novation contingent, I pondered privately about my potential for winning the prestigious award. When the event started, the first agenda item was to present the winner for the Corris Boyd award. As the presenter proceeded to mention the traits of the unannounced winner, I was amazed how similar that person sounded to my own values. He then stated "And the winner is… Lamont Robinson." I immediately began to clap along with the crowd to congratulate the winner, not realizing *my* name was Lamont Robinson. After seeing everyone clapping and looking in my direction, I realized it was *me* who had won the award! Nervously, I approached the stage to accept the award, passing through the faceless sea of supporters while feeling overwhelmed at the attention and responsibility that came along with the honor.

The award was made more special to me because of who it was named after. After entering the stage to receive the award, I was asked to say a few words about the honor. Since Corris meant so much to my professional life, I was excited to speak. I talked first about the honor of the award, especially for a child that grew up on the West Side of Chicago. I couldn't have dreamed of being honored in front of 4,000 executives on a national platform in D.C. I talked about how my humble background served as the fuel for my fire.

After briefly discussing my background, I was then moved to acknowledge my respect for Corris's impact on my life. I assured everyone that Corris's legacy was not going to die and that I would proactively do everything I could to bring sustainable opportunities to disadvantaged companies and communities. While speaking, I felt not only the legacies of Corris and Will but also the presence of my brother. I could see and feel June's smile shining down on his little brother. While the award ceremony was probably received like a typical event for the attendees, I knew how special it was to me. Many thought my speech was prepared beforehand, but the award was a complete surprise and the speech came directly from my heart with help from the spirits of Corris, Will, and June.

Shortly following the Corris Boyd award, I continued to receive individual and company awards. I was honored by *DiversityPlus* magazine as one of 2011's Top 30 Champions of Diversity. The *Minority Business News USA* magazine followed by honoring me as one of the top 100 supplier diversity professionals from 2000-2010 as well as one of the top eight catalysts for diversity in 2010. Under my leadership, our supplier diversity program was also honored by *MBN USA* magazine as one of the top 101 supplier diversity programs in 2010. DiversityBusiness.com provided our program with their Div50 award in 2012. Other Novation employees often greeted me with congratulations as well as facetiously attempted to guess the timing of my next award. The awards and honors weren't special just to me; they were celebrated by the company. Our senior executives proudly mentioned the awards while they participated on various industry panels. Many of the minority population at Novation sent me encouraging and supportive words, often telling me how proud they were of my success and that I was succeeding for all of them at the company. I took these supportive words seriously since I knew how hard it was for my culture to succeed in corporate America.

As throughout my life, I struggled to find ways to enjoy successes while dealing with pain. The more bad news I received, the harder I worked. The harder I worked, the less pain I was feeling from the bad news. Success became my drug. I was able to escape reality by enjoying current successes or focusing on future dreams in the same way music, television, and movies allowed me to escape the violent world around me as a child. While this helped with maintaining my equanimity and sanity, it did nothing to resolve the problem. I realized I could have done a better job of proactively connecting with my siblings to help with their challenges. However, I also understood that in order for them to completely overcome their struggles, they needed to want to change, which is something I hadn't seen up until that point. Knowing I couldn't help my siblings, I started to focus more on bringing enjoyment to my mom's life.

Always in my corner, my mom made it a point to acknowledge how proud she was of my accomplishments. I arranged for her to travel to Texas to visit and to watch my sons during an extended business trip. When she arrived at the house, immediately she became extremely emotional. I knew that she was seeing the fruits of all of our family struggles in the form of the home. While others would view this as materialistic, being able to afford a large home is seen as an achievement not only for me but for everyone that sacrificed to make me successful. I was happy to be able to provide joy in my mom's life because of the struggles she had to endure while raising me and my siblings.

Our family had plenty of positive memories, but we felt like the Evans family in the television show *Good Times*. Just when it seemed like life was turning around for us, we were hit with another blow that unsuccessfully attempted to cripple us. Fortunately, our resolve helped us build an unbreakable resilience and keep fighting. Our hope expanded with each downfall, knowing that life couldn't get much worse than all of our negative experiences. While many others have grown up in homes much bigger than mine, most haven't had the same struggles to realize any levels of success. I didn't grow up with a blueprint for success. The home represented to my mom and family that anything was achievable.

Growing up, we only saw success in television and movies and never thought it could be achieved in our own family. My home was a culmination of hard work, dedication, perseverance, sacrifice, blood, sweat, and tears. Seeing my mom enjoy our Texas surroundings was one of the first times I saw her with a look of contentment. My success was her success, just as her problems had been all of ours. She was the reason I stuck with the plan and didn't allow anything or anyone to deter me from reaching greatness.

After my mom returned to Chicago, I continued to focus on raising my sons while succeeding at work. However, my life hadn't necessarily reached all forms of success. Michelle and my daughters were still living in Illinois, which provided significant emotional and financial burdens. I was paying for two mortgages as well as utilities for both homes. While finally enjoying a comfortable salary, my financial obligations easily erased any feelings of financial achievements. We still lived paycheck to paycheck and often had to be fiscally innovative to buy necessities. There were moments when we were close to losing our Illinois home because of our lack of paying the mortgage. We also fell behind on our car payments, home owner's assessments, insurance, and utilities, which all had negative impacts on our credit. Michelle often incorrectly assumed me and the boys were having a great time spending our money in Texas. It was difficult to not be able to enjoy going on vacations like the other families we knew or buying the latest gadget that entertained the friends of my children. We also couldn't afford to furnish the beautiful home we had in Texas because of our financial obligations.

As we continued to struggle financially, my personal struggles would soon improve. My big break came when Jacqui decided that she was moving to Texas at the beginning of the 2010-2011 school year. I was very excited to hear Jacqui's decision but knew that she was concerned about the impact on Michelle. However, Jacqui also realized that there was a better life for her in Texas. She would have a greater chance to have friends, attend better schools, and happily live with her father and brothers. I'm sure she also hoped her decision would positively impact Michelle's decision to move as well, since she wouldn't have three of her four kids with her on a daily basis.

Against Jacqui's and the rest of our wishes, Michelle decided to return to Illinois after Jacqui's decision. Even though I continued to struggle juggling my career and raising three kids, having Jacqui, Malik, and Antonio with me was a tremendous blessing. I could tell that Jacqui was enjoying her freedom as a young woman while meeting new friends and doing things girls her age were enjoying. Also during this time, I decided to be more proactive with taking control of our financial situation. Before this time, Michelle had been responsible for paying the utilities and any other costs associated with the Illinois home. I decided that in order to reach our goal of becoming financially independent, I was the one that had to take charge.

Being responsible for all bills would also give me a clearer perspective on the decisions that needed to be made. To be simple, my financial goal was always to increase my income and decrease my expenses. To increase my income, I needed to continue to build my brand within the supplier diversity community. I strongly believed that following my passion would lead to success. I also knew that greater success would lead to financial recognition either at Novation or another company. To decrease my expenses, I knew that I had to find a way to reduce the financial burden from owning the Illinois home. I also established and staunchly followed a budget to ensure my income was covering my expenditures.

Another financial decision I made during this time was to eliminate credit cards. When I was younger, I saw my mom enslaved by debt accumulated from her usage of credit cards. I saw her freely purchase an item using her credit cards then struggle with making the monthly payments. While at Lake Forest, I accumulated debt while purchasing items I wanted but didn't necessarily need. I refused to grasp the concept that purchases made via credit still needed to be paid. As an adult, I made a conscious decision to not use credit cards as a way of extending my income, instead opting to pay cash for everything. I felt that using cash would increase my sensitivity regarding the way my income was being used to acquire goods and services that were actually needed versus wanted. A financial plan was a necessity to support our dual lives in Texas and Illinois.

As I enjoyed my life in Texas with Jacqui, Malik, and Antonio, Michelle made a difficult decision for her and Payton to move to Texas on February 14, 2011. Her decision wasn't necessarily permanent because she continued to maintain her Illinois license plates and driver's license. The condition of the Illinois home was also left as if she planned to return. She frequently reminded me that her stay in Texas wasn't permanent. However, I was happy to have everyone back together again even though we were wasting money each month paying for expenses for a home none of us occupied. I also thought the move to Texas could potentially help to strengthen our marriage. I believed that the kids needed to see us together again for them to build their own confidence. However, I also knew that there was a chance that living under the same roof could exacerbate the challenges we had already been facing during our entire marriage.

Michelle and I continued to struggle because of our various refusals to commit. I believed that her noncommittal approach towards the move displayed her lack of commitment as a mother, while my addictions began to resurface, which impacted my lack of commitment as a husband. Temptation was very strong in Texas while I lived alone without Michelle. My struggles also contributed to Michelle's decision to not move to Texas as she feared the family would be broken up after the move and she would be left without a strong support system. However, I believed our panacea would be for all of us to be under the same roof. Strength comes in numbers. I also understood that supporting each other's shortcomings could either strengthen our family or have the potential to exacerbate our problems.

While Michelle and Payton were physically with the family, emotionally they were still in Illinois. Payton often complained about not being around her Illinois friends while Michelle continued to refuse to call Texas home. We also maintained the home in Illinois which continued to negatively impact our financial health. Having everyone in Texas during the year encouraged me that better times were ahead of us. Even though Michelle and I continued fighting on a daily basis, I knew that I was in a better mental state with everyone in Texas. We were able to go on vacations and enjoy family weekend moments and family movie nights. I also didn't have to keep answering the awkward questions from concerned Texas friends regarding whether or not my entire family was going to be in Texas. Even though I knew life wasn't going to be easy, it would be impossible to improve our situation unless we were all together.

Rejuvenation

WITH EVERYONE FINALLY IN TEXAS, I was able to focus more on growing my career at Novation and building my brand. My success at Novation garnered many speaking engagements as well as additional recognition not only among supplier diversity professionals but also healthcare executives from other organizations. Many of the executives I spoke to as well as diverse business owners approached me about opening up my own consulting firm, since I was already the de facto consultant for supplier diversity in healthcare as a result of the exposure I had been receiving. I also enjoyed helping others and solving problems, which are both traits of successful consultants. To prepare for my next career phase, I started a business plan to open my own consulting firm. I also incorporated the firm in the state of Texas and paid tribute to my father's family name by calling the firm Robinson LaRueCo Consulting. I talked to other consultants to understand the various challenges I would potentially encounter on my own. I wasn't going to make the move until I knew I would be able to at least match the salary I'd been receiving from Novation since I had five other people I was responsible for financially.

As I moved towards starting my own firm, my plans took a detour. I was approached by a recruiter from Nielsen, the market research giant, to interview for their newly created Vice President of Supplier Diversity position. The position intrigued me for several reasons. Rarely do companies make a strong commitment to support supplier diversity by creating a vice president position. Also, I had been working in healthcare for thirteen years and felt it was time for a change. Nielsen supported media, advertising, entertainment, manufacturing, retail, sports, and expositions, which were all industries I was unfamiliar with from a business perspective. Although I had been a consumer all my life for the areas Nielsen supported, I had never been exposed to those industries in my career.

The Nielsen opportunity also excited me because of the chance to improve their program. Throughout my professional career, I have never been interested in status quo. I believe this is one of the main reasons I decided to terminate my dreams of becoming an accountant. I am more interested in creating or enhancing something for which others may view as broken than stepping into a role that was already successful. Before I joined Cardinal, our relationships with key customers were damaged. After I left, I was able to improve those relationships as evidenced through winning awards with two of our most openly critical customers. At VHA, I arrived after relocating to create their supplier diversity program. I was able to successfully increase the internal and external awareness of the program. At Novation, our satisfaction scores among our supplier diversity advisory group members were embarrassingly low in comparison to the other Novation councils and advisory groups. After taking over the program, I was able to successfully implement programs and other initiatives that resulted in our program being considered one of the best, while winning awards and gaining myriad recognitions. The Nielsen opportunity could give me the chance to improve their supplier diversity program while showing I could succeed outside of healthcare.

Becoming a vice president with Nielsen could also provide an important personal benefit. As a child in Rockwell, I often rode my bike downtown with other Rockwell friends. Once we arrived, I frequently looked at the businessmen and women traipsing the downtown streets dressed in suits and accompanied by their expensive briefcases. I knew then that I wanted to be a businessman working downtown. My dreams were renewed each time I sat in my Rockwell apartment window looking at the businesspeople speeding towards downtown in their luxurious vehicles. The eastward movement on the imaginary yellow brick Eisenhower expressway seemed to lead to the Chicago Land of Oz, which featured the Willis (Sears) Tower and other amazing skyscrapers blanketing the downtown landscape. I viewed the businesspeople as achieving a desired level of success and understood that I would have to work harder than most of them because of how far behind I started in regards to education and environment.

I was fortunate to receive the chance to be interviewed for the Nielsen opportunity. As with any interview, I prepared myself by researching everything I could about Nielsen and the industry. I also developed an initial strategic plan based on my experience and what I knew was needed to create a successful program. Another pre-interview strategy was to develop a list of questions for each interviewer based on their specific areas of focus within the company as well as any personal history I could find while conducting my research online. I had to convince the interviewers that I was the only person for the job and that I had the confidence to lead them. Since the position was at a vice president level, I increased my preparation more than for any previous position. I strongly believed that I was the perfect fit for Nielsen and that the opportunity was exactly what I needed in my professional life.

During the interview, I was confident that I answered all questions directed towards me by the two senior vice president interviewers who were also the managers for the position. In addition to answering their questions, I interjected strategic thoughts on how to build a successful supplier diversity program. I offered thoughts on how supplier diversity could become a revenue-generating opportunity for Nielsen. I talked about ways to utilize the researching assets and capabilities at Nielsen to establish a brand within the supplier diversity community. I also articulated my strategy for working with our clients and suppliers to build a successful brand alongside other Nielsen staples. I was confident that Nielsen viewed me as a strong candidate. The only challenge with the potential job was that it was located back in Chicago.

On July 3, 2012, I received a phone call from Dee, the original Nielsen recruiter who approached me about the opportunity. She gave me the great news that I was being offered the position at Nielsen! She also provided me with even greater news that I would not have to move for the position. Nielsen was going to allow me to work from my home in Texas, which would be a new experience for me. Although I was personally prepared to move for the job, I wasn't excited about going through the painful process of relocating my family again. I knew that an additional relocation could potentially be the final nail in the coffin for our marriage. I received the great news with an emotional response similar to Will Smith's at the end of *The Pursuit of Happyness* as I realized this was the biggest opportunity not only in my life, but for any of my family members or Rockwell friends.

The first family member I called after receiving the news was my mom. I knew that she would understand how much the job meant to me in regards to a reward for the sacrifices I made with education and other job changes. She would also understand the needed boost to not only my professional career but personal situation as well. Lastly, she would see this opportunity as another confirmation that anything in life is possible through working hard, overcoming fear, having determination to succeed, and maintaining faith. If I had decided to bypass the ABC program, I may not have realized the successes in life that occurred after graduating from Lower Merion. If I had decided to remain in accounting because it was my childhood dream, I wouldn't have been successful or happy because it wasn't my passion. If I hadn't spoken up to Ron after the church meeting, my career at Hospira could have remained stagnant. If I hadn't had the courage to move my family and tackle Michelle's lack of desire to leave, I would have either remained status quo at Cardinal after relocating my family to an unknown area or be unemployed in Chicago.

While I am extremely confident that I will build a successful program and career at Nielsen, I am realistic in knowing that nothing is guaranteed. I know that I must continue to plan for my next career phase regardless of my potential Nielsen success. I also realize that I was starting to live the dream I always had as a child. Mr. Bottom's favorite phrase is still my motivating quote to believe in myself. In early 2014, I was able to reconnect with Mr. Bottom. After telling him about my life, which included personal and professional successes, he expressed how proud he was of me. I was able to tell him how his influence on me resulted in overcoming fears to continue to enter uncharted territory to find that next level of success. I can't rely on anyone else to bring me success. My success has to be built through my own efforts. While others could play vital roles in introducing me to potential opportunities, my own confidence in my abilities will ultimately determine whether or not I achieve success.

The year I started at Nielsen was the same year President Obama was seeking reelection. The economy was coming out of a recession but still struggling. Unemployment had been high for the past several years. Republicans in Texas as well as the Mormon church made their hatred towards Obama clearly known. Since Mitt Romney, a Mormon, was Obama's opponent, many members of the church were extremely boisterous about their feelings against the president. I felt that members focused more on anti-Obama instead of pro-Romney movements. My struggles within the Church intensified as I heard the horrible labels to describe the president, which was something I had never heard to describe any previous president. I felt more like an outsider each time members openly articulated their vitriol. However, I continued to attend church mostly because I didn't want the kids to see their father quit. I also continued to attend because I still believed in the foundation of the church. I still appreciated the way the church valued the family structure, which I didn't want to break up had I decided to leave.

I also continued because I still had a lot of friends in the church, many of whom were the very ones criticizing Obama. I had to try very hard to separate the church and its foundational values from the opinions of others. This is the beauty of America. We have the ability and freedom to express our own opinions. As much as I didn't agree with Obama's critics, I would be a hypocrite if I didn't accept their opinions while wanting them to accept mine.

When Obama was reelected, the same sense of pride I had in 2008 returned even stronger in 2012. I felt rejuvenated within my job and as a black male in America. I didn't care about the unprecedented insults and accusations made about him by members of the church. I enjoyed his acceptance speech, especially his statement which focused on "the young boy on the South Side of Chicago who sees a life beyond the street corner." I thought about the struggles I had as a kid to become successful. While I knew that my career was just beginning, I also accepted the reality that I had already realized a level of success most black men wouldn't in their lifetimes. My purpose in life was being fulfilled, and the knowledge I gained from living in the violent Rockwell environment was now an asset for me to survive corporate America. I felt that there would be a renewed focus on supplier diversity more than ever before.

My life experiences have shaped me into who I am today. Performing in front of others while in dancing or rap groups gave me confidence with public speaking. Also contributing to my oratory ability was my hard work in trying to improve my vocabulary while at Lower Merion. I also developed a habit of learning new words while reading magazine articles, then forcing myself to occasionally use those words. I knew that if I was going to be successful, I had to speak and act as if I had already reached that desired level of success. From my first speech as the top student at Grant School to speaking in front of thousands while accepting the Corris Boyd award, my nerves pushed me to strive to entertain audiences.

The foundation for my passion for diversity began the moment I realized there were no African-American business owners in my neighborhood. Another driver for diversity developed from my exposure to other cultures and religions while attending Lower Merion. I fully understand that diversity is essential for any society because it encourages members of historically underutilized cultures to achieve success. Being able to assist companies owned by minorities has been a blessing. My success is achieved when I witness their growth, especially when it leads to those companies adding jobs to communities that were similar to Rockwell.

My dedication to becoming a strong father resulted from having an example of a strong single mother who didn't allow our limitations to impact us negatively. Not having a father or strong male role model in the home provided my immovable need to assure my children that I would always be in their lives. Watching Bill Cosby's character on *The Cosby Show* gave me the initial blueprint for the type of father I wanted to be, while the church provided great real-life examples. I couldn't use the excuse of not having a father in my home to shirk any responsibilities for taking care of my children. It was up to me to change the cycle and to make a difference in the generations that followed me in regards to being the ideal father. While I am realistic in knowing many times I fall short with this tremendous responsibility, I know that overall I am succeeding.

As with most kids that survive living in the housing projects, the impetus for my competitive zeal came from Rockwell. There is an edge that you have to maintain while living in violent environments, regardless of whether you were in a gang. You are trained to be aware of your surroundings at all times. Also, the weight of my family and the neighborhood encouraging me to succeed contributed towards that competitive spirit. Failure was not an option because of the enormous amount of invested time and emotional support I received from my family and neighborhood friends. They wanted me to succeed and needed to see me succeed to prove that such a violent and depressing area could still produce greatness.

I was also motivated by those that doubted my ability to succeed. I remind myself of the perception Pat from Hospira had about me without fully understanding my background or what drives me. Pat didn't understand that I will not allow *anyone* to derail my goals to succeed. He didn't understand the solid foundation established by my strong-willed mother. He didn't understand the confidence Rockwell instilled in me. He didn't know about my own internal battles to prove others wrong not only about me but about all black men in America. However, the irony of it all is that I owe much of my success to Pat because of his doubt. He forced me to reach deeper inside myself to find ways to follow my passions to obtain success, even if that meant leaving Hospira. I wasn't afraid of leaving Hospira; I was afraid to fail. Fortunately, I knew that in order to succeed, I had to have an unrelenting approach to becoming the most successful supplier diversity professional I could be.

To shape myself into a professional brand, I frequently observed other executives. I developed a voracious habit of researching business etiquette from various books and business magazines. I subscribed to the *Wall Street Journal* and magazines such as *Businessweek, Inc., Forbes, Entrepreneur, Barron's,* and *Fortune* to be able to speak about the current business events and teach myself about various ways to invest. I constantly watched business-related television channels such as CNBC, Bloomberg, and Fox Business Network. I also purchased biographical books about the lives of successful business people such as Donald Trump, Henry Kravis, John D. Rockefeller, Henry Ford, and Chris Gardner. To improve my vocabulary, I forced myself to learn most of the words included in the multitude of business magazine articles and books I read, and I listened to audio dictionaries while driving in my car. To augment the reading material, I watched how executives dressed, spoke to others, behaved at company events, conducted meetings, presented to various audiences, and traveled. I read stories about well known business executives and envisioned myself in their shoes.

Rejuvenation

I have always strongly believed that in order to become successful, you have to be associated with others that have achieved a desired level of success. I also believed that you should always work on building your brand, which is how others perceive you. I worked hard to make sure that my brand included the perception of being professional, well-groomed, articulate, considerate, and influential. To maintain my perspective and motivation, I never try to convince myself that I have achieved success for fear that I would become complacent and stop striving for greatness. As long as I viewed success as an unreachable goal, I knew that I would always strive to obtain it. If I thought success was within my reach, I feared that I would always find excuses to stop or slow down my pursuit of it.

My professional life has taught me that the status quo and complacency will always be a detriment to success. It is imperative to think, act, and perform differently than others, constantly seeking to identify and mold your differentiation. I was fortunate to have survived the housing projects. The experience in Rockwell will always remain and provide confidence to accept any challenge in corporate America. I also have never had a feeling of entitlement. I have always believed since inequalities exist and will always exist, it is the responsibility of each individual to work hard to change them and to fight hard to succeed in their midst. If we allow the concept of inequalities to pervade our minds, we cheat ourselves of allowing it to be our motivator instead of our detriment.

Success doesn't have to be defined as someone who has become wealthy; success could merely be defined as an individual who has not only escaped a situation in which most fail, but was still able to find a positive path providing options for greater future successes. Too often, individuals from underprivileged areas believe success is achieving financial independence. When individuals believe in this mentality, they often fail to realize that their survival of violent environments exceeds any achievements made by business people who may have been born into successful families. A more dangerous impact of this mentality is that youth in underprivileged areas convince themselves to not strive for more achievable successes if it's obvious they may not become the next popular rapper or NBA superstar.

As I stated in the beginning, this is not a rags-to-riches book; this is a story of a boy who was determined to not allow stereotypes to determine his future, even though he was never provided a blueprint for success. It is a story of not giving up when most in similar situations would have acquiesced to the status quo. This story is about not allowing family influences to dictate the structure for your own future foundation. It is also about not allowing your fear of the unknown prevent you from seeking unknown fortunes.

This is also not a unique story, as it has been, and continues to be, lived by many men, women, boys, and girls. There are many raised in similar or worse environments who have exceeded professional boundaries I'm still waiting to reach. However, I am proud to say that my story is unique. I was inspired to tell my story for those individuals that could relate with my upbringing, obstacles and successes; to give them a voice as they continue to struggle through life to find their own muse. I also hope that those currently going through similar adolescent experiences continue to fight for survival and seek their own successful paths outside of the standard, myopic approach of their environment. Success is not about how much you've made; it's about how much you've *left*. It is about the legacy you leave behind for others and the standards you have raised for them to exceed.

As much as I eagerly followed what I considered the American Dream, my perception of success changed, even while writing this book. For most of my life, success revolved around career achievements. I found great joy in being honored as one of the best in my profession, the top student in elementary, the first in my family to achieve educational merits, and the first to write a book. However, my personal success was redefined as being able to overcome fears and impossible obstacles to raise children who are all successful in their own ways, and hopefully leaving behind an inspirational path for others to emulate.

Although this book focused on my ability to survive and succeed, it is important to know how the characters overcame their own struggles. I consider my maternal sisters to be successful. Although they'll always have obstacles, like all of us, in overcoming their addictions, they continue to fight in finding life's enjoyments. I'm proud of my sisters and look forward to seeing them continue to improve while leaving behind the dangerous and destructive paths they were heading down.

Rejuvenation

My father's success is realized in his ability to change from a violent and self-absorbed person to one that loves his children and grandchildren. The pain of not seeing or hearing his own father's love is overcome by his ability to verbalize his prideful heart when discussing his family. He also has found serenity in his life by moving to Alabama to be near Sheila, Shanee, and his grandchildren instead of suffering a somewhat reclusive life in Houston. He has committed to eliminating alcohol and cigarettes while also striving to live an emotionally healthy life. We both realize that our best years are ahead of us in terms of building our relationship as father and son as a result of his commitment to becoming a better person.

June was successful in finding light at the end of his tunnel. He left this world as a free man and was able to expand his horizons with a new relationship. The majority of his life was spent inside penitentiary walls. When he left prison, he committed to exploring the life he lost and rebuilding the relationships he missed. It was great seeing him get acclimated to the technology and other innovations created during his extended stint in prison. As devastating as it is to realize he is no longer alive, it is a blessing to know that he passed away after being able to enjoy his freedom.

Bob is discovering the enjoyment of retirement. He enjoys the flexibility his new life provides while continuing to be an inspiration to others on the south side of Waukegan. He continues to be the single most inspirational person in my life regarding my desire to succeed in corporate America. Bob's long-standing service to help the citizens on the south side of Waukegan is a great example to other civil servants as he sacrificed his time, life and finances to improving the lives of the common man.

My mom's success is manifested in overcoming all of the obstacles placed ahead of her in life. She overcame abusive relationships to discover the beauty she never thought existed but was always there. She sacrificed a lot, including the involvement in unwanted relationships, to raise her four kids in the middle of a perilous environment. She overcame the painful process of witnessing her firstborn son survive a penal career, only to be taken cruelly away from this earth while finally being a free man. She survived the painful period of seeing her youngest son leave home to live in an area a thousand miles away just to receive a better education. She survived the horror of any parent in seeing her daughters physically and mentally deteriorate as a result of drug addictions. She struggled to discover her inner strength and fortitude while making a bold, and unpopular, decision to leave behind everything and everyone to finally live the life she earned. Mom's survival is the definition of success.

For most of my life, my maternal siblings believed my mom loved me more because of the way my life turned out versus theirs. What they failed to realize was that my journey included more obstacles than theirs. Unlike my siblings, I didn't live in the same household as my father. I struggled through life not fully understanding my full identity because of my paternal mystery. My mom shielded me from her world so that I could live my dreams. She didn't want me to be impacted by the events surrounding me because she saw something special in me that she may not have seen in the others. She didn't love me more than my siblings, but after she realized I *wanted* a different life, she protected me, which is also what I would have done for my child. My mom knew that I was building my brand even at an early age. She knew that I had the discipline needed to escape from the only world she and my siblings knew. She wanted to live her life vicariously through my achievements, and I'm honored to have her along for the ride.

My decision to not follow the paths of my maternal siblings regarding drugs and violence was a result of personally seeing the negative consequences from the choices they made in life. I saw firsthand how the usage of drugs could physically and mentally kill you. I saw the effects of incarceration as well as being on constant edge not knowing if your enemy was waiting for you around the block. My life is different because I made a choice early in life to avoid most of the same pitfalls that unfortunately befell my siblings.

Even though my siblings decided to go a different route, I am not without blemishes. My struggles through pornography and various levels of infidelity negatively impacted my relationship with Michelle. While I blame a lot of my struggles on inappropriate early childhood exposures, I am accountable for my decisions. Because I'm human, I know that I will continue to have vices, which is why I won't judge my siblings for theirs. However, because of my siblings' experiences, I am confident that my vices and shortcomings would not come at the hands of drugs or violence, as long as I received the proper counseling. Fortunately, I received the proper counseling to help me with overcoming my struggle with pornography. I needed to be reminded of how my early exposure and experiences impacted my decision to view pornographic material. The breakthrough for me resulted from realizing consequences of a simple decision to view the filth. Unfortunately, as long as society downplays the severity of pornography, we will continue to struggle with our perception of the role of women or our thoughts on the sanctity of marriage.

I realize that not everyone has the same desire to obtain as much education as possible; some of the greatest contributors to modern society have achieved success without a college degree. Arguably, education provides more optional roads to success, but what defines a person's greatness is their ability to impress their own soul. When a person knows they have done all they could with the talent they've been blessed with, they have left behind their own legacy and are able to leave this world as a success.

One of the most memorable and impactful eulogies I heard was delivered in 1999 by the Reverend Jesse Jackson, Sr., during the memorial services of Chicago Bears legend Walter Payton at Soldier Field in Chicago. During his message, Reverend Jackson talked about the importance of understanding the significance of the "dash" placed on tombstones between a person's birth and death dates. While we can't control our birth date, and sometimes the day we leave this earth, that dash represents the impact we've had on others in our lives. Regardless of whether a person's dash is longer than others because of the duration of their life, it is up to them to leave this earth with a dash that has great depth.

When I am faced with my own mortality, I pray that my "dash" will display the life of someone who attempted to help others escape impoverished lives. I can only hope that my dash is strengthened as a result of my descendants having a greater impact on society than I was able to accomplish. I can also only hope that my dash inspires someone from a similar background to strive for greatness after realizing that in order to achieve anything in life, he or she would have to make necessary and difficult sacrifices for it to happen.

The 12 Disciplines

EVEN THOUGH I'VE HAD TO endure many painful events in my life, I have been blessed with opportunities presented to me that others may not have received. However, I had to be keen enough to identify those opportunities when presented with them, and then work hard to achieve success. Some of us have multiple distractions to detract us from clearly seeing doors opened ahead of us. Some of us have involuntary responsibilities that take away from our internal quiet moments to ponder our next steps. Ultimately, success involves luck regardless of whether it's a major or minor element.

Success is also based on our willingness to make sacrifices and keep our eyes on the long journey, even while obstacles create internal doubt. While going through that journey, you need reminders of why you've originally accepted the challenge. Based on my experiences past and present, I have staunchly adhered to the following twelve disciplines throughout my life to keep me on that path towards success:

1. **Identify your own level of success.** Success comes in many ways. Some view success materialistically while others may see it more as achieving personal goal. Before you head down the road to success, first define what that means to you. You cannot allow others to determine what makes you successful. Too often we get caught up in chasing someone else's dreams of success instead of pursuing our own. One of the worst things you could do in life is to fail while seeking to achieve someone else's dreams instead of maintaining an unrelenting drive to pursue your own. You also cannot compare your successes with those of others, which could create frustration. And that person whom you viewed as being more successful may actually think the same about

you. While speaking to a mentor, I expressed how impressed I was with his achievements. He quickly replied that he viewed me as more of a success because of what I had to endure to get to where I was versus what had already been handed to him.

After we've identified our own level of success, we can never allow ourselves to believe we have reached a pinnacle. Once that occurs, we become complacent and may not have the drive to continue to push ourselves toward additional levels of success. It is more beneficial for us to keep our own internal carrot dangling in front of our eyes and leading us to continue moving forward. The more we keep reaching for that virtual carrot, the more we move beyond our own imaginable boundaries.

2. **Surround yourself with ambitious people.** Stay away from the chronic complainers! They are never happy for your achievements because they're too afraid to take the risks to challenge themselves in order to realize their own level of success. They will sometimes secretly pray for your failure because misery loves company. Conversely, forward-thinkers not only challenge you to achieve greatness, they expand your mind into strategies you may not have been able to identify on your own (or while in the midst of chronic complainers). This isn't to suggest that you un-friend chronic complainers, however, just avoid strategic and forward-looking conversations with chronic complainers. Their vision of the future isn't positive, mostly because they failed to witness present successes. Their "half-empty" mentality permeates their daily thoughts and actions and becomes chronic and unproductive for forward-thinkers. As a forward-thinker, challenge your intellect by being around people you believe are smarter than you.

3. **Emulate success.** If you want to be successful, imitate those you'd classify as being at the desired level of success by reading their magazines, watching their movies, observing their behavior, expanding your vocabulary, and dressing like success. The more you place yourself virtually in the shoes of someone with the level of success you've desired, the closer you'll get to reaching your goals. My penchant for reading business magazines and books gave me the ability to effectively conduct small talk in the circles I wanted to be associated with, which

is a necessary skill for networking. As I read intellectual periodicals, I wrote down words I didn't know, searched for their definition, and then tried to use them in sentences to try to build the word into my typical vocabulary. I also challenged my kids to understand the word.

Even though I wasn't exposed to many corporate leaders early in my life, I received great advice on investing, decreasing expenses, and increasing income by reading business magazines. The more expansive my vocabulary became, the more confidence I had to communicate with anyone, regardless of whether it was the janitor or the CEO. The more my dining etiquette was improved, the more comfortable I was during business meals. I enjoy reading biographies of successful people to understand their impetus to succeed. Successful people breed success because they're constantly thinking about their next steps while investing in their own knowledge and surrounding themselves with other successful people.

4. **Pass on your knowledge.** Whether or not you are a parent, look for ways to provide youth with knowledge in areas you did not receive as a child. Growing up, I wasn't well versed in the stock market or other ways of investing. The only method of investing we were taught was to save money in a personal bank account and allow the slow-moving interest to build over time. When I became a parent, I knew it would be my responsibility to teach my kids what I didn't know about the stock market. To make it fun, I purchased games called *Pit, Stock Market Tycoon,* and *Stock Rush!* to play with my kids. Instead of just playing the games, I used it as an educational opportunity to teach them investment strategies and how various events impact stock prices. Although I know these games will not build stock market gurus, I hope having an early exposure to the stock market and other investment strategies will increase their desire to pursue additional financial literacy.

5. **Don't be afraid to be different.** We often make the mistake of allowing ourselves to be grouped into specific labels or buckets for fear of being different. Differences change the world! After observing the behaviors of successful people, I wasn't afraid to add my own flair, which served as my differentiator and provided me with a platform to show my brand. Even though I knew it was not going to be a favorable

decision among my family, joining the Mormon church gave me the fundamentals and networks to break many negative cycles endured by generations within my family. I knew that most times I would be the only African American in my ward, but I didn't let that deter me from joining because I also knew the good it could bring to me and my future family. I knew that going to the A Better Chance program was going to alienate me with some family and friends, but I saw the doors it would open for me later in life. Leaving home to attend Lower Merion gave me the exposure into other cultures that expanded my world, which helped me later in life. I know that I am a better person because of those experiences.

6. **Always keep your inner fires flickering.** Rockwell gave me an internal and eternal edge that is effectively used, when needed, and never dissipates. That environment gave me a chip on my shoulder that I dare others to knock off. When some in corporate America discover my background, confrontations are sometimes avoided because of their fear of the unknown. They don't know how I'll react in adverse situations because of their perception of someone from my upbringing. Be proud of your past! Embrace it and use it as motivation, not as a detriment. Because of my Rockwell background, I'm not typically fearful of most challenges presented to me in corporate America since I've been through a lot of trials and tribulations already. It's ok to keep your inner fire burning; it's even greater to let others know it's inside of you.

7. **Embrace risks.** A person who refuses to take risks is a person who remains stagnant. Calculated risks are the blueprint for success. I can't imagine my life without taking my greatest risk, which was leaving my comfortable, but violent, home to enter the scary, but necessary, A Better Chance program. My mom was also taking a major risk of letting her son leave home to live a thousand miles away with strangers in order to obtain educational success.

The key with risks is to research, ponder, and pray before making your final decision. You should never rush a decision without meticulously researching any necessary backgrounds, pondering the pros and cons and praying to receive confirmation of your decision before moving forward. An ignorant risk is a dumb risk. However, being afraid of taking risks is cheating you of future blessings and rewards.

8. **Be the only one to define your brand.** As you go through life you are establishing your brand, which is the perception that others have of you. You cannot allow someone to place you into a bucket that is outside of your brand. If I had listened to others telling me that my passion was in accounting, I would have never gone down the more successful path of procurement, which led to my true passion of supplier diversity. If I had allowed Pat from Hospira to convince me that I wasn't management material, I would have never left Hospira to take the risk of succeeding as a director at Cardinal. I knew what I needed to do and where I needed to go because I had prayed and pondered about my future. Allowing someone else to define who you are is doing a tremendous disservice to your hard work in building your brand and firming up your foundation.

9. **Recognize the pattern and break the cycle.** Too often we fall into the trap of accepting the status quo or mediocrity because it is woven into the fabric of our environment's culture. We also fear the unknown if we attempt to break the cycle. We should use the "garbage in, garbage out" theory to explain why we should break the cycle. If we want our kids to be successful, we shouldn't teach them garbage by introducing them to bad habits or not emphasizing the importance of the role of education in their futures. I was able to survive because I didn't accept the pattern established before me. I knew there had to be a better model for being a great father and husband. Initially, I used the fictitious Cliff Huxtable to show me the way before seeing real-life examples from the church. I was then able to actually be a great example to my own father later in life.

10. **Own your decisions.** Never make a decision unless you are completely confident in standing behind it. Rarely are decisions popular to everyone. It is acceptable to receive negative responses after making decisions as long as you know you've made them after thorough pondering and understanding of the consequences. You can't live your life afraid to make choices because of your fear of the ramifications. We grow as a result of small failures, and it's difficult to succeed without failing at least once. In order for you to defeat challenges and obstacles, you

have to work hard to overcome your fears and doubts.

As with all decisions, I've been impacted by their consequences whether the decisions were made by me or someone else. My mom's decision to raise me on her own had positive and negative consequences on her life as well as mine. My struggles with overcoming pornography addiction had its own consequences on my life and my family. Being accountable for both positive and negative choices is the first step toward overcoming struggles. Without a sense of accountability or ownership, it is impossible for a person to move forward without placing inaccurate blame on others for his or her own shortcomings. Understandably, admitting ownership and accepting accountability is a daunting but necessary step in any healing process.

Everyone is afraid of something. It is OK to be afraid. Fear can also be used in to create something positive. Instead of using avoidance as your tactic, use your fears to motivate you to succeed. Fear makes you focus. The greatest career move I made up to this point in my life was based on fear. I saw the vision and knew opportunities would be presented to me if I moved to Texas instead of remaining in Illinois, even though that wasn't a popular decision in our home. Without moving to Texas, I would not have been able to succeed at Novation/VHA, which would not have allowed me to be recruited by Nielsen. And my opportunity at Nielsen is an undefined but vital part of my master success plan.

11. **Be patient and allow plans to work.** We are often quick to rush decisions while expecting immediate results. The best laid plans are sometimes those that take time to manifest. I'm a true believer that everything happens for a reason. We all have master plans while we are here on Earth. As we progress through life's journeys, we experience purposeful moments within our plan. While we should be patient, we should also develop an awareness that lets us know when we need to act on situations placed ahead of us. I wasn't supposed to know my dad before the moment I met him, which could have impacted our relationship if we met a couple of years earlier. I wasn't supposed to be accepted into Lane Tech High School, which would have taken away from my life-changing experience as an ABC student. I believe I wasn't

supposed to leave Rockwell until my fourteen years of experience was fulfilled before going away to Lower Merion, which provided me with an unrelenting need to be successful. While it's extremely important to create plans, allow those plans to work without losing focus on your role to execute those plans.

12. **If it is to be, it is up to YOU.** Succeeding shouldn't be easy. Failure actually *is* an option as long as you're using it to push yourself as far away as possible from other failures. In order for us to achieve our own defined level of success, we have to understand that it is up to us to push ourselves towards greatness. While positive and successful people may help to motivate us, we cannot succeed unless we have that internal fire flickering and take chances others may willingly shy away from. Instead of avoiding the unknown, challenge them head on.

My story is obviously repeated in other cities, suburbs, small towns, and countries. I know that others have gone through more hardships than I have had to endure. I also know that someone reading this book may not see my life as a success because I'm not famous by society's definition. My path was destined for me, just like yours is waiting for you. You are responsible for running your own marathon and shouldn't compare your journey to someone else's. In order to find your path, the key is to be keenly aware when critical opportunities approach you. Without being in tune with who you are and what you want, your blinders will prevent you from witnessing key decisive moments surrounding you on a daily basis. You will be blessed as long as you have hope and take action towards delivering on that hope. Dreams are only the vision and beginning toward a successful journey, while the hard work to achieve those dreams is what creates the success.

I realize that my ever-evolving life story is incomplete. I will continue to push myself to move beyond boundaries. I also know that every facet of my journey, whether positive or negative, was purposeful in shaping me into who I am today and provided a framework for what I want to be. Finally, I know that it was up to me to make it to "be;" to grow into a successful man after entering into this world as what society would view to be an unfortunate bastard. Life has no excuses for anyone, and every decision we make has repercussions. However, the negative influences are often the ones that lead to greater individual growth as well as opportunities to challenge and overcome our internal fears. The moment we truly embrace our negative experiences is when the plan to accomplish our dreams is revealed to us. Until we reach that stage in our lives, we will continue to make excuses for the obstacles that, on the surface have held us back, but, in truth, have led to our growth and success.

Who would have thought that a bastard child raised in one of the most dangerous neighborhoods in the United States would have found a way to overcome the odds to become a success? Who would have believed that the same unwanted child that was almost aborted would be given the chance to become a father himself, working hard to provide a life for his kids that was only a dream when he was a child himself? Although the journey witnessed through the eyes of this bastard would be one filled with pitfalls, he was able to look beyond the ominous clouds to reach for the tiniest ray of sunshine which contained the most powerful motivator of mankind. Hope.

About A Better Chance

A Better Chance's mission is to **increase substantially the number of well-educated young people of color who are capable of assuming positions of responsibility and leadership in American society.** Since 1963, this guiding principle has driven A Better Chance to place talented young people of color into the leadership pipeline through increased access to academically rigorous secondary schools. Its signature College Preparatory Schools Program annually recruits and places 500 new Scholars and supports a total of 2000 Scholars at leading college preparatory schools across the country. Over the course of the last 50 years, A Better Chance has been a driving force in the effort to increase educational attainment among youth of color. Its record of success is evident in the more than 14,000 Alumni who have become great innovators, thinkers and leaders in their respective fields. Their success is a direct result of the educational access that they received through A Better Chance.